McLuhan's Children

The Greenpeace Message and the Media

McLuhan's Children
The Greenpeace Message
and the Media

Stephen Dale

Between the Lines
Toronto, Canada

Published by:
Between The Lines
720 Bathurst Street, #404
Toronto, Ontario
Canada   M5S 2R4

Cover design: Stray Toaster
Interior: Steve Izma
Cover b & w photo © Robert Keziere/Greenpeace, used by permission
Backcover author photo by Laura Macdonald
Printed in Canada

Between The Lines gratefully acknowledges financial assistance from the Canada Council, the Ontario Arts Council, and the Canadian Heritage Ministry.

Canadian Cataloguing in Publication Data

Dale, Stephen, 1958–
McLuhan's Children

Includes index
ISBN 1-896357-04-0

1. Greenpeace Foundation. 2. Mass media and the environment. 3. Environmental protection. 4. Nature conservation. I. Title.

P96.E57D35 1996   363.7'0577   C96-931502-3

Contents

ACKNOWLEDGEMENTS

THIS BOOK IS A HYBRID. IT IS PARTLY A COMMENTARY ON the mass media and partly a study of how one organization – Greenpeace – has built its worldwide profile and influence on an information-based strategy.

To the extent that it delves into Greenpeace history, the book is a bit like one of those unauthorized biographies: Greenpeace itself did not commission or gives its blessing to the work, and many of the people interviewed are former employees or associates who now feel no need to uphold the party line and in many cases tend to dwell on disagreements with former colleagues. Despite the "unauthorized" tag, however, I'd like to think that my approach to Greenpeace is quite different from, say, Kitty Kelley's run at Frank Sinatra. The people who spoke to me during the course of my research – many of them present and former Greenpeacers, some of them willing to talk to me about their work for many hours at a time – by and large looked at this as an opportunity to reflect openly and honestly upon serious issues (such as how reliance on mass media can distort the public perception of ecological crisis, or the tendency of media-based campaigns to accentuate North-South schisms) rather than as an opportunity to propagandize.

First of all, then, I'd like to offer my thanks to the people, both insiders and detached observers, who poured their reflections and recollections into my tape recorder. I hope that within these pages they can recognize themselves and the issues that confront environmentalists trying to navigate their way across the ever-changing electronic landscape. One person who merits a special thanks is David Peerla, who introduced me to many interesting people and regularly brought crucial information to my attention. David's keen insight and on-the-ground experience (which he was always willing to share) played a key role in shaping the approach of this book.

A number of the interviews used here were originally conducted for an earlier project, a two-part radio series, "Greenpeace and the Politics of Image," broadcast on the CBC's *Ideas* program. This book would probably not have been written were it not for the work of the CBC radio team. My thanks to Bernie Lucht for commissioning the radio series and for his hands-on work with the product. Max Allen was a masterful script-doctor; as well, I'm highly appreciative of all the encouragement he has given me over a number of years. A special thanks go to Doreen Brule for her great artistry as a radio producer, her dedication, and her good humour. Jennifer Norfolk's archival research was a great boon to both the radio program and the book. Thanks also to Marc Laurin, Pierre Millette, and Liz Nagy for significant contributions, technical and otherwise.

After the project crossed over into the realm of print, a number of people made invaluable contributions. Members of the board of Between the Lines reviewed various drafts of the manuscript and provided excellent suggestions and commentary. Marg Anne Morrison has been great to work with: my thanks to her and to BTL staffers Pat Desjardins and Paul Eprile. Jamie Swift provided encouragement, valuable insight, and a healthy dose of levity. And I'm sure that very few first-time authors have the privilege of working with such a skilful, sensitive, and insightful editor as Robert Clarke, who greatly improved the flow and organization of the material and also brought his keen intellect and broad knowledge to bear on the subject-matter.

Laura Macdonald and Benjamin Macdonald-Dale, as always, made our house a happy place and gave me good reason to turn off the computer every now and then. They were huge in the moral support department; it is always my greatest joy to be in their company.

Finally, I gratefully acknowledge the generous support of the Ontario Arts Council and the Canada Council; without their financial assistance this book could not have been written.

CHAPTER 1

INTRODUCTION

WHEN I BEGAN THIS PROJECT, WHAT INTRIGUED ME MOST about Greenpeace was its remarkable ability to transform itself. When Greenpeace was hatched in Vancouver in 1971, it seemed unmistakably a product of its time, indelibly marked with all the quaint cultural trappings of an era that is now like a distant, vaguely amusing dream. Looking at old photographs of an early Greenpeace crew – a rag-tag collection of long-haired, bearded men standing on the deck of a ship flashing peace signs – is like popping a copy of *Woodstock* into the VCR: what leaps out from those images and into the present is a determined sense of idealism that, today's cynics would say, was clearly doomed to dissolve as the world turned harder and the drugs wore off.

In my basement is a mildewed copy of a Greenpeace newspaper from 1976. Its contents describe a movement driven by a burning, instinctive impulse to change the world – a movement of heart and spirit, though without much of an intellectual road map, perhaps. The magazine is light on science, uncomplicated in its analysis, and unconcerned with the social and economic ramifications of environmentalism. No matter. In the 1970s those things were quite beside the point: like other countercultural creatures of that time, Greenpeace saw its first task not as indulging in intricate argumentation but as challenging the fundamental logic and seemingly unstoppable momentum of some dark and dangerous forces. Greenpeace's enemies were an industrial mind-set that pursued material prosperity

1

with a blind, savage contempt for the natural world, and a war machine that didn't consider the end of life on Earth too great a price for ideological triumph. Launching its campaigns against these compelling forces, Greenpeace concerned itself with broad strokes, with changing the paradigm, with mobilizing support for the key realization that – to borrow from Joni Mitchell – "we've got to get ourselves back to the garden."

A quarter-century later, many of the products of this period of experimentation – from back-to-the-land communes to a multitude of new political organizations – have died, been rendered marginal and obscure, or have sold out to a system that continues to plunder the planet and murder its people for the sake of material profit. But not Greenpeace. The seemingly rag-tag outfit has not only survived into its third decade, but also managed to project its influence into new corners of the globe. Many (though certainly not all) veterans of the early days would say that Greenpeace has been able to maintain its relevance without sacrificing much of its original idealism.

And that's what I meant when I said I was intrigued by Greenpeace's ability to transform itself: it struck me that Greenpeace was able to make the leap into a new world by embracing new ideas and learning new languages, both figuratively and literally. Beginning in the late 1980s, Greenpeace started to factor issues such as globalized trade and North-South disparity into its environmental reasoning – making it the first major environmental organization to do so. Since the early campaigns of the 1970s it has also greatly enhanced its capacity for scientific inquiry and enlisted its own brigade of negotiators to champion the cause of the environment within the rarefied realm of global treaty-making. In many respects, in the 1990s Greenpeace is a very different organization than it was in the 1970s: more cosmopolitan, more concerned with the details than with sweeping manifestos, certainly more hard-headed. While Greenpeace used to be a pair of bell-bottomed blue jeans, today it is more like a three-piece pinstripe suit.

Now here comes a U-turn. Part way into my research I began to wonder whether I was barking up the wrong tree, whether the staying power of Greenpeace arose not so much from its adaptability as from its consistency. It dawned on me that – in spite of all the changes in its approach and ideas – the engine at the centre of this thing called Greenpeace has always been its prophetic understanding of the nature of mass communications, which a handful of

Greenpeace's founders picked up from the writings of Marshall McLuhan. This insight has been the driving force behind a strategy that has anticipated, with uncanny accuracy, the shape of today's world: a world increasingly without borders, a world in which the mass media perform a function akin to gravity – keeping everything in its rightful place, maintaining a sense of order, and mediating the distance and relationships between objects. Looking back, you can see that Greenpeace workers were able to foretell emerging trends that would eventually broadside other groups. For one thing, Greenpeacers believed what McLuhan said about the "global village" and so set their sights on international environmental issues at a time when most other people and organizations were still rooting around in their own backyards. While many campaigning organizations have tried to get their messages out through the mass media, few have had anything like the success of Greenpeace.

The key tool has been the international news services – at first the print newswires and later the satellite distributors of TV news footage. The organization has also based the more pro-active aspect of its strategy on the realization that our global society is controlled not just by powerful transnational corporations but also by transnational agencies – ranging in stature and importance from the International Whaling Commission to the World Trade Organization – which are not democratically accountable but are still susceptible to the glare of negative publicity.

Greenpeace has cultivated its political influence using a two-pronged approach: attempting to change the public climate through mass media, and at the same time launching focused political campaigns aimed directly at international treaty-making. The diplomatic prong was present as far back as the 1971 campaign against U.S. nuclear testing in the Aleutian Islands and was a key element of the first campaigns against French nuclear testing that followed a short while later.

Clearly, Greenpeace's multifaceted strategy – an interconnected web of direct-action spectacles, mass media campaigning, and diplomatic lobbying – was not created ad hoc. Rather, it seemed to have emerged, fully formed, from the imaginations of its founders, with a little help from McLuhan.

It is, I believe, the organization's insight into the patterns of global social change – and into the relationship of global communications structures to political power – that accounts for its disproportionate influence in the world. There is an image today of Greenpeace as a kind of environmental megacorporation, an organization that has grown so prosperous that it can buy political change. Supporters take consolation in this image because it shows that real power can spring from the grassroots. Detractors use it to discredit Greenpeace as an organization that has become complacent and self-serving: primarily concerned with its own survival and expansion. But the image of Greenpeace as a fat-cat institution is misguided. In 1994 the budget of Greenpeace International – the entity that supports all of Green-peace's international campaigns through dues from national offices – was U.S.$28.3 million. This is a lot more than most non-govern-mental organizations (NGOs) have to work with, but it is minuscule compared with the resources of the corporations and governments that Greenpeace regularly opposes.

The business pages tell me that in 1995 each one of Canada's five major banks posted profits about twenty-six times the size of Green-peace International's annual budget (about a billion dollars Canadi-an). And General Motors Canada, a major automobile company in a secondary market, recorded profits (not sales, but profits) about thirty-five times higher than the Greenpeace International annual budget figure. These profits indicate a scale of cash flow that is bound to translate as enormous economic and political clout and would qualify these corporations as headline newsmakers any time their CEOs might decide to pronounce upon some matter of public importance. The higher up the food chain you go, the more impres-sive the arithmetic. With post-Cold War spending levels now cut down to about $280 billion dollars a year, the U.S. military is subsist-ing on an annual budget about one thousand times greater than the Greenpeace budget – giving the military a financial heft whose bene-fits are distributed widely enough across the corporate hierarchy to ensure a sympathetic hearing by the news media. Even within the specialized sphere of mass communications, Greenpeace is clearly (in budgetary terms) a minor league player. Voice of America, the U.S. government's international shortwave radio service (a signifi-cant but by no means major force in the information age), has an annual budget of $359.3 million, about thirteen times more than the amount that Greenpeace International spends on all aspects of its operation.

So the relative wealth of Greenpeace cannot explain its influence over international opinion and the international decision-making processes. Having a few million will allow you to rent space in the exclusive neighbourhoods of global communications and diplomatic deal-making, but being able to do something once you're there depends on less tangible factors: an ability to focus on key pressure points, perhaps, or a knowledge of what holds the system together.

★ ★ ★

None of this is to say that underdog status implies sainthood. In the 1990s Greenpeace has been having a rough time of it both internationally and in Canada, the land of its birth. Its public image has become increasingly tarnished by factional squabbles and generalized discontent. As the euphoric years of financial boom faded into history for Greenpeace shortly after the United Nations "Earth Summit" held in Rio de Janeiro in 1992, the press on several continents began airing the complaints of ex-allies and ex-employees. The refrain heard time and again was that Greenpeace had become mired in its own bureaucracy and had lost touch with the grassroots, that it had become a cumbersome, sluggish organization that decreased in effectiveness as it increased in size.

Consider an episode that we can call "the Stan Gray affair." When I first started talking to people at Greenpeace's Canadian head office, many of them would speak to me excitedly about the breakthrough that had been achieved with the hiring of Stan Gray, an organizer with a long and distinguished career of working on health and safety issues for labour unions. Gray brought a kind of class analysis to Greenpeace that had previously been absent. He saw environmental concerns as a working-class issue, a matter of everyday importance to the people who had to work with toxic chemicals or live in poorer neighbourhoods close to industrial areas. Gray saw the conflicting imperatives of jobs versus a clean environment – which the corporate masters had harped on so effectively to keep the environmental agenda off the main political stage – as no conflict at all. For him, the issue was a clean environment *and* jobs.

A practical kind of guy, Gray had done the calculations showing that by shifting state subsidies away from capital-intensive but environmentally risky industries (such as nuclear power, or the asbestos industry) and into newer, labour-intensive, and environmentally benign industries (such as recycling enterprises) the government could seed all kinds of new initiatives that would both generate employment and lessen environmental strain. This kind of thinking put practical flesh on the abstract theorizing of environmentalists who had recently become obsessed with concepts like "sustainable development" and with the need to marry economic instruments or thinking to environmental goals. Gray's co-workers at Greenpeace Canada made a point of telling me, unprompted, that his work was pushing Greenpeace onto an important new frontier, addressing questions that the environmental movement would eventually have to deal with. It also won Greenpeace an enthusiastic endorsement from the Canadian labour movement, which in the past had more often than not been at loggerheads with environmentalists.

This bold experiment went up in flames when a high-ranking official with Greenpeace International sent an e-mail expressing alarm that Greenpeace would be compromised by any such close alliance with labour. Subsequently Gray and another well-respected activist, Gordon Perks, were given the boot from Greenpeace after it was discovered that they had also led a successful union organizing drive. A law suit, charges that Greenpeace had engaged in union-busting, and a series of explosive newspaper stories followed; eventually a cash settlement bought peace and brought an ambitious and promising experiment to a sad end.

After Greenpeace Canada's labour problems came to the fore, people I know began to ask me what I really thought about this organization in human terms. Are the people inside really as ruthless as they have been portrayed in the newspaper reports? I wish I could act like a real journalist and give a straightforward, unequivocal answer, but in truth this episode had such a complex story line, was fraught with such complex emotions, that it would be hard for a mere mortal (and an outsider, at that) to cast a judgement on it. But I do have some ideas about the possible systemic causes of this and other unpleasant episodes in Greenpeace's recent history.

At the root of these matters, I believe, is the question of control. Who can use the secret password? Who is allowed to hold Aladdin's Magic Lamp? Greenpeace is a name that carries tremendous power – an "open sesame" allowing access to the global airwaves and a passageway into the homes and minds of millions of people around the world. To be welcomed into Greenpeace's global extended family is to be given a surname that's as marketable as "McDonald's" or "Coca-Cola," and it is to be made an heir to a mythology that would be the envy of many nation-states. Being part of Greenpeace means gaining access to a very potent kind of knowledge: of how the global news media work and how to use them. The people at the head of the Greenpeace clan are concerned that succeeding generations don't squander this legacy.

Part of what they worry about is that newer members of the family will start keeping the company of those who would sully the family name, causing Greenpeace to lose the sheen of non-partisanship that has helped it stay in favour with global news peddlers. For that reason, Greenpeace tends to be jealous of its power and protective of its identity. As Stan Gray found out, Greenpeace is not terribly fond of sharing decision-making with labour unions – whether within its own workplace or as long-term political allies within coalitions. In a wired world, image is everything. And Greenpeace wants to keep its own image separate from the images of other organizations that the mass media find easier to ignore.

The conflict between Greenpeace Canada and Stan Gray is, I believe, only one minor example among many of how Greenpeace's media strategy – brilliant as it may be – is now routinely bumping up against its own limitations, particularly in the Northern, hyper-technologized countries. Paradoxically, while media play was essential to the early development of environmentalism, today that reliance on the media is probably restraining the movement's influence over human affairs.

Environmentalism has a tremendous amount to offer our world. An emerging, socially concerned environmental philosophy (a good chunk of which has sprung from the heads of energetic and imaginative Greenpeacers) offers solutions not just to the physical poisoning of our planet but also to a more general malaise in politics, economics, and the personal lives of individuals. If any group of people can effectively and coherently challenge the prevailing logic of an economic system that, in the search for ever-increasing trade, has been willing to subjugate human, community, and natural values to a few abstract economic equations – if anyone can offer an antidote to the religion of consumerism that has swept the globe – it is environmentalists.

The problem is that while environmental organizations such as Greenpeace have become more expansive in their thinking, they must, at the same time, try to squeeze their message through the eye of a needle – that is, through the highly restrictive lens of the electronic news industry. The result is that the increasingly complex and nuanced arguments of environmental thinkers are compromised by the breathtaking limitations of the electronic mass media: by the tight formats of television news, by the inability of television to think historically, by the ideological disposition of the medium itself and the increasingly tight control exercised by media conglomerates. There has been a lot of utopian talk about using new media such as the Internet as a way around all of this. The use of narrowcasting networks, so the techno-visionaries tell us, will lead to the break-down of a mass media system that demands simple, unambiguous story lines. In the process it will restore literacy and the art of informed debate, and it will create a new class of tuned-in citizen. Sadly, given the current level of treatment of issues at large – whether it's the "race" to the U.S. presidency, the continuing "deficit hysteria," or the epidemic of drug and crime coverage that consistently fails to note the economic and social underpinnings of those problems – it is difficult to see any great influence that these new media might have on the character of mainstream public debate in our late twentieth century.

So, when we are talking about Greenpeace and its involvement with issues ranging from whaling to global warming, inevitably we are led to a discussion of whether the mass media are up to the challenge of helping us find a way out of our current mess. Indeed, despite what its title may suggest, this book is largely about the media, rather than a history of Greenpeace or a discussion of the ideas of Marshall McLuhan. Its intent is to examine a number of important events in the life of this one organization and to ask what they say about the use of mass media as a tool for protecting the environment, for citizen political action in the age of globalization, for the future of protest movements. In doing this I make use of the insights of a variety of people – most of them Greenpeace activists from the past and present, but also media practitioners and rival environmentalists – a group of people who I believe have been candid and thoughtful in assessing the larger significance of their work.

★ ★ ★

In close to a generation of environmental campaigning, Greenpeace has gone from a small Vancouver office to a head office in Amsterdam and about thirty offices around the world. It has gone from anti-nuclear, anti-whaling, and anti-sealing campaigns to focus on issues of chemical contamination and waste disposal and, more recently, the international trade in toxic wastes. It has seen its flagship *Rainbow Warrior* sunk in New Zealand by French agents in 1985. The explosion killed one crew member, provoked international outrage, and triggered a funding boom that would change the scope and shape of the organization.

That was, apparently, when a certain amount of organizational chaos and problems in direction set in – after the *Rainbow Warrior* was sunk, when millions of dollars in fresh support started pouring in. Like the banks, which were drowning in petrodollars during the Arab oil boom of the 1970s, Greenpeace engaged in a frantic search for new projects to invest in, setting the stage for a major expansion that included the opening of new offices in Latin America. In the 1990s, Greenpeace became known as a champion of a North-South perspective on environmental issues and played a pivotal role among NGOs at the Earth Summit. Soon after that meeting a financial crisis took hold, forcing Greenpeace to retreat from some areas of campaigning and fuelling disputes over the future direction of the organization. And like the global debt crisis that hit when the banks began to demand enormous interest payments on their loans, when boom turned to bust Greenpeace found itself wielding an axe over the heads of those to whom it had originally offered financial support.

Prior to Greenpeace's 1994 annual general meeting it appeared that the organization was about to explode: members of the board flatly rejected the budget proposed by Greenpeace's upper management (read: the old boys' network), which the board interpreted as simply calling for most of the funding for the new, non-self-sustaining branches in Latin America and elsewhere to be lopped off. This triggered an immense conflict between board members and managers; Greenpeace's e-mail system was burning up with invective.

The debate over how financial cuts should be divided up – and the impact that move might have on the power differential between the Northern and Southern flanks of Greenpeace – dominated once again at the 1995 AGM, provoking the same feelings of crisis and discord. Blair Palese, at Greenpeace International's Communications office in London, England, acknowledges that it will take a long time to remedy this malaise, but protests that the situation is not as bad as the papers portray it. The work goes on, she reports, and Greenpeace offices in Mexico, Guatemala, and Brazil continue their productive and enthusiastic campaigning. Besides, organizational problems are fairly widespread these days. "All you have to do is look at the European Union," she says, "to see that everyone is having difficulty figuring out how to be an effective international institution." Meanwhile, a board member who attended the 1995 AGM says that things are getting better. People are talking to each other, they are being calmer and less confrontational – the result of mediators being called in to help get Greenpeacers talking to each other once again. And then, in 1995, Greenpeace appeared to emerge from its long period of painful self-reflection with a massively successful campaign to alert the world to the resumption of French nuclear testing in the South Pacific.

The recent turmoil at Greenpeace may seem like an unfortunate episode in an otherwise charmed organizational history: after two decades of continual expansion and ever-widening influence, Greenpeace had finally sailed into waters too choppy to navigate. The truth of the matter is that the struggles of the 1990s represent nothing new. Bitter internal strife has been a major theme in the Greenpeace story since the very beginning. Heated conflicts, stormy departures, coups, rebellions, and expulsions: these are the markers of close to a quarter-century of Greenpeace history. There have been a few recurrent issues – money, power, ideology – at the centre of these regular storms, and they make the disputes of the past seem familiar today.

This state of simmering internal strife has been a blessing as well as a burden: the same combustible cocktail of fierce ideological commitment and personal combativeness that has at times threatened to rip Greenpeace apart has also powered its political drives and propelled it into new and uncharted territory.

Many of the events in Greenpeace history have been landmarks in the worldwide environmental movement. But as with many things in our wired world, the events themselves have sometimes been less important than how they were recorded, and how those images have embedded themselves in our consciences and rattled along the alleyways of power.

CHAPTER 2

FROM THE CONTROL TOWER

MORE THAN A GENERATION AGO, A PREVIOUSLY OBSCURE
Canadian academic named Marshall McLuhan won international
celebrity by presenting a set of ideas that, at the time, seemed highly
novel and perhaps a trifle paranoid. McLuhan's central belief was
that any new technology – operating as an appendage to the human
body – changes both the people who use the technology and the
world it operates in.

For instance, the wheel, a mechanical extension of the human
foot, had a profound impact on economic processes and therefore
upon human society. The ability to move goods around much faster
than people could walk set in motion a great surge of building, buying and selling, and other forms of economic activity. And because
the wheel enabled people to travel more quickly and easily between
places, it also changed how people looked at the world. So the introduction of the wheel not only physically altered the landscape and
retooled human relations, but also irrevocably changed human consciousness.

McLuhan believed that the new electronic communications systems of the late twentieth century would similarly reshape human
society and rewire the human mind, but much more dramatically
and quickly than the technologies of the past did. In his 1964 book
Understanding Media, McLuhan described these new communications
networks as a new "central nervous system" for a globalized human
society.[1] Indeed, McLuhan also said that in an age of electric

communication humankind wears its nervous system on the outside; a person's nerves are constantly exposed to the outer world. He saw the planet as a "global village" in which events and impressions from around the world are absorbed by microphones and camera lenses and teletype machines in the same way that sense impressions are gathered by the eyes, ears, and skin of the human body.[2] All of this information is analysed, contextualized, and interpreted in the brain of mass media image factories and sent back out through that electronic nervous system to the various appendages of human society around the globe. According to McLuhan, this creates a "unified field of experience." People in opposite corners of the Earth see their own experiences placed in the context of a manufactured composite image of global events and are told how to react to the outside world, in much the same way as the limbs of a human body are instructed to react to impressions gathered through the eyes, ears, nose, or some other part of the anatomy. The electronic media made it possible to imagine a world that thinks – and acts – in unison.

Was the advent of this electronic "central nervous system" a good or a bad thing? In McLuhan's view, it signalled perhaps the biggest and most rapid change in human history and had the potential of being extremely dangerous. It was quickly undermining long-established national cultures, and because it made next-door neighbours of people who watched the same images on the nightly news in north and south, east and west, it increased the chances that those neighbours would feel their own value systems threatened by those who were now too close for comfort. In that way, it increased the chances for global conflict and war. These new technologies also had the power to erode from within: McLuhan saw the Western tradition of linear argument being broken down by communications media that presented information visually, non-sequentially, and in a form that appealed more to the intuitive right-brain than to the logical left-brain.

McLuhan shied away from passing any final judgement on the meaning of these changes. In a conversation broadcast in 1967 on the CBC radio program "The Way It Is," novelist Norman Mailer challenged McLuhan to make a moral pronouncement on the globalizing effects of electronic media. McLuhan responded, "Norman, do you remember a phrase of Edmund Burke's – 'I do not know how to draw up an indictment against a whole people'? Now, I wouldn't know how to value the Western world, which we are demolishing by our new technology, or the Oriental world, which we are westernizing – we're demolishing the Oriental World and demolishing the Western World. I don't know whether that's good or bad because I wouldn't know how to make a value judgement on such a scale."[3]

More than twenty years after that conversation, history has proved Marshall McLuhan correct about the scale of the change. Instantaneous electronic communication has helped to rewrite the terms of international trade, erode distinct national cultures, and introduce an international political language based on a common set of television images. McLuhan's electronic "central nervous system" now penetrates virtually every corner of the globe: the Cable News Network is beamed by satellite to five continents, telling people in the metropolitan vortices of power and in supposed stagnant backwaters alike what's worth knowing about the world. During the Gulf War of 1991, the Pentagon used CNN as its prime carrier of disinformation because it knew that Saddam Hussein was watching.

Meanwhile, computerized stock-market trading and electronic transfer of funds have made capital instantly mobile and given multinational corporations the pick of dozens of competing countries as sites for their operations. This has radically altered social and political relations within individual nations across the globe. And it has made workers in Asia, the Americas, Europe, wherever – the people who produce components for a common inventory of consumer goods – co-workers on a global assembly line. Yet what these people know about each other isn't likely to come through personal contact but over the newswires and through television outlets like CNN.

All of this, of course, is the familiar backdrop to almost all social and political issues in the 1990s – a scenario that today's opponents of the status quo have a lot less trouble passing moral judgement over than Marshall McLuhan did. Opposition movements have a decreased influence over policy in this new world, and they are largely invisible to the global news media whose transmissions hold it together. This is partly because of the obvious fact that, by and large, the entities that control commerce in the wired world also own the media outlets. To operate a global news empire requires the financial might of a Ted Turner or a Rupert Murdoch and a substantial flow of multinational corporate advertising dollars. In the past, national opposition or reform movements – say, labour groups seeking a reduction of the workweek; the women's movement campaigning for daycare funding; or consumer advocates who want unsafe products banned

– have been able to focus public attention on their goals and thereby work to achieve change. But as their various gains have been eroded in a hypercompetitive global business environment, those groups have been largely shut out of the public discussions over global economic restructuring, international labour standards, transborder environmental protection, and other issues. Perhaps that's partly because of who constructed and who owns that global nervous system.

A somewhat less conspiratorial view is that today's opposition movements have little access to the media because, objectively, they don't matter as much as they used to: as decision-making has shifted from national to international forums they have lost influence. While opposition movements could once at least sway national policies by going on strike or rallying the electorate against the government of the day, these threats are of less concern to governments today than the spectre of mobile corporations exporting capital and jobs to other countries if they don't like their current hosts' legislative programs. Add to this the fact that important decisions are increasingly being made not by elected governments but by international tribunals sheltered from public pressure and the democratic process, and McLuhan's "global village" begins to look like the fiefdom of transnational corporate power, from which voices of dissent have been banished. While citizen groups continue petitioning increasingly weak national powers, the real decisions are being made outside the national arena.

Greenpeace, though, is an apparent exception to the rule. It is an organization that has established both its image and a concrete presence in the global community by specializing in the construction of sharp little media moments that the newswires and television outlets can't seem to resist. As a kind of mirror-image of today's transnational corporation – media-savvy, global in scope, pragmatic, and unencumbered by industrial-age concepts such as national borders and ideology – Greenpeace seems to offer a model of hope for opposition movements that have been shut out of McLuhan's electronic world.

Greenpeace has been able to deal on more-or-less equal terms with its corporate nemeses by operating in much the same way they do. It can follow footloose corporations from country to country when they try to dodge national environmental laws or environmental pressure groups; it has the established media-clout and logo recognition to get picked up in the international media alongside the official sources; and it has even been able to lift the shroud of secrecy surrounding a number of normally impermeable international bodies, helping to bring about changes in international conventions.

Greenpeace has been able to do this because its Canadian founders took seriously McLuhan's early pronouncements about the power of the media in the new globalized world. Bob Hunter, a founder of Greenpeace, says: "One of McLuhan's big lines was 'It was time for intellectuals to get out of the ivory tower and into the control tower,' and the control tower seemed to us to be the studio and the newsroom." More precisely, the founders of Greenpeace decided in the early 1970s to move *out* of the studio and the newsroom – where many of them had been working, acquiring the practical knowledge of how news is selected and packaged and sold – and into an activist role where they could use those skills to advance the cause.

★ ★ ★

In the fall of 1971 an embryonic Greenpeace organization sailed a creaking fish boat – a chartered halibut seiner named the *Phyllis Cormack*, redubbed *The Greenpeace* for the purposes of this mission – from Vancouver towards the site of a planned U.S. nuclear test at Amchitka in the Aleutian Islands. At the time the crew members were very likely not aware that they were conducting a historic experiment to prove the enormous power of mass media images in the age of instantaneous communications.

Like other opposition political groups of the times, the Greenpeace crew was torn by dissension and racked by self-doubt. The twelve members of the Greenpeace crew fought constantly, and according to crew member Bob Hunter some of its members teetered on the brink of madness.[4] Shortly after the Amchitka voyage, Hunter delicately described the group as "anti-heroes rather than heroes. We were Dustin Hoffmans and not John Waynes." Another early Greenpeacer, Ben Metcalfe, more bluntly described Greenpeace as "an absurd, pathetic little group," which was nonetheless free to attempt the impossible since it was composed of people who had "given up on this convention of hope" and so felt that they had nothing to lose.

Towards the tail end of the Vietnam War era, when a multitude of antiwar protest groups existed in any given city, Greenpeace appeared to be just one of the bunch, with nothing concrete to offer that would give it extra leverage over the U.S. nuclear establishment. Indeed, going up against the world's most powerful government, modern science's most deadly weapon, and the largest military machine in human history, Greenpeace could barely afford fuel for its thirty-year-old rented fishboat.

But the masterminds of the operation, keen students of the mass media, did realize that Amchitka as an issue had enough broad appeal to sustain the attention of editors and journalists and to enlist the support of several different public constituencies. Since the planned nuclear test happened to be, fortuitously, both a crime against nature *and* an enterprise of the same U.S. military machine that was blasting Vietnam back to the stone age, the cause had the potential to bring together both the antiwar movement and the new ecology movement then sprouting on Canada's west coast. Amchitka also rang the kind of nationalist alarm bells that appealed to more conservative segments of the Canadian public, which would not necessarily find fault with the Americans' anticommunist rationale for the Vietnam War. Greenpeace organizers were counting on mainstream opposition to the Amchitka test on the grounds that it violated Canadian sovereignty, and they tried to cultivate that reaction by emphasizing the speculation of scientists that the underground atomic blast could unleash tidal waves on Canada's west coast.

The goal of the Greenpeace organizers was to marry this mainstream opposition with the anti-Amchitka sentiment that had arisen from the student protest movement. Thousands of students had taken to the streets in 1969 to protest the detonation of a bomb code-named Milrow; shortly afterward, the U.S. government announced its decision to detonate a second bomb, Cannikin, in 1971. Three organizers, Irving Stowe, Paul Cote, and Jim Bohlen, decided to harness the energy of the first protest by forming the Don't Make a Wave Committee (a reference to the tidal wave threat), which at first operated as a committee of the Canadian wing of the venerable Sierra Club, based in San Francisco. Ben Metcalfe credited that trio with keeping the Amchitka issue alive: "People just came to them like iron filings to a magnet," he told CBC radio in 1973.[5] Meetings took place at a Unitarian church in Vancouver, and at some point it was decided that the Don't Make a Wave Committee, soon to become Greenpeace, should sail a boat out to the site of the nuclear test, as both a symbolic representation of Greenpeace's opposition to nuclear testing and a focus for media coverage.

The voyage had "two philosophical bases," according to Bob Hunter. "One was the Quaker idea of 'bearing witness' – which is supposed to change the observer and increase their level of activism, compassion, anger, whatever it is. The other part of it was to try to focus the mass media on the issue, which is otherwise like a mugging going off in a back alley."

Most of the early members of Greenpeace had some experience in media. David Garrick, who began his tenure at Greenpeace doing support work during Amchitka, recalls that most of the Vancouver office during the first three campaigns had worked for the city's highly successful underground newspaper, *The Georgia Straight*. The architects of Greenpeace's first campaign, the Amchitka protest, included Hunter, who was writing an ecology/youth culture column for the daily *Vancouver Sun*, freelance radio commentator and former public relations consultant Ben Metcalfe, and Bob Cummings, the *Georgia Straight*'s publisher.

Hunter himself has moved back and forth between media work and activism: after leaving the *Sun* he became president of Greenpeace in the mid-1970s, and after that wrote books and television scripts before landing a job as an environmental reporter for a TV station in Toronto. A seasoned journalist before arriving at Greenpeace, Hunter was as cynical about the profession as his fellow reporters on board the Greenpeace boat, and like many ex-Greenpeacers, he will still go on at length about the foibles of the mass media and its propensity for re-creating reality in some absurdly twisted forms.

Flawed as the media may be, the founders of Greenpeace recognized the truth in McLuhan's assertion that these new electronic networks now directed the course of human events and represented one of the few sources of true power still accessible to ordinary people. "The line I used was that the only delivery system we had which could possibly fend off the military's nuclear weapons delivery system was the mass media," Hunter says. "Our idea was that we would fire off press releases instead of ballistic missiles. So in a way this little old fish boat became a kind of media battleship."

★ ★ ★

The Amchitka campaign was not the first attempt to interfere with the U.S. nuclear test program by sailing a boat out to the scene of the crime. The Quakers themselves had initiated earlier efforts, twice sending boats out to the Bikini Atoll in the South Pacific to protest nuclear testing. While those attempts may have achieved the first goal of conscientizing the participants, they had not ignited much media interest. "In both cases," Hunter says, "because they were American boats and American citizens, the American military just grabbed them and hauled them away."

The Quaker voyages had ended before the participants could rally widespread public concern, and the media were not interested in covering a trip to the centre of a nuclear test, a trip that had no hope of reaching its target. But the Greenpeace voyage had a key difference. Heading off from Canada, in a Canadian boat, with Canadians on board, the crew knew that any attempt by the U.S. military to detain their vessel would be seen as an act of piracy. Violating that naval taboo promised an even greater public relations disaster for the Americans than letting the protesters go ahead. And so Greenpeace was free to play out the story like a daily radio serial or TV soap opera, with the momentum building, each plot detail unfolding in the shadow of the big question of what would happen if the daring Greenpeace crew managed to sail into range when the bomb was detonated.

The David-versus-Goliath spectacle of ordinary people defying a morally bankrupt and intellectually unsound enterprise rallied a remarkable amount of public opposition to the U.S. nuclear test. Although the crew of the Greenpeace boat, which had left Vancouver on September 15, 1971, had by October 12 abandoned hope of reaching the Amchitka test site in time to be physically present when the bomb went off, they had created enough public interest that their support team in Vancouver was able to raise the funds to send out another, bigger boat – *The Greenpeace Too* – to continue the voyage that rough water had forced the original crew to abandon. As the first Greenpeace boat limped back to port and its replacement steamed towards Amchitka, media coverage rose to a deafening crescendo, stirring widespread protest across Canada that put significant pressure on the Nixon administration in Washington. Canadian syndicated radio hosts Charles Templeton and Pierre Berton delivered the world's longest telegram to the White House: a petition with 188,000 signatures on it, urging President Nixon to call off the test.

The Canadian Parliament also got into the act, passing a motion that made the same request. This is a remarkable occurrence for the

Vietnam War era, an uncomfortable time in U.S.-Canada relations when Canada stuck to a policy of "quiet diplomacy" – a convenient but quite transparent piece of double-think whereby Canada refrained from commenting publicly on its objections to the war. The device allowed the Canadian government to tell the domestic electorate that it disapproved of the Americans' war, without having to directly condemn its closest neighbour and biggest trading partner, to which Canada happened to sell large quantities of war materiel.

At street level, meanwhile, massive protests blocked Canada-U.S. border crossings at Sarnia, Windsor, Niagara Falls, and Cornwall, while eight thousand protesters surrounded the U.S. consulate in Toronto.

Not bad for a dozen misfits on a barely seaworthy boat. Of course, the public response had very little to do with those twelve people or that old boat, or the new Greenpeace boat, or how far either of them were from the nuclear test site. It did, however, have a lot to do with the power of mass media images and of the emotional charge that Greenpeace sent through McLuhan's mass media "central nervous system." The realization that Greenpeace had found a pressure point that gave it some power over Goliath was a turning point; a moment that foreshadowed the birth of a new movement.

What were the concrete results of all this media sound and fury? The Americans certainly weren't persuaded to cancel the test. On November 6, 1971, before *The Greenpeace Too* could reach the site, the U.S. government detonated its nuclear device at Amchitka. Shortly afterward, however, U.S. authorities announced that they would terminate their testing program in the North Pacific and turn Amchitka into a wildlife sanctuary. Without a doubt, they did this to make up for the enormous public relations battering they had received; to recapture some of the high ground that Greenpeace had taken from them. In packaging its protest of the Amchitka test, the upstart peace group from Vancouver had managed to avoid the polarization of opinion that surrounded the Vietnam War. Amchitka had become a mainstream issue – it was all about an American bad-neighbour policy that infringed upon Canadian sovereignty and threatened the environment of Canada's beautiful Pacific coast. It wasn't hard to find people who wanted to save British Columbia from a government-sponsored tidal wave. You didn't have to be a student radical to want Amchitka stopped. You didn't need to have an opinion on the march of communism in Vietnam; on whether the Vietnamese were best liberated by Ho Chi Minh or by tons of U.S. explosives. Defending Canada from the effects of a nuclear test was not radical, but patriotic. And the members of the Greenpeace crew who set out to protect the Canadian coastline were not just underdogs but heroes in the mould of all those sailors who had departed from Canadian ports during wartime, risking death if their vessel could not stand up to the cruel sea, or at least risking radiation exposure if the bomb test vented in the direction of the Greenpeace boat.

Accordingly, Greenpeace members were treated with a kind of cordiality by the media that certainly was not forthcoming for the actions of the Yippies or Black Panthers. Old radio interviews from the Amchitka period provide a jarring glimpse of how Greenpeace had managed to win the media's support during its first campaign. After interviewing Greenpeace organizer Chris Bergthorson just before *Greenpeace Too* set sail from Vancouver, "As It Happens" radio host Barbara Frum – generally known, at least when it came to oppositional politics or anything from the left – for an abrasive scepticism that bordered on rudeness – signed off by uncharacteristically bidding her guest "good luck to you." During that interview Bergthorson told Frum, "The media in Vancouver has been very good to us." He cited the positive coverage as the main reason why Greenpeace – besieged by telephone calls throughout the previous night – had to turn away three hundred people who volunteered to serve on the boat.[6] The Canadian national media's reverent respect for Greenpeace continued for at least another two years.

The print media as well offered a tone of (sometimes grudging) admiration for Greenpeace's early ventures. Even *Time* magazine, generally recognized at the time as an organ of apologia for U.S. foreign policy, found it difficult to dismiss Greenpeace as part of some radical fringe. The magazine described the campaign against Amchitka as the "most vigorous" protest "ever lodged against nuclear testing, both in the U.S. and overseas."[7] It opined: "Seldom, if ever, had so many Canadians felt so deep a sense of resentment and anger over a single U.S. action. For once the cries of protest were not confined to the radical left, but came from a broad spectrum of Canadian society distressed by the environmental risks and other possible hazards of the test."[8] Like its main competitor, *Newsweek, Time* carried a lot of its coverage of the Cannikin test in its environment section, which may account for the uncharacteristically even-handed reporting on the opposition.

Yet while the U.S. newsweeklies' coverage of Greenpeace was fair – even generous – it was still nothing like the luminously positive ink found in *The Vancouver Sun*, which paid Bob Hunter to write a daily column about the expedition he had helped organize. If Greenpeace was a brigade of patriotic eco-sailors, standing on guard for Canada, Hunter became a typical war correspondent, an unapologetically partisan chronicler of the fight for right. "Years later [magazine columnist] Alan Fotheringham would say that Greenpeace owed its existence to *The Vancouver Sun*," Hunter says. "And there is some truth in that."

CHAPTER 3

CULTURAL SHIFTS AND NEW SPACES

GLOBAL STRATEGIES AND GRIDLOCK

THE RESOUNDING SUCCESS OF THE FIRST GREENPEACE campaign has been felt within the organization ever since. If the power of mass media imagery was (to invoke Hunter's analogy) a weapon for Greenpeace on a par with the U.S. military's nukes, then the original Greenpeace crew members who witnessed the harnessing of that media power during the anti-Amchitka campaign were, like Robert Oppenheimer and the Los Alamos gang, pioneers gazing upon the birth of a new era.

Greenpeace's media stunts and public relations drives have not only become the centrepiece of its campaigns but also the models for other social movements striving to maintain a presence in the electronic age. The campaigns in turn have been responsible for a number of striking successes on particular issues and for Greenpeace's own enormous growth. The images of derring-do have moved through the planet's electronic nervous system to touch people on opposite ends of the Earth, paving the way for new Greenpeace chapters that are the markers of a vast new international movement.

Most of the growth had taken place during a financial surge in the late 1980s, before the onset of recession in the 1990s burst the bubble for both Greenpeace and the environmental movement in general. The successful outcomes of Greenpeace campaigns against whaling, sealing, and French nuclear testing – in addition to the organization's visibility in new areas such as toxic substances – had, by the mid-1980s, positioned Greenpeace front and centre when environmental concerns began to take off as every Western politician's pet issue and as the main focus of the mass media's migrating angst. A donations boom accompanied the heightened public attention, fuelling Greenpeace's expansion beyond its traditional base in Western Europe, North America, Australia, New Zealand, and Japan. New branch plants were opened in Latin America, in the former Soviet bloc, and in smaller European countries, leading some members to contemplate that future moves into Southeast Asia and Africa would complete the transformation of Greenpeace into the first truly global environmental organization.

My first opportunity to witness the immense geographic and cultural span of the present-day Greenpeace came in the summer of 1993, after a media liaison in Toronto suggested that I could snare some interviews for a radio documentary on Greenpeace by showing up at a series of "skill-sharing" sessions being held at the organization's New York office.

These sessions were being held barely a year after the renowned "Earth Summit" – the United Nations Conference on Environment and Development (UNCED) – had been convened in Rio de Janeiro in June 1992. That Rio Summit, attended by over one hundred world leaders and thirty thousand participants, was touted as the event that would put environmental concerns on an equal footing with economic and political issues. Activists, the media proclaimed, hailed it as the beginning of a new era. Non-governmental organizations had held their own forum in Rio at the same time – though it was located miles away from the main UNCED meetings.

In New York in 1993 the fallout from that conference – both good and bad – seemed to cling to the participants who had flown in for the confab. There was still a sense of elation – lots of talk about the historic juncture that environmentalists found themselves in – but also a certain edginess. It was like the day after a big party, when everyone seems tired, perhaps a bit confused, but residually exhilarated from the events of the night before.

Besides providing a sense of the electricity of Rio, the New York sessions also offered a glimpse of the new Greenpeace's cosmopolitanism: representatives from the distant outposts of the Greenpeace eco-empire had descended upon the organization's sixth-floor open-plan office in a converted warehouse in Soho, New York City's Bohemian district. The choice of real estate said a lot about how Greenpeace had changed over the years. With sightlines leading into the floodlit artists' studios of the surrounding buildings and down onto rooftops with their ancient wooden water towers perched on top, with the perpetual wash of car horns and engines and crazy, coke-fuelled conversation flooding in through the windows with the summer breeze, this place was clearly an illustration of how Greenpeace had been repotted in urban soil.

Certainly the local foot-soldiers who strolled through the Greenpeace offices – doing the legwork for a city demonstration while the international campaigners met in stale adjoining offices – seemed more a product of the brooding, post-punk culture on the streets below than of that exuberant, back-to-the-land impulse that had given rise to Greenpeace back in the early 1970s in Vancouver. They worked the phones, painted posters, and made frequent elevator rides down to the street to smoke cigarettes. Toiling quietly, this brigade of volunteers in their teens and early twenties seemed somehow quarantined from what was going on around them – under the friendly façade was a sense of disconnectedness, something sullen and slightly forlorn.

According to Blair Palese, then head of Greenpeace's media unit in Washington, D.C., and the person in charge of logistics at these New York City encounter sessions, the faces in Greenpeace USA change about as fast as those at your neighbourhood McDonald's. "The United States tends to have younger activists," Palese says. She attributes the phenomenon to the ingrained American drive to secure the kind of monetary and status rewards that Greenpeace USA is unable to offer. "I found that people who work in our international office have been there a number of years – ten or twelve years sometimes – whereas in Washington, or anywhere in the United States, if you've been there for six or eight years, you're very much a veteran."

Applying that kind of arithmetic across the whole lifespan of Greenpeace, one can conclude that three or four generations of activists have passed through the North American wing of the organization in the close to twenty-five years since that first crew of hippies and draft-dodgers boarded *The Greenpeace* to stop the nuclear test at Amchitka. That sets Greenpeace apart from many of its contemporaries. For while all manner of institutions that were formed or transformed during that earlier era of sixties/seventies counterculture – from *Rolling Stone* magazine to the social science faculties of most universities – have remained in the grip of the baby boomers,

Greenpeace (particularly in North America) has had the chance to evolve. New ideas have come into the organization; new contexts and political landscapes have shaped its worldview.

This change was evident at the New York City meeting, where the agenda was clearly different from what it would have been in the 1970s and 1980s, when the post-Amchitka campaigns to stop the Newfoundland seal hunt and to save the whales established Greenpeace as an international, household name. Most of the activists meeting in New York were involved in some aspect of Greenpeace's campaign to disrupt the transnational trade in toxic substances, an issue that revolves not around wildlife and wilderness concerns but around human and social issues, and which is inevitably bound up with subsidiary political questions such as the nature of international trading arrangements, the postcolonial relationship between North and South, and discrimination on the basis of class and race (an issue that's become integral to toxic trade campaigning, because toxic substances invariably seem to be dumped in the backyards of the world's poor and – within the North – often in minority communities).

With this change of thematic focus has come a distinct cultural shift. That first generation of eco-buccaneers – living through what Bob Hunter terms "the dawn of the New Age" – was guided on its voyages by mystical illumination and a pantheistic rapport with the natural world they sought to protect. They had a finely honed sense of how to stage media events, but they also had a kind of wild-eyed missionary fervour that helped them confront the powers that be. At times the early Greenpeacers had, by their own accounts, depended on the well-timed appearance of a rainbow or some other omen to point the way across ocean waters.

In the New York City Greenpeace office of the early 1990s there are few reminders of this colourful past. The international Greenpeacers who have gathered here come off as a more sober, pragmatic bunch: they'll speak to the environmental effects of the intellectual properties provisions in the new GATT, define their concept of "social equity," interpret the power struggles at the Earth Summit, all without so much as a passing reference to whales, seals, or rainbows. Few of the local staff at the New York office now have occasion to walk aboard a Greenpeace boat. Their daily routine is more likely to include a subway ride to the South Bronx to help organize the fight against a medical waste incinerator that city bureaucrats want to build in a predominantly Latino section of that notoriously troubled borough.

The overall approach of the organization, it seems, has shifted more to the logical left-brain in recent years. Palese acknowledges this shift cautiously, demonstrating a publicist's knack for pre-empting any suggestion of conflict or discontinuity. She says Greenpeace's roots "are very much in the same place" as before, "but the issues we are dealing with have become much more sophisticated." She points to complicated free trade agreements and other international treaties and conventions that have an impact on the environment all over the world. Greenpeace has had to hire staff people – economists, or specialists in international trade, for instance – who understand and can deal with those issues on a diplomatic level. She says, "We're able to track things now that, ten or fifteen years ago, we would have had no ability to understand or campaign on. The toxic trade campaign is a good example of that."

Listening to her measured, reasoned responses, I realize that Blair Palese is herself indicative of a change in the approach of Greenpeace. Her career path is very much in the classic mould of Greenpeacers before her. She says she worked as a journalist for a few years after college before jumping into activism with the realization that "I wasn't interested in being objective in any way." The big difference is style. The old-timers tend to shoot from the hip: most are given to emotional, eruptive responses – often angry and sometimes profane. The current crop of Greenpeacers like Blair Palese seem cooler, less confrontational, more professional, and often more rehearsed.

But after a couple of days of watching these people emerge from their marathon meetings bleary-eyed and ashen-faced, yet with their willingness to discuss the issues intact, I find myself thinking the lower-key style of presentation may not really signify any great change in spirit. Perhaps it's just that the newcomers belong to a generation that has grown up entirely within the clutches of McLuhan's "cool" medium. They have seen wars and riots and apocalyptic famines transmitted live on television, unmediated by any consistent human expression of horror or outrage, and it may be understandable that their public personas should take on that same aloof air.

Beneath the surface impressions, outrage and indignation remain the core emotions of the Greenpeace experience. A number of young activists have told me that what attracted them to Greenpeace was its attitude of hopeful defiance; its maverick stance; its determined commitment to the idea that individuals with the courage of their convictions can say "no" and that righteous anger can bring about change. Such a spirit is indelibly encoded into the "direct actions" that remain Greenpeace's signature. Those actions are also Greenpeace's most potent advertising tool, with the power to reach the nascent anarchists within people who have long felt that they have ceded control over their lives to anonymous bureaucrats and scheming politicians. As Greenpeace USA president Barbara Dudley told me: "People remember the actions. It's the same image that's been going for Greenpeace for twenty years, and it still works." According to her this image says to everyone, "We're not going to take it anymore," and "We're not going to let you get away with this, we're going to follow you wherever you go and we'll make you stop."

The early Greenpeace direct-action spectacles of the 1970s may have served as a kind of time-delayed, electronic recruiting poster for today's activists. "I guess I would have learned about Greenpeace when I was very young," Blair Palese says. "It would have been back in the mid-seventies. I would have been ten years old or something like that. I learned about the whaling actions and I thought it was very creative, that it wasn't your standard way of going about making change. Not just that it was heroic – that people were putting their lives on the line – but that it was very creative."

The message was all the more powerful because it appeared on TV, normally the conduit for sitcoms, cop and lawyer shows, and, in general, celebrations of suburban complacency. When Greenpeace's antics were beamed into that cathode world, they introduced an ideology of personal responsibility harkening back to the tradition of Thoreau and Ghandi and King, a direct challenge to the message of passivity of television and its Madison Avenue masters. Greenpeace's anti-whaling campaign "gave a hopeful message about what we could do," Palese says. "It took ideas from other places that said your common person could get out there and put themselves into an issue and bring about a change. That had a big influence on me, I think."

Another attendee at the New York skill-sharing sessions, Kalle Hesstvedt, had also been infected by Greenpeace's spirit of determined defiance, but that was across the Atlantic Ocean, in his native Norway. "I think that what I thought when I first encountered them is, 'Here is a group of people who are willing to go out and do something – not only sit around and talk,'" Hesstvedt says. His speech is measured and calm, but his demeanour speaks of determination and certainty. "It's like they say, 'Everybody talks about the weather, but nobody does anything about it.' Well, Greenpeace not only talks about the environment, but it does something about it as well."

When we spoke in New York, Hesstvedt was preparing to move into a new position as co-ordinator of Greenpeace International's global warming campaign in Amsterdam. After working for eight years in the oil industry he had an insider's knowledge that would benefit a campaign largely directed against oil companies. Like Blair Palese, he had kept the environmentalists' message in a separate mental compartment for several years, but couldn't contain it forever. "I actually felt quite bad working in the oil industry, knowing the consequences of what we were doing. I think that many people in the oil industry feel that what they do is wrong, and they'd feel much more comfortable if their industry moved to a more sustainable path." His own discomfort led him gradually to defect to the opposition. "I made the shift over a number of years, first mentally and then physically," he says. "I was lucky to get a job at Greenpeace. I can really say in a heartfelt way that the only bad feeling I have is that I should have done it years ago."

Before moving to the global warming position at Greenpeace International, Hesstvedt spent two years working on national campaigns in his homeland (where an office was established in 1988). It proved to be a thankless task, because Norwegians have responded coldly to the organization. Greenpeace generally does better in hyper-urbanized, industrial areas (where the population is in closer contact with toxic contamination and more remote from nature, which they tend to romanticize) than in predominately rural countries like Norway. Apart from this generic culture clash, Norwegians have a specific gripe with Greenpeace: Norway is a whaling nation, which means that Greenpeace's anti-whaling campaign has elicited the same kind of hostility that the anti-sealing campaign stirred up on the east coast of Canada. Most Norwegians view Greenpeace not as saviours of helpless animals but as killers of the local economy. This situation has been worsened by the fact that, in Norway, Greenpeace's opponents have captured the momentum in the media wars.

According to Hesstvedt, the negative view of Greenpeace held by many Norwegians was bolstered by Magnus Gudmundsson's film *Survival in the High North*, which portrays the organization as a terrorist outfit specializing in faking film footage. The movie was released to great public fanfare just after Greenpeace opened its Norwegian office. Greenpeace won a defamation suit against the filmmaker, but Hesstvedt complains that, typically, the retractions have not been as widely publicized as the original reports.

Most of the other new branches established in recent years have benefited from the significantly more positive connotations attached to the Greenpeace moniker and logo in those other countries. Their comfortable niches in new surroundings may have as much or more to do with Greenpeace's approach to media – its communication style and its image – as with the issues it raises or the generic appeal of environmentalism. In Latin America and Eastern Europe in particular, the crumbling of repressive structures and the tentative moves towards more open and free societies have blended well with Greenpeace's use of information and images as its weapons of choice in the struggle for change. In those uncertain and often dangerous contexts, Greenpeace has carved out a fairly secure operating space by conveying the issues in much the same way that it did during its first campaign against the Amchitka nuclear test. The classic Greenpeace approach of trying to strip the issues of their ideological baggage, of trying to reach the broadest possible cross-section of people by appealing to self-interest, national pride, and common sense, seems to have become – in some of Greenpeace's newer venues of operation – an essential ingredient not just of success but of survival.

Marcie Mersky, co-ordinator of the new Central American office based in Guatemala City, says that in the region where she works there's a need not just to accentuate the mainstream, universal aspects of the issues, but also to downplay the confrontational tactics that Greenpeace has traditionally used.

"In Central America there's a very long history of internal civil wars, of repression, of political violence, and that of course makes the environment very complicated in terms of how we're perceived, in terms of how we work," she says, squeezing a few minutes of conversation into the space before an 8:30 a.m. meeting at the New York City office. "Actions that may involve minimal risk in the United States or in Germany may involve enormous risk for us. And so we've had to tailor how we make decisions to these conditions. But we're moving forward."

While the authoritarian traditions of most Central American nations have for the most part precluded the use of civil disobedience and other confrontational techniques, Mersky says they have not stopped Greenpeace from making effective use of the news media as a device to pressure politicians to adopt pro-environmental policies. I found this a surprising claim, given the common conception that neither the press nor the electorate in most of Central America has the clout to influence policy. The majority of countries in Central America are, after all, considered by most people to be merely nominal democracies, where elected politicians perform the rituals of governing but true power remains in the hands of the military and shadowy death-squads. A free press is not a long-established tradition in these countries: newspaper stories that challenge the established order or the interests of the wealthy have been known to win their authors a trip into exile or a bullet in the head.

But when I asked Marcie Mersky whether the historical absence of strong civilian institutions had limited the effectiveness of Greenpeace's campaigns in Central America, she responded that, on the contrary, the current resolve to fortify those institutions had put Greenpeace in the right place at the right time. Since the Esquipulas peace plans had committed Central American nations to democratize, many people within those societies have been searching for ways to stretch the "democratic openings" mandated by the peace accords, to establish free and open civil institutions by putting the rhetoric of democracy and freedom into practice. Environmental issues provided just such an opportunity to strengthen civilian authority and democratic accountability by setting practical tasks for those institutions.

According to Mersky, the environmental agenda challenges governments and legal systems to take action in response to public pressure, but at the same time the challenges it presents are sufficiently mainstream and apparently "apolitical" enough not to prompt a crackdown by the military. This process, she says, benefits not only the environment but also contributes to the democratic growth of society by helping to strengthen the rule of law.

"I think there's a very strong movement throughout the region in favour of having laws obeyed," Mersky says. "In the midst of civil war, legal systems disintegrated, judicial systems disintegrated, and in a number of countries in the region people are actively involved trying to reweave those systems. Having functioning courts and functioning laws is a really significant part of constructing any kind of democratic society. So I think in the arena of environmental legislation and activism – which I see as going hand in hand – it's kind of one piece of the reconstruction of society. We can make a contribution around solving specific environmental problems, and at the same time we can help move these societies forward."

That's not to say that the environmental issues raised by Greenpeace are themselves peripheral or insignificant. Mersky reports that in its first two years of operation Greenpeace's Central American office helped expose over fifty schemes to import and dump toxic waste in the region, and now none of those plans have been able to proceed because of public opposition. This success comes despite limited resources and person-power. Mersky (an American, and one of the few foreigners to be parachuted into Latin America, given Greenpeace's decision to staff its new offices with local people) oversees an office in which a minimal staff co-ordinates activities in seven countries, and that relies heavily upon its contacts with a network of grassroots environmental groups in the region. But the power of Greenpeace and its allies has been magnified by their facility for circulating information. News reports on toxic trading schemes have touched raw nerves and activated public opinion.

"What we've found," Mersky explains, "is that trying to dump garbage – and particularly hazardous garbage – on poor countries is seen as morally unacceptable throughout the region. So our experience has been that, if we can find out about these proposals, and get them to the press, and get them to public opinion, in fact they can be stopped."

And so, in a way that's strikingly similar to the Amchitka campaign, Greenpeace's new office in Central America has (two decades later) built a successful strategy around the appeal to national pride, to a sense of sovereignty and moral rectitude that transcends class divisions and ideological disputes. Mersky says that the deeply polarized politics of Central American nations has not been a significant factor in its campaign against toxic waste importation.

"It's been a very good entry issue," she says, "because nobody's going to get up and defend waste trade. No government is going to say 'We want the trash of the First World to build our countries on.' And so you have a lot of potential allies on this issue. At the same time, we've been able to raise other toxic issues around this one soft issue."

By Mersky's account, Greenpeace won a foothold in Central America partly by appealing to the vanity of local elites, who don't want their countries seen as the dustbins of the industrialized world. According to Ricardo Wilson-Grau, this is not the only way in which Greenpeace has secured some operating space within a repressive political environment. Wilson-Grau is a Guatemalan human rights monitor who signed on with Greenpeace International in Amsterdam – working on the toxic trade issue – but left the organization after a protracted dispute. Sometime before the New York City conference (and before his departure from Greenpeace) he explained to me that the very nature of toxic trade as a North-South issue helps avoid head-on political conflict; that to avoid pointing the finger of blame entirely at local authorities, who tend to react violently to such challenges by civilian groups, Greenpeace had consciously adopted an issue in which culpability lies partly in Northern countries. Wilson-Grau said the danger of not allowing those in power the chance to skirt blame is illustrated by Greenpeace's anti-nuclear campaigns in the southern cone of Latin America: when Greenpeace began campaigning directly against nuclear power and nuclear-powered submarines in Brazil and Argentina, it began receiving death threats.

Still, Marijane Vieira Lisboa, a Brazilian sociologist who took on the job of co-ordinating Greenpeace's toxic substances campaign in Latin America, believes that Greenpeace's clear public image as an organization committed to non-violence provides it with some kind of protection. In the countries she works in – again, not known for their democratic traditions or political stability – Greenpeace has not had problems with the armies, police, or governments. "They see us as a different type of organization," she says – that is, different from dissident groups, other non-governmental organizations, or civil pressure bodies. Lisboa's colleague and fellow Brazilian, regional anti-nuclear co-ordinator R. de Goes, isn't so sure about how sturdy a shield a strong media image can be, but he's sanguine about the threat of reprisals. When the topic comes up he simply shrugs and says, "It's all just a part of the job."

Latin America is not the only place where a new climate of political opportunity and change has enabled Greenpeace to apply its communications-based strategy to good effect. In Greece the experience of dictatorship is further back in the public memory, and the dangers of political activism are not as overt. Still, just as in Latin America, Greece is home not only to a growing public impulse to open up a closed political environment but also to a new awareness of ecological issues. The convergence of those two factors has again been fruitful.

Stelios Psomas, toxics and oil campaigner from Greenpeace's new office in Athens, tells a story that is strikingly similar to Marcie Mersky's accounts. Psomas believes that Greenpeace became the most popular NGO in Greece only a year after the May 1991 opening of the Athens office, mostly because of its effectiveness in forcing elected officials to respond to negative publicity. Like the experience in Central America, Greenpeace's investigation and publication of the environmental damage created by oil companies in Greece have focused public outrage and forced governments to respond. In this sense, Psomas believes, Greenpeace's impact on Greece extends beyond the environmental agenda and into the functioning of the political system.

Psomas believes that Greenpeace has helped to open up "new spaces" for civil rights. "After some actions we had against the oil industry, it was the first time in Greece that both the industry and the authorities were obliged to start a public discussion about certain things. And it was the first time that environmental impact assessments made by industry were really confronted, even on a technical basis." As in previous campaigns, Greenpeace took complex, technical issues and framed them in ways that made them important – and understandable – to ordinary people.

"We really believe that information is the key," Psomas says. "Nobody can really judge what is right or wrong if he or she is unaware of the problem itself." Another factor, he says, is that people in Greece – like elsewhere – don't trust the political parties any more. So instead of the "big words and the language that politicians use" Greenpeace spokespeople use "very plain, simple language" and take an "everyday approach" to get to the core of the problems.

The effusive progress reports from Marcie Mersky in Central America and Stelios Psomas in Greece show how Marshall McLuhan's prediction of a generation ago – that information flow was becoming as tangible a political force as guns and money – has indeed come to pass. But the chief impact of this reality is not how communications systems have remodelled the political landscape within individual nations, but that nations themselves have taken on different roles within this new world system, where information flows across borders without restriction. It follows from this that the success of Greenpeace as an international movement should be judged not by its ability to capture public attention in particular countries, but by how effectively it operates between and across national borders.

Marcie Mersky is convinced that Greenpeace has scored well by this test as well. She cites an example involving a chloralkaline chemical plant called El Pesa, in Managua, Nicaragua, as an illustration of how the organization has put together a formidable transnational machine that can routinely match the moves of its corporate nemeses. After a twenty-year campaign against the plant – which dumped toxic chemicals into Lake Managua, one of the most polluted bodies of water in the world – the local community was finally successful in having the plant ordered closed. Then the company announced that it would stay open, thanks to new technology being imported from the North that would clean up the plant.

Through connections with unions in the United States, Greenpeace found out that equipment from an Olin Chemical company plant in Niagara Falls, New York, was being shipped to Central America; a little cross-referencing then led to the conclusion that the Olin technology was destined for El Pesa. "What we discovered was the Olin technology was actually older and dirtier, and would have made the situation worse," Mersky says. Armed with this knowledge, Greenpeace helped the local community keep the closing order in place and subsequently countered the company's PR line when it attempted to move the Olin technology into Honduras and later into Guatemala.

In this one case, Greenpeace won an immediate victory by blocking a company's attempt to deceive the public into allowing it to reopen a dirty and dangerous plant. But Mersky believes that the most lasting impact of this episode is that it helped refine a new process of transnational work; that citizens in the North and the South responded together to deal with the problem, based on a mutual understanding that toxic waste is a global issue. She feels that this type of co-operation will be essential in the future; that in order to deal with an industrial machine that's at home in both North and South, citizens' groups must be tuned in and functioning harmoniously on both sides of the divide.

If you only apply pressure points in the North, Mersky says, "There's no accountability in the South – in the receiving countries, there's no public knowledge of the problem." What you have to do, in the long term, she says, is "build up partnerships of peoples across the planet who have to work together to solve these problems together, and to build the kind of knowledge and activism around issues in Southern countries that really need to transform those societies and the way they relate to and use the environment." This is the aim, and the potential of Greenpeace as a "budding international organization" – "this one-two combo of North and South working together."

Despite Mersky's glowing report on North-South co-operation within Greenpeace, some critics argue that its increased geographic scope has led to an organizational nightmare and horrific misunderstandings. The organization hasn't had a rational process of growth, they say, to ease the transition from a small, tightly knit band of zealots (usually engaged in no more than one campaign at a time) to a multinational, multi-issue NGO working on a series of overlapping and sometimes conflicting efforts.

Originally the organization was structured as a group of autonomous campaigning cells, which were given a budget and carte blanche to achieve their goals without a cabal of managers looking over their shoulders. But a huge increase in cash flow after the French government's sinking of the *Rainbow Warrior* in Auckland Harbour in 1985 led to two contradictory and generally destructive developments, according to insiders. The first was that a corporate hierarchy began to rob the campaigns of their spontaneity. The second was that the way in which decisions were made did not change to fit the new circumstances. Managers continued to make decisions casually, like old friends around a kitchen table.

According to Greenpeace's international ozone co-ordinator Mike Affleck, whom I met about a year after the New York skill-sharing sessions and a few hundred miles upstate in his home in a suburb of Syracuse, the people who were making the decisions were often not qualified to lead a multimillion-dollar organization.

"The problem of Greenpeace," says Affleck, reflecting on the organizational crisis gripping the organization at that time, "has been that the people who had the imagination and hard work and dedication and creativity to get the organization to the point where they were ready to sail into a French nuclear test zone were not the kind of people, by inclination, training, or any other measure, to handle an organization that was getting millions and millions of dollars in support and had legions of new staff and volunteers on a worldwide basis. And so what they did was say that anyone who came up with a good idea could start a campaign. There was money, so the analysis grew, and the campaigns and research activities and all sorts of stuff just exploded all over the place."

But while Greenpeace was doing more things in more places, and thinking about bigger issues on grander scales, the way it was organized remained the same as when everybody knew each other and had regular personal contact. After the rapid expansion of the post-1985 period there were no objective processes of evaluation put in place and no co-ordinated structures for decision-making. Insecurities began to grow because decisions, and value judgements, continued to be made on the basis of an indecipherable system of personal allegiances, old habits, and the privileges that come with longest tenure.

"Organizational theory is just about worth the paper it's printed on, when it comes to Greenpeace," Affleck says. "You'd have decisions being made on the basis of personal relationships, money, backroom deals, personality conflicts – that kind of stuff. Absolutely the worst combination of managerial efforts that you could imagine."

Several problems arose from this increasingly labyrinthine and irrational style of organization, and campaign gridlock was one. To undertake any action or to initiate an activity, Affleck says, campaigners had to run a gauntlet of involved officials whose territories all overlapped and whose interests had not been placed within any meaningful hierarchy of priorities. According to Affleck, if he, as an international co-ordinator, planned to do an action at a chemical plant in the south of France, he would have to get the permission of the Mediterranean co-ordinator, the executive director of Greenpeace France, the French ozone campaign leader, as well as people in marine services, communications, and the direct-actions department – all of whom might resent the competition for attention with their own activities.

"To do one thing you have to get all these people to agree," Affleck says. "The problem is that you will get equal and opposite messages; messages that are diametrically opposed but have equal organizational weight. So someone will say 'save money' and someone else will say 'take a chance.' Someone will say 'increase your flexibility,' and someone will say 'you didn't get my permission.' Someone will say 'you didn't check with the Greenpeace media department,' but we ended up getting a front-page story, so we were a media success.

"So you will be criticized for a failure and praised for a success at the same time. And so you're always in conflict within the organization because nobody knows who has the most authority. The media people think they're most important because everything, finally, is a media story. The direct-action people think they're most important because they take the risks. The finance department thinks they're more important because we're going to go broke. When nobody can figure it out they pass it over to the national offices just to get rid of the problem."

Affleck also believes that the huge (and some said, potentially fatal) fight in the 1990s over how financial cuts should fall can also be traced to the disorganized manner in which Greenpeace grew following the sinking of *Rainbow Warrior*. According to Affleck, an inherently unstable situation was made worse by the fact that Greenpeace didn't have the talent to expand in any other way but ad hoc. And despite the fact that some of the organization's most important work was being done in Latin America, Affleck questions whether the entrenched Greenpeace leadership back in Europe and the United States had been completely committed to the Southerners who joined in the late 1980s.

Certainly, the peculiar organizational structure would have worked to keep them apart: with the old friendship-based power network still intact – the newcomers tenuously connected to it by such impersonal media as e-mail – the necessary bonds of trust and understanding had little opportunity to grow, he says. And given that Greenpeace had ventured into new territory partly out of the desperate need to absorb surplus cash flow, Affleck wonders whether the idea of Greenpeace as an international organization remained a practical construct more than a deep-seated ideal. "Is there an intrinsic commitment to a kind of worldwide effort, or was that only the result of the financial ability to explore those areas and persuasive arguments to do it? As soon as the money goes, do the ideas go too? I get no sense that Greenpeace USA feels they should split half their money with Greenpeace Latin America and be assured that the organization there is the same. When it comes down to it, it's 'screw 'em. We'll take care of our own business. We've got enough to do here.'"

The changes that have taken place within Greenpeace in two decades had become obvious to me several minutes after arriving at the New York City Greenpeace office. An infusion of young blood and the arrival new voices from outside of Greenpeace's original terrain had given the organization a new take on the world and remodelled its agenda. But what's less obvious to the outsider is the factors that constrain that wave of change and work against that new agenda being carried to its logical conclusion.

Greenpeacers will hint at this – mostly when the tape recorders have been switched off and the conversation has turned casual – by referring euphemistically to the "vigorous debate" that routinely erupts between segments of the Greenpeace world. Tales of these "stimulating" and "useful" clashes inevitably pit the Third World newcomers and the young, urban North Americans – the most enthusiastic supporters within Greenpeace of a new, socially defined brand of environmentalism – against the older, more prosperous, and more conservative burgers of Western Europe.

Those two sides do not necessarily debate from an equal footing. Just as at the United Nations across town, merely being at the table doesn't necessarily mean you get to make decisions. Most people within Greenpeace agree that the real power centre of the organization lies across the Atlantic Ocean, in industrialized Western European nations like Germany, England, and the Netherlands. The organization, like any other, has a power differential based on wealth, history, political cunning, and accumulated prestige – and, alongside the campaigns and media interaction, that power differential began making waves in the 1990s.

Clearly, by the time of the UNCED conference, Greenpeace had arrived at a historical crossroads. Years of screaming about environmental threats had succeeded in increasing public awareness and led to a new and fundamental question: what to do about it? By taking that question seriously – by pondering not just the problems but also potential, systemic solutions – Greenpeace had come face to face with the massive, thorny, and clearly divisive questions of how the very structure of human affairs was promoting environmental destruction and how that could be changed. This raised yet another basic problem at a tactical, strategic level: was it possible to take a much more sophisticated and encompassing approach to the environment and still command a mass following?

CHAPTER 4

GLOBAL VILLAGE OR DIVIDED
PLANET?

PAUL HOHNEN MARVELS AT THE POWER BASE THAT
Greenpeace has built in Europe. By his own self-description, as an
"older, more conservative creature more at home in a suit and a
stripy tie," Hohnen comes across as a bit of an anomaly within
Greenpeace. An eighteen-year veteran of the Australian foreign service, he worked as that country's representative to the Organization
for Economic Co-operation and Development (OECD) before
becoming political director of Greenpeace International (in charge of
ozone and atmosphere policy) at its headquarters in Amsterdam – a
posting that places him close to the geographic centre of Greenpeace's core of support.

Since the days when he stalked the halls of Old World power on
Australia's behalf, Hohnen has been a keen student of the European
psyche. He is still amazed at how well Greenpeace can speak to the
anxieties and aspirations of urban Europe. West Germany, he reports,
has been the bedrock of Greenpeace's European support, both financially and in terms of membership numbers. But in per capita terms
the Netherlands provides the most remarkable illustration of the
kind of political clout Greenpeace has developed in Europe. In the
Netherlands more than eight hundred thousand of the country's fifteen million people are Greenpeace supporters – a ratio suggesting
that one in five Dutch households contains a Greenpeace supporter,
which would make the organization more popular than any one of
Holland's fourteen political parties.

Those same elements that made Greenpeace a sensation in Vancouver in 1971 remain central to Greenpeace campaigns and are key
to its popularity in Europe: the campaigns are still scripted to high-
light conflict, drama, and environmental self-interest, and to appear
mainstream and practical. Hohnen marvels at Greenpeace's continued ability to tailor its media images to fit the public mood.

I met Hohnen during those same 1993 skill-sharing sessions in
New York, in the hotel where Greenpeace had warehoused its conference participants – a less-than-elegant structure just off Times
Square with pipes visible on the ceilings and an elevator that
laboured arthritically up to the sixth floor. The reason that Greenpeace is more popular than most political parties, Hohnen tells me,
is that it has perfected the art of communicating with Europe's infor-
mation-saturated, television-addicted, and increasingly anxious population. "Television," Hohnen says, "has limited not only the NGOs,
but also the politicians, to effectively thirty-second advertisements –
sound bites. Unless you can say it in one sentence people don't listen; the attention span has gone down."

For years Greenpeace had used much the same effective formula,
of combining dramatic visuals (like having people hang off
smokestacks, or buzzing a nuclear warship in rubber dinghies) in
conjunction with short, exclamatory slogans. "The actions were full
of life and vitality," Hohnen says. The media could focus on the simple message "of David going up against Goliath." The messages tend
to be crisp and precise: Halt Global Warming, Halt CFC Production
Now, Stop Whaling. "I think people are sick of longer, hollow messages from politicians that are seen to contain very little in terms of
commitment."

But Greenpeace's appeal in Europe is a matter of psychology as
well as style. Hohnen feels Europe has been receptive to Greenpeace's
environmental messages because they touch on the practical concerns
of urban Europeans. The continent's long history of industrialization –
along with its dense population and limited land mass – has made ecological issues immediately felt. "People have come to terms with the
reality that there is no 'away' as far as waste is concerned," Hohnen
says. "That the waste you throw into your backyard is in the frontyard
of somebody else. The River Rhine is the perfect example of that,
where the French and the Swiss and the Germans have been throwing
rubbish into the River Rhine for a long time, and by the time it gets to
Holland you can develop your film in it."

Europeans therefore see their own self-interest tied up with environmental concerns, so Greenpeace today doesn't have to look far afield to demonstrate the public's stake in the issue – it doesn't have to amplify, for instance, scientific speculation about a nuclear-triggered tidal wave, as it did during the Amchitka campaign. With ecological concerns so immediately felt, Greenpeace doesn't have to work all that hard to portray itself as an agent of common sense and conventional wisdom, rather than as a collection of radical ecological kooks. Hohnen describes Greenpeace's European support base as middle class and mainstream. Although Greenpeace's popularity in Europe grew in the 1980s in sync with the rise of the anti-nuclear, anti-Cruise missile movement, Hohnen believes that the two movements had only a few "co-travellers" in common, and that Greenpeace supporters are generally more conservative in outlook.

Certainly, Hohnen's explanation of why he left the Australian foreign service to take up a lobbying position at Greenpeace ties in nicely with Greenpeace's European appeal to a conservative constituency. Just like the first Greenpeace brigade, which was seen by the Canadian media as struggling on behalf of Canadian sovereignty, Hohnen speaks of himself (and by extension, of the organization that hired him) as patriotic rather than subversive.

"I suppose the motive that brought me to Greenpeace," he says, "was the same impulse that brought me to the foreign service in the first place. That is: a perception of a certain national interest and the desire to protect that national interest. It became clear to me in my work over the years in the OECD and the European community that the national interest was not only threatened by strategic or economic events in the external world, but increasingly by environmental degradation. With global issues such as ozone depletion and global warming, the Australian national interest – and indeed, the interests of all countries in the world – was increasingly and compellingly being threatened."

By aligning itself with a mainstream and broadly defined "national interest," Greenpeace won huge public support and a degree of media credibility, which have, in turn, given it significant political clout over national and international environmental issues.

Yet the danger for an organization that chooses to dwell in the fantasy kingdom of Western media culture is that it could wind up – in subtle ways, perhaps – propagating the assumptions and ideals of that culture and shying away from positions that might challenge or offend its target audience; that it begins to take on the characteristics of the mass media that it had sought to exploit. By portraying itself in Europe as a mainstream organization with a non-controversial agenda for the middle classes, Greenpeace risks downplaying ideas that *are* controversial and confrontational: the idea, for instance, that systemic solutions to environmental problems require an overhaul of the world's economic system and a new division of wealth, a position that enjoys considerable support within Greenpeace but generally doesn't play well on the television networks of industrialized nations.

By packaging environmental issues as short dramas for the nightly news – with the self-interest of potential donors inevitably presented as an underlying theme – Greenpeace may inadvertently be reinforcing the chauvinist notion among affluent television-watchers in the North that it is they who are the victims of environmental atrocities committed elsewhere. If it's true that there needs to be a change in the attitudes and behaviour of the people in the industrialized North – the people who consume most of the world's resources – then maybe it is more appropriate to launch an all-out challenge to those attitudes and behaviours.

★ ★ ★

Some insiders will tell you that there *have* been times when Greenpeace's smart packaging of an issue has created a stir in the Northern media but at the same time distorted the broader social and political context of the issue. One such example is still fresh in the mind of Kay Treakle, a fifteen-year Greenpeace veteran who left in 1991 to work for the Washington-based Bank Information Centre, a watchdog group monitoring the World Bank. Treakle's association with Greenpeace began in the late 1970s in Seattle when, she recalls, a "merry band of activists from Canada" – who were at the time campaigning against Russian whaling – "brought their dumpy little boat into port and gave tours and showed films, and it was all very exciting." After signing on as a volunteer at the Seattle office, she went on to work on international campaigns against nuclear weapons and nuclear power.

In the mid-1980s Treakle returned to school to earn a degree in agricultural ecology, an accomplishment that, it turned out, made her the right person to take the reigns when Greenpeace decided, in

1987, to launch a new agriculture campaign focusing on pesticide use in Third World countries. The campaign, it was decided, would apply Greenpeace's media expertise in support of the research and lobbying work already being done by groups like the Pesticide Action Network.[1] Treakle recalls that the proposed campaign was contentious: many Greenpeacers were wary of launching a land-based effort that left Greenpeace's rag-tag "navy" with no role, while others were nervous that this first foray into the South would take Greenpeace into strange territory, a place with unfamiliar ground rules and political customs. Ultimately, though, Greenpeace decided that it would campaign against the use of dangerous pesticides in the Third World by focusing on the Northern actors that promoted their use, such as the financial institutions promoting pesticide-dependent agricultural schemes and the Northern-based companies exporting the actual product.

One of the first goals of Greenpeace's pesticide campaign was to achieve a ban on the export of hazardous agricultural chemicals from the United States to the Third World. And so – even though this was one of the first campaigns that took Greenpeace to a new terrain outside the club of industrialized nations – it still centred on American public opinion and political processes, because the goal was to change U.S. law. Over time, Treakle recalls, the necessity of crafting a public relations strategy to suit the U.S. public mood – and especially to enable the issue to play well within the theatre of congressional politics – would drastically rearrange a story that the campaigners, at the outset, had seen as a tale with clear villains and victims, a straightforward story line, and an obvious moral imperative.

"The original intent of the campaign," Treakle says, "was to look at pesticide exports – in particular the exports from the North of pesticides that are banned or severely restricted or not even registered for use in Northern industrialized countries. But they are exported and used in the South under pretty bad conditions with very little regulation and very little, if any, worker protection in the field." In the Third World, Treakle says, somewhere between 100,000 and 200,000 pesticide poisonings were occurring every year, which included about 20,000 pesticide-related deaths.

This tragedy, she explains, did not arise accidentally, but was the result of policies consciously adopted in the North: "Pesticide producers, the manufacturers, are out in the rural areas," she says, "with big promotion packages saying 'miracle drugs, just use these and all your problems will be gone.' For us, it was a moral issue: if these pesticides are banned in industrialized countries – if they are banned because they are carcinogenic or they cause birth defects or they are acutely toxic – then why are we sending them south?"

But moral issues – so the information experts say, and so Greenpeace was prepared to accept – would not play well in the North American mass media. There had to be some appeal to public self-interest – to back-home concerns – to get the attention of assignment editors and television news producers and to reach out to public opinion. In the case of the pesticide campaign, public opinion was particularly important, since the centrepiece of the effort was a bill before the U.S. Congress seeking to ban toxic pesticide exports from the United States. The script doctors were duly called in, and the pesticide issue was rewritten in a way to make it fly on the nightly news.

The blunt response to the issue of the politicos on Capitol Hill, according to Treakle, was that Americans don't care about the Third World. "What they care about is their own skin or their own backyard issues or their interest in the matter. So it was basically because of that – because we wanted to get the legislation passed – that we began to look at issues called the 'circle of poison.' What that says is basically that 'we sell pesticides to farmers in developing countries that are banned here, and those farmers use the pesticides on food that's grown for export, which then finds its way back to our dinner tables.' While this is a legitimate issue, it's just hard to play it that way knowing that the interpretation will be that the enemy is the Third World farmer, not the producer who sells the stuff overseas, or not U.S. law that allows this practice to continue."

Kay Treakle disagrees with the premise (which most media gatekeepers use as a yardstick to judge whether a story is newsworthy) that public outrage can only be aroused when self-interest is at stake: the whole American civil rights movement, she says, depended upon white society's altruistic feelings for another social group. But when it came to getting the anti-pesticide message out, Treakle and her associates agreed that they would have to play by the accepted rules of the game, which in this case meant casting American consumers in the lead role in this little drama.

The result was that, by the time the media began to report on the "circle of poison" issue, reality had been turned upside down: the victims were now the culprits, and the villains were the victims. The story was no longer a case of the United States creating problems for the Third World by exporting pesticides banned at home; but of Americans being targets of yet another sinister international conspiracy. While there was initially an opportunity to understand more about the environmental problems faced by people in the Third World, it had soon been turned into an opportunity for more xenophobia.

"During the period that the legislation was being introduced," Kay Treakle recalls, "there was quite a bit of coverage, and really it was funny, people would call us up and say 'Could you explain how much residue is on the food? What kind of food? Where does it come from?' The questions were not, 'How many farmers were poisoned? Do you know any examples?' and so on. So I think the tendency here is to look at the story from the point of view of the Northern consumer. That kind of angle, and that kind of thinking – that 'it's the Third World farmers' fault, because they're sending us food that's poisoned' – I think it can feed a certain attitude in Americans that is unhealthy and unhelpful and is wrong."

Despite her lingering discomfort over how the narrative conventions of the Northern media reframed the pesticide issue, Treakle remained associated with Greenpeace long enough to see it transformed into an organization in which context – the big picture – had become as important as the immediate goals of campaigns. Treakle – like others I've talked to – attributes this change to the opening of new offices in the Third World and the recruitment of Southern staff, who tend to view the world and its problems through a different historical lens than the Europeans and the North Americans. In Latin America – where most of Greenpeace's new offices are located – environmental issues are rarely discussed separately from economic and political issues. The common assumption there is that environmental destruction has been encouraged and exacerbated by an economic crisis, a world trading system, and a model of economic development that has forced Southern countries to ravage their environments in the quest to earn the hard currency that would allow them to pay off their debts and restart their economies.

According to Josh Karliner, the head of Greenpeace's delegation to the 1992 UNCED conference in Rio, the opening of the new Southern bureaus beginning in the late 1980s has had an impact upon the perspective of Greenpeace as a whole. "The great thing about

Greenpeace is that we're beginning to hear different voices within our own organizational structure," he says. "Unlike some other environmental groups, when we take on an issue that involves the South, we have offices in the South that are run by people from those areas, and they tell us what the issue means on the ground."

At the Earth Summit, Greenpeace's new fixation with the economic and historical underpinnings of eco-destruction was abundantly evident. For a brief instant Greenpeace moved away from its traditional style of campaigning: in place of the simple slogans, arresting media stunts, and snapshot summaries of the issues were complex and intricately reasoned tomes on such abstract, difficult, and profoundly unglamorous issues as Third World debt, the mandates and philosophical biases of such institutions as the World Bank and International Monetary Fund (IMF), and the anti-environmental structure of the international trading system. One publication, *Beyond UNCED*, exemplified the new style and approach. The book has no snappy photos or wildlife shots, and the text deals with broad issues in a way that demands patience and concentration; long historical preambles and definitions of terms have replaced the short, pithy slogans that Greenpeace was famous for.

The objectives outlined in *Beyond UNCED* are similarly ambitious, amorphous, and quite unlikely to arouse any self-interested concerns amongst the news media or the general public in the affluent North. The book calls for the cancellation of the Third World debt (which it says is far outweighed by the debt owed to the South by the North, by virtue of centuries of resource plunder). It calls for the radical reform of the international trading system and for increasing the level of citizen political participation in everything from international trade panels to civic governments. These moves, it suggests, will increase the power of citizens to protect the environments that sustain them and will make decision-making agencies more accountable.

Yet despite its migration to loftier intellectual ground at Rio, Greenpeace was still unmistakably Greenpeace: an anti-authoritarian and audacious outfit that couldn't resist thumbing its nose at the powerful. Josh Karliner says his most enduring memory of Rio was when Greenpeace invited some Brazilian street kids onto the famous Greenpeace ship *Rainbow Warrior* for a tour – a gesture of openness starkly distinct from the mood of the assembly of world leaders and bureaucrats across town, whose festival of pomp and privilege was cordoned off from real life by an impenetrable shield of military might.

Kay Treakle believes that Greenpeace made a major contribution at the UNCED conference by countering a massive corporate PR blitz that at points had been threatening to turn the meetings into a huge propaganda fest for multinationals suddenly transformed into evangelists of green. One publication, *The Greenpeace Book of Greenwash*, offered detailed dossiers on how many of the highly visible transnationals at UNCED were scamming the media by (among other things) shifting dirty business out of the media-saturated North and into the South, through bogus "recycling" schemes and other means. Treakle also feels that Greenpeace – with its international character and its new fluency in the political vernacular of both North and South – played an effective role as liaison between Southern NGOs and Northern environmentalists.

Yet even though Greenpeace was a valuable presence at UNCED, Treakle says its role and approach were highly contentious within the organization itself. Many people, she says, were concerned that Greenpeace was starting down a path that would carry significant political costs. For in addressing vast and contentious political and economic issues, Greenpeace was turning its back on a long-successful public relations strategy: of focusing on specific, attainable goals; of campaigning on issues easily understood and conveyed in the pictorial language of television; of staying away from political controversies or ideological debates in which the organization could lose public sympathy. Treakle says the split over these issues, true to form, pitted the Europeans – who worried about policy approaches that undermined their (highly marketable) public face as a politically non-partisan and eminently reasonable organization – against Greenpeacers from North, South, and Central America, and from New Zealand and Australia. It's the difference, Treakle says, of looking at one specific environmental issue – say, "where one particular transnational corporation is producing a particular kind of chemical that is inherently deadly" – and looking at the larger "root causes of problems."

Admidst this geographic split, policy people – who felt they were merely following environmental issues to their logical conclusions – also clashed with Greenpeace's fundraising and marketing staff, who wanted pointed images and clear-cut issues that would put money in the bank. The fundraisers and PR wizards saw concerns such as

Third World debt, the power of multinational corporations or the World Bank, or the nature of the GATT treaty as a publicist's worst nightmare. To sell these issues to the public, Treakle says, a bumper sticker that said something like "Save the Whales, Forgive the Debt" wouldn't work. The connection Greenpeace could make between those issues would be "nebulous to most people."

"Greenpeace had always dealt with specific environmental problems," Treakle says. "There is an incinerator and it's going to be built in your backyard, and it's going to dump dioxin into your atmosphere, and it will get into your drinking water and your soil and so on. Very concrete issues had been addressed by the organization, that were, I guess you could say, very black and white. The issues that were developed around the UNCED process were not black and white. They're very complicated."

It is much easier to raise alarm bells than it is to draw a detailed road map out of a crisis. Fear, anger, and the sense of personal threat or impending doom are much more compelling forces for most people than abstract arguments and political programs. Many insiders believe that the source of Greenpeace's power is its ability to make the issues *personal*. And they are reluctant to move away from their forte.

★ ★ ★

Long after the UNCED conference faded from public memory, this basic conundrum continues to challenge environmentalists. The issues, post-Rio, remain complex. Many campaigners in Greenpeace are convinced that to be effective in the coming years, environmentalists have to move the ecological debate to higher ground. "I am convinced," Greenpeace USA director Barbara Dudley says, "that the nexus between economics and environment is a crucial issue that we have to resolve as we move into the next century."

The creation of Greenpeace International's economics unit, a think-tank branch of the organization dedicated to exploring the relationship between fiscal flow and environmental fiascos, shows that Dudley's view is widely endorsed within the organization. There may be deep divisions as to whether this unit should be looking at how to manage the microeconomic connections between specific trade arrangements, business activities, and environmental problems, or whether it would have more impact by questioning the environmental friendliness of our economic system as a whole. But there is little disagreement that economics is far too vast a subject to be comfortably squeezed into twenty-second sound bites and some striking visuals on the television news. And so, while Greenpeace activists gush about the need to push forward onto this new frontier of environmental economics, their work in that area proceeds very much in the background, overshadowed by issues that are flashier and more easily understood and less likely to create controversy and dissent.

Michael M'Gonigle, a long-time Greenpeace activist, isn't surprised that Greenpeace has been shy about publicizing its interest in economics. The subject "poses tactical problems for every environmental organization," he says, "and it certainly poses tactical problems for Greenpeace." The major risk, M'Gonigle believes, is that environmentalists will fracture their broad following as they delve into the deeper questions of "why?" and "how?" It's the matter of specific issues and political boundaries again. "Whether you're a Communist or a capitalist, you can like whales. You can want whaling to stop," M'Gonigle says. But if you go beyond this to get into "structural causes, or root causes of problems," it makes you look political, look like you are allied with sectoral political interests.

When M'Gonigle refers to people who want to save whales – not because of any political judgement but simply for the love of whales – he is actually referring to himself. He recalls being entranced by whales ever since he was a small boy growing up on the Pacific coast of Canada; and the whaling issue first drew him to Greenpeace. M'Gonigle remembers the day in 1976 when he walked into the original Greenpeace office on Fourth Avenue in Vancouver and offered to put his academic training in international law and political economy to use by representing Greenpeace before the International Whaling Commission (IWC). It took the three Greenpeace organizers in the office at the time – Patrick Moore, Paul Spong, and Bob Hunter – about ten minutes to decide on accepting his offer. The result was that Greenpeace plunged into the diplomatic arena, with M'Gonigle serving as the organization's chief arm-twister at the IWC from 1977 until the early 1980s, at which time a whaling moratorium was imposed. M'Gonigle left Greenpeace International in the mid-1980s, but returned at the end of that decade to serve as volunteer chair of the board of Greenpeace Canada.

Yet while M'Gonigle's motivations for joining the environmental

movement were at first personal and apolitical – based solely on his
love of whales – today he is adamant that environmentalists must
stand for more than this. To have an impact on the global dynamics
driving ecological destruction, he argues, they must be clear about
the economic and political forces at work. These are questions
M'Gonigle now spends much of his time pondering. Employed as
professor of resource management at Simon Fraser University in
Vancouver, M'Gonigle spends a big chunk of his time out of reach of
phones and fax machines on a secluded section of Vancouver Island,
contemplating and writing about the intricate and arcane connections between ecology, economics, and political life.

His work now is not the stuff of a Greenpeace media stunt.
Indeed, some of the themes M'Gonigle writes about are barely popular enough to reach the newspaper op-ed pages. In 1991, for
instance, M'Gonigle cast his sights on Canadian politicians' attempts
to hammer out a new constitution. Skirting the mainstream public
debates about the respective roles of the English and French "founding nations" in Canada, M'Gonigle instead advised the federal and
provincial governments to take a broader view and rethink some key
assumptions underlying Western liberal democracy, such as the sepa-
ration of economic and political life that allows the global economy
to develop unrestrained by the civil ideals defined in political consti-
tutions; and the definition of the liberal state as merely a collection
of free and autonomous individuals. M'Gonigle posited that the
Canadian constitutional debate – as dry as it may have appeared to
most in the outside world – was of clear significance to all those
environmentalists whose utopian visions of a green society grew
from the conceptual soil of "bioregionalism" and decentralization.
Canada could take a practical step towards giving those concepts a
place in the real world, M'Gonigle believed, by crafting a new constitution that recognized the rights not just of individuals but of
communities, which gave those communities some control over the
resources they depend upon, and which made the big players in the
economic sphere (who under free trade have been given virtually
limitless power) more accountable to the citizenry and subject to
local regulation.[2]

After challenging the politicians with this notion of an "eco-con-
stitution" at the beginning of the decade, M'Gonigle has since co-
authored *Forestopia: A Practical Guide to the New Forest Economy*, a significantly less abstract exhortation to change that envisions the

replacement of British Columbia's current resource-based economy (an economy that chews up primeval old-growth forests such as Clayoquot Sound, while simultaneously destroying jobs through mechanization) with an employment-generating and wealth-creating system based on selective logging and the development of value-added, labour-intensive secondary industries.[3] M'Gonigle's road map begins with the idea that it is not only time to start thinking about alternatives to the current economic system, but also eminently practical, in today's world, to start building a new, greener economy.

I met Michael M'Gonigle – in a manner of speaking – via a microwave line linking two radio studios in Vancouver and Ottawa. Our conversation was itself oddly exemplary of a key problem that M'Gonigle was trying to grapple with: the question of how environmentalists can communicate complex and contentious issues (such as green economics) to a mass audience whose connection to environmentalism has often come through simple images of birds and dolphins and open spaces. M'Gonigle's primer on the interchange between economics and ecology was punctuated by his frequent apologies for violating the grammar of the mass media. ("This is a bit long-winded," he said more than once. "I hope you can use it.")

Like anyone who has worked for Greenpeace, M'Gonigle is acutely aware that expansive expositions are taboo on the airwaves; that rather than drawing out the connections between phenomena you've got to simplify things, to reduce the issue to snappy sound bites. But M'Gonigle, the academic, the thinker, is also aware that people need to see the big picture before they can embrace his vision; that it takes detailed and persistent argument to break down the conventional wisdom and put something new in its place. Hammering away at the anti-ecological impacts of our current, growth-oriented economy, M'Gonigle now builds his case with a patient eye to detail and a passionate persistence, like some crusading lawyer.

A *prosecuting* lawyer, to be sure: for at the centre of his argument is a blistering indictment of the-way-we-do-things-now, and a fierce commitment to the idea that a fundamental change in our social and economic thinking – not just surface reform – is the key to protecting the environment. "Personally, in my own analysis of things," M'Gonigle declares, "the market – the very nature of the free market – is inherently anti-environmental. Free trade and the growth mechanism ... we can tag all the environmental caveats [onto them] that we want, but the direction of ever-increasing free trade is, by its very nature, anti-environmental."

Why is M'Gonigle driven to utter such fractious words? He says that honest environmentalists won't be able to finesse their way around this fundamental conflict. The emerging movement known as "ecological economics" or "green economics" holds principles that are directly at odds with conventional, free-market economics. A cursory glance at the defining standards of the two disciplines confirms this, he says. Greens will interpret measurements that signify economic health for classical economists – such as gross national product and the rate of economic growth – as indicators of waste and environmental strain and predictors of future doom. Thus begins our introductory seminar on green economics. Its fundamental premise, M'Gonigle explains, is that "every time you build something, you use energy. And inevitably, every time you build a building or a car, you create a lot of environmental disturbance by the use of this energy. So, for example, they'll say a car that weighs two thousand pounds – a ton – uses ten tons of materials and energy in the process of being assembled, and that goes out as waste. Ecological economics talks about the cost of economic flow. The flow itself, the economic activity itself, causes environmental problems. Therefore we need an economy which maintains a stable and solid stock of economic goods with as little flow as possible, with as little throughput as possible – a certain stock of wealth.

"The problem is that our economy is oriented in exactly the other direction: gross national product, growth, the actual frenetic activity of economic transactions, is the measure of an economy's health. So that the very nature – from an ecological economic point of view – the very nature of our flow economy, our growth economy, causes more damage than it can contain."

The economic and social problems associated with conventional economic theory, M'Gonigle believes, are only intensified by a regime of expanded global free trade. The economists may speak of how "competitive advantage" and the national specialization involved with free trade allow goods to be produced more cheaply, but they don't calculate the hidden costs – for the environment and for humanity – of keeping goods and raw materials in circulation between countries and of keeping this huge transnational economic machine in working order.

M'Gonigle sees this pernicious cycle at work each time he goes out to buy groceries. "When I go down to the market in Vancouver," he says, "the only vegetables you can get are 'Cal' or 'Mex' – California or Mexican. Well, shipping tomatoes from Mexico, anybody knows, is ridiculous. Maybe on some purely abstracted, profit-based economic calculation there's some justification for it, but there is no justification for it when you think of the huge trucks and the diesel and the refrigeration for hauling these things all the way from Mexico. So there's enormous environmental costs.

"Plus, free trade in products like this also have environmental costs at both ends. The local, small producers – the family farms which are an essential layer of our culture – go under in Canada. Meanwhile in Mexico, the small producers there who could be producing for local consumption get pushed out of the way by big multinationals who then consolidate the agricultural holdings and pour on the pesticides and develop these hybridized tomatoes that can travel well, and pour on the fertilizer and export them. So in both the producer and the consumer countries, the social fabric is being ripped apart as well as instilling a very inefficient economic system."

This may sound like the basis of an apocalyptic critique – the foretelling of a social unravelling that (if one now accepts the construction of a new global trading regime as a fait accompli) will be inescapable. Yet M'Gonigle insists that green economic theory actually has a positive message, that it posits an alternative vision that is bright and highly saleable. And, he says, you can begin working towards this kind of future with most of the structures of today's economy still in place.

Consider one of the practical offshoots of green economics: the potential for new jobs. If efficiency, reduced "flow-through," and reduced energy use are the cornerstones of a green economy, there is plenty of employment to be generated in the short term by retooling the current economy to meet those criteria. At the simplest level, items like low-efficiency refrigerators could be retired and replaced with energy-saving models, a huge-scale initiative where there's money to be made and jobs to be created. But M'Gonigle says that it's when you start looking at the larger systems of human society that the real ability of a green economics to engage human ingenuity and effort (to become, itself, the basis of economy) comes into focus.

"Pro-environmental strategies make sense right across the board," he says. "One of my favourites is the concept of 'green cities.' There are all kinds of strategies there, in terms of rapid transit, energy-efficient architecture, use of open spaces for gardening, much more efficient energy uses for lighting and cooling, much better use of water, more recycling. All of these things could turn our quite black cities into green cities, and they all make large economic sense. There may be some difficulty now making profits from some of those industries, but that's only because the infrastructure is so locked up by the big businesses and existing suppliers of cars and gasoline and plastic tomatoes. So there is a lot of potential for job growth and for reduction of harm to the environment, and for just better local economics, by making this kind of eco-conversion in all kinds of areas."

M'Gonigle believes that even after the short-term boost from converting the social infrastructure from "black" to "green" is over, green economics could retain its populist appeal, because the concept of sustainability at its core applies as equally to the question of employment as it does to the ecological consequences of growth. Free-market economics – which has mandated enhanced efficiency through continual technological innovation and the globalization of production – has been snuffing out jobs and creating new marginalized classes in both North and South, leading to a worldwide employment crisis with no end in sight. On the other hand, green economics – with its emphasis on local self-reliance and non-technological fixes – may provide an antidote. "Over the long term," M'Gonigle says, "it's very important to put in place different types of jobs and a whole layer of employment in society that is inherently sustainable. For instance, I don't think there's any question that fifty years from now, a far higher percentage of the population is going to be employed growing food. People have been fighting for centuries against being displaced from the land, by the enclosures in Britain in the thirteenth century all the way through to the demise of the family farm today, where people are being replaced by energy-intensive machinery and large-scale agro-industries. So there is, I think, an economic strategy that leads to different types of occupations, different types of employment, that are much more sustainable over the long term."

All of this upbeat postulation sounds like the basis for a comprehensive political program. Greens like Michael M'Gonigle, it seems, have arrived at a vision of the future that speaks to a public angst not just about the fate of the Earth but also about the source of tomorrow's bread and butter (which is invariably a more immediate political issue). In the face of paralysing fear and uncertainty – of a widespread, gnawing sense that the world is drifting on automatic pilot towards an undesirable destiny, guided only, perhaps, by some immutable and unforgiving Law of Economics – here is a re-evaluation that opens up fundamental questions about the *purpose* of economic activity, reaffirms the power of human beings to choose their own future, and provides a road map for the trip to a more humane, sensible, and stable world. With evangelical conviction, M'Gonigle foretells a time not far away, when people will wake up to the fallacies of the current system and reach out for something better.

"There's a huge potential," M'Gonigle prophesies, "to get away from this trap we're in, of increasing productivity and then throwing everyone out of work and then trying to expand the economy some more to find some more jobs for these people who have just been thrown out of work, but then we have to expand the economy in a way that's productive so we have to throw more people out of work. . . . We're on this treadmill of productivity and internationally competitive economic growth, which is driven by what? Why do we need this? Is it necessary that some machine can pick fruit and grow vegetables more quickly than human skill? Why is that? Is that written in stone?

"The only reason is the free-trade nature of our economic system. And, unfortunately, the costs there are mounting, mounting, mounting, and one day we're going to realize – and I think people already are beginning to, with the reaction in Europe to the EC [European Community] and the reaction against the free-trade deal [in North America] – that this international competitive, productivity-driven, job-shedding economy is working for fewer and fewer interests. And a more balanced economy that develops local markets and has much less international trade, in fact, much reduced international trade, would be preferable to the direction we're going in now."

Why then, have influential environmental organizations like Greenpeace not done more to promote green economics and to challenge the prevailing ethos of growth-at-all-costs?

The reason, M'Gonigle submits, is that environmentalists would have to give up something first. They'd have to disavow that part of their public image that casts them as being above the partisan fray, as untainted by ideology, unsullied by the cut and thrust of political debate. True, many environmentalists (included many within Greenpeace) still say that they have no allegiance to any particular set of

ideas or intellectual masterplan; that they will do whatever is needed
to serve the purely practical end of saving a piece of the planet. In the
past this approach has guaranteed a certain unity among environmental organizations: different groups have been able to match up
their respective skills and work together on specific issues when their
goals were concrete and immediate and did not propel them towards
any Great Clash of Ideas.

But this apparent unity among environmental groups (which the
public perceives as a consensus on the issues, something that lends
additional weight to environmental causes in the political arena)
becomes much more fragile as environmentalists begin to offer
opinions on subjects like economics. Suddenly a dangerous quagmire appears before them. Environmental groups may voice their
approval of green economics as an abstract set of principles. They
may rally around such nebulous terms as "sustainability" and "efficiency" as the keys to a green economy down the road. But this ami-
cable consensus is likely to dissolve into open warfare when those
groups are pressed to define what the buzzwords actually mean –
when the abstractions have to be interpreted and applied in the context of real world events and situations.

★ ★ ★

A cluster of Canadian environmental groups (Energy Probe, Environment Probe, and Probe International) puts a decidedly different
policy spin on many of the concepts that M'Gonigle champions. The
head-scratchers at Probe, for example, agree with M'Gonigle that
"efficiency" is central to a more ecologically sustainable economy.
But they move off in an opposite direction when challenged to
define what economic systems are "efficient" or "inefficient" or
what route should be taken to ensure a sustainable, or green economy. While M'Gonigle sees free trade as fundamentally unecological
– promoting the squandering of resources, the destruction of local
economies, and the production of mutant tomatoes – Environment
Probe threw its support behind the Canada-U.S. Free Trade Agreement of 1988. Its rationale was that free trade would protect the
environment by outlawing the state subsidies that encourage inefficient use of resources and shelter environmentally destructive industries.

This approach – attacking state support for environmentally

destructive industries, challenging them to hold their own in the private marketplace – was used to good effect in Canada in the 1980s by another cell of the Probe group, Energy Probe, which argued that if the nuclear power facilities in Ontario were privatized and forced to buy insurance on the private market, they would become economically unviable and shut down. (Greenpeace took the same approach to the nuclear power industry in Britain, casting the organization as an unlikely ideological ally of Margaret Thatcher in her campaign to privatize government enterprises.) For the Probe organizations, targeting state support for nuclear power was not just a tactical decision, but a matter of ideological conviction. The principles underlying the groups' anti-nuclear power campaign have become reference points for all of its efforts: invariably, the fundamental litmus tests that Probe organizations use to judge the environmental soundness of a variety of activities are whether they receive state support, and how well they can fend for themselves in the open marketplace.

Political scientist Laurie Adkin describes Energy Probe, which splintered from the organization Pollution Probe in the early 1980s, as an "ecocapitalist" organization. She writes: "While Energy Probe has been a keen critic of public utilities for their lack of accountability and has viewed energy policy as undemocratic in that it has been implemented in the absence of informed public debate and serious consideration of alternatives, it has in recent years moved away from democratic discourse and toward a preoccupation with what research director Norm Rubin calls 'the discipline of the marketplace.'" Adkin finds fault with the group's preoccupation with market solutions on several grounds, mainly that this reliance on market forces "ignores the social and economic consequences" of environmental issues (such as employment); and that placing power over environmental decisions in the hands of "consumers" and "taxpayers" makes the process of determining environmental policy less democratic, because people who have been economically marginalized will have no role in that decision-making. Furthermore, Adkin argues that reducing environmental concern to an economic equation (in the belief that the marketplace will ultimately choose the most environmentally safe options because it is more costly to pollute the environment) leads to a "lesser of two evils" approach to environmental planning in which environmental planning becomes a simple business decision; say, shall we have nuclear power or coal? By contrast, philosophically broader forms of environmentalism call for "a profound rethinking of the goals of production, of consumption norms, and of the meaning of work and leisure" and aim to provoke a participatory form of debate, Adkin says.[4]

Recently Probe has become more preoccupied with the magical ability of the free market to solve all of life's problems and is less focused on the environment. A slick, expensive-looking magazine called *The Next City*, co-published by the Energy Probe Research Foundation with Donner Foundation money – its editor/publisher is Probe researcher Lawrence Solomon – came onto the market in 1995. The one issue I've seen is full of articles railing against the manifold forms of government regulation: one story advocates the privatization of street parking; one tells why the poverty in Brazilian *favellas* is better than Canadian public housing; and another argues against Canada's gun control bill.

Probe International has brought this type of analysis to the problem of the Third World environmental destruction caused by infrastructural megaprojects such as hydro dams. The fundamental culprit in this matter, the group believes, is the welfare mentality of foreign aid: ill-advised dams, hydro generators, and smelters get built not because multinational corporations want access to cheap resources, but because foreign and domestic governments throw money at those projects without the requirement that they generate the revenue to pay for themselves. At one point this idea that it was the influx of foreign money that was causing environmental problems in the South led Probe International's director to write that the Third World debt crisis was a *good* thing, since it diverted funds away from the construction of megaprojects and taught Third World leaders a lesson about fiscal responsibility. For instance, Probe International's Pat Adams told me that the group was not in favour of relief of Third World debt, because "the problem is money." She says, "I'm worried that if we could wave a magic wand and do away with the debt, the banks would go rushing back in and much of the problem would be re-created."

Adams also states that there is no evidence of the debt causing environmental decay and poverty and the problem is one of internal policies in the Third World. While she says Probe supported groups that sought to repudiate their countries' debt where the decisions were made undemocratically, "to the extent that these governments incurred the debt legitimately, in the name of their people, I do believe they should pay it back."[5]

It is ironic that a public interest group would want to punish "democratic" countries while letting "undemocratic" governments escape from the debt burden. That contradiction aside, the Probe position infuriates other commentators who see the debt crisis as damaging health and social programs while prioritizing infrastructural megaprojects that promised to serve the export market and so generate foreign currency to pay debt service charges. International development groups (backed by organizations such as UNICEF) say that conditions imposed on indebted nations by the International Monetary Fund in the 1980s led to deprivation, hunger, and death for the poor. These conditions in turn led to populations of desperate people who had little choice but to hack down forests and otherwise ravage the environment, just in order to survive.

Environment Probe also saw the pro-market, anti-subsidy provisions of the Canada-U.S. free trade deal as a saviour of Canadian forests: it argued that, under the deal, the government could no longer allow Crown lands to be logged for pennies a tree, since this would be considered an unfair subsidy to Canadian exporters. In short, free-market treaties are good because they outlaw government subsidies that encourage waste and inefficiency. The market will protect the environment because it is not cost-effective – not profitable – to waste resources and pillage the land.

For Michael M'Gonigle, the right-wing environmental economists' approach to the current challenges "may make some sense" in theory. "But in practice, it is completely fraudulent." What's "naive" about the idea that free-market policies can save the environment, he says, is the assumption that the marketplace exists as a pure and independent entity; that the marketplace and the state can somehow be separated. "The history of the rise of the market is a history of a thousand years of state intervention," he says. "The only way the wool trade got going in England in the twelfth, thirteenth, and fourteenth centuries was because the state – the nascent state – kicked all the people off the land so that the private owners could start exporting wool. The only way that the fur trade got going in Canada was because of a state charter from Britain to the Hudson's Bay company." He sees current international efforts to bring down trade barriers as just more of the same: another initiative sponsored by governments (and now, transnational trade bodies) to benefit the corporate elite. Rather than providing a "level playing field" where all the players can exercise their rational economic impulses (unencumbered by regulatory interference), free-trade treaties like NAFTA and GATT are really about entrenching the rights of powerful economic forces and forestalling change.

"Free trade is really a misnomer," M'Gonigle says. "I call it mandated trade. The reason free trade is a misnomer is because it makes it illegal for local industries to develop. If we wanted as a community to protect our local farms and have a dynamic local trade in our own produce – even though that may cost more than buying imported tomatoes from Mexico – that's made illegal. What free trade does is that it forces consumers, even if they would like to buy local products – it forces them to buy tomatoes from Mexico because that's all they can get. The other markets have been essentially shut down."

And so – somewhere in the middle of M'Gonigle's blistering public attack on a prominent Canadian environmental organization – what becomes most apparent is the fragility of the façade of solidarity amongst environmentalists. Venturing out of that enchanted land of glowing, universalist visions of a green tomorrow, we have circled back into a volatile, partisan, and contentious debate. This drift illustrates perfectly M'Gonigle's point about environmentalists being "reluctant to get into structural causes, or root causes of problems because it tends to make them look political." Ecologists may protest that they are "neither left nor right but out in front" – but when they line up on particular sides of political issues, they are sure to be judged by the company they keep.

The problem does not exist merely between different environmental groups with distinct ideological dispositions. Ever since it began expanding into Latin America in the late 1980s, Greenpeace itself has been divided by the question of how closely to adhere to a broad economic or political framework. The ongoing, unresolved tactical question, M'Gonigle says, is "how far you can stray from specific environmental issues into larger economic questions, without losing your rudder, and becoming more of a political group rather than an environmental group." How one is likely to answer that question depends upon what M'Gonigle diplomatically refers to as "legitimate differences of experience."

Brazilian campaigner Marijane Lisboa, for instance, cites the destruction of tropical forests in her country as an issue that can't be resolved separately from the general conditions of economic crisis and poverty, because the plundering of the forests "is very directly related to the economic misery in the region," which forces poor people to find some means to survive. Her colleague and fellow Brazilian R. de Goes, Greenpeace's Latin American anti-nuclear campaigner, also cites nuclear power as an issue inseparable from broader questions of trade, economics, and politics, because large outputs of electricity are needed to produce aluminum, which is exported and used to pay foreign debts. "This is a product of the whole model of development," he says.

In Europe the response to ecological crisis can be notably different. Greenpeace's Swedish office, for example, refrained from commenting in general on the European trade arrangements, but did take aim at a specific clause within one deal that might have forced Sweden to accept other countries' nuclear waste. "We have been very careful with not really taking a stand against trade agreements," explains Lena Ahlby, co-ordinator of the campaign work for Greenpeace Sweden, "but instead really try to make concrete what issues we don't like."

If an issue like economics can create divisions between and within environmental organizations, it can surely drive a wedge between the environmental movement and supporters in the general public, who tend to live in affluent countries and don't necessarily hold radical ideas about how the world economy is constructed. Michael M'Gonigle's experience with Greenpeace may have led him to the conclusion that the market is fundamentally anti-environmental, but he's not suggesting that Greenpeace tell its supporters that. "If Greenpeace were to campaign against the market, or against free trade per se," he says, "a lot of eyebrows would go up, and people would get angry, and donations would go down."

And there's the rub: Greenpeace's strong presence in the mass media not only allows it to educate the public, but also to raise funds. There is an obvious incentive to be prudent with your public image when it is the main lever on a multimillion-dollar fundraising machine. Greenpeace is certainly not the only environmental organization that has learned this lesson.

In his book on the African conservation movement, *At the Hand of Man*, journalist Ray Bonner provides a disturbing example of how fiscal concerns can widen the distance between an organization's professional view of an issue and the representation of that issue as presented to the public through the media and direct-mail campaigns.[6] During a debate in the late 1980s over whether the United States should ban the importation of African ivory, a number of prominent conservation groups lobbied for a total ban on ivory, even though they believed that such a ban was not a good idea. The World Wildlife Federation (WWF) agreed with most scientists that policies of "sustainable utilization" and controlled culls of African elephants were necessary both for preservation of the species and for the health of nearby human communities, but the organization tried desperately to hide that belief from the donating public. Bonner quotes an internal WWF-US memorandum that explains, "Although we support sustainable wildlife utilization projects . . . these concepts are not understood by the vast majority of the 450,000 WWF-US members."[7] Similarly, the African Wildlife Federation (AWF), a Washington-based organization working to protect African species, initially resisted calls by its direct-mail contractor to make a strong pro-ban statement, but eventually jumped onto the pro-ban bandwagon.

These organizations supported policies they didn't agree with, Bonner says, because they stood to make a lot of money by tapping the U.S. public's emotional attraction to elephants. Past experience told conservationists that the elephant was a more potent fundraising symbol than any other species. And because animal rights organizations had seized control of the elephant issue in the United States by calling for a total ban on ivory imports, groups like the AWF and WWF decided that they also had to take a strong stand if they wanted to protect their basis of support from these upstarts.

According to some observers, the norm now is for the tail of fundraising and publicity to wag the dog of environmental policy. In his book *Confessions of an Eco-Warrior*, Earth First! founder Dave Foreman complains that, for many environmental outfits, the "viability of the group" overshadows its "conservation mission." That viability, of course, hinges on the organization's ability to maintain a strong public image that puts money in the bank. And so, Foreman argues, the emphasis has shifted from what an organization can do to protect the environment to what it can be *seen* to be doing: "Instead of trying to truly win a battle, the group merely wants to get credit for a victory, no matter how hollow it may be. Wilderness Society and Sierra Club staff receive specific directions from their supervisors to beat each other in the media race, to get more 'sound bites' and 'face time' than their counterparts in the other group."[8]

Mike Affleck, a former Notre Dame theology professor and anti-nuclear activist who joined Greenpeace International in 1990 to direct its ozone campaign, believes that the environmental movement has become trapped by the conventions of its own publicity machine. Organizations like Greenpeace have arrived at new conclusions about the roots of environmental crisis, he says, but they are unable or unwilling to use their enormous PR machines to transmit these ideas to the public. Rather than providing public education, the groups generally crank out material designed to appeal to the public's existing mind-set, to press the emotional buttons that will open their wallets.

"Raising the number of miles per gallon on a car is a good thing to campaign for," Affleck told me during a wide-ranging conversation at his home on the suburban fringe of Syracuse, New York. "But in reality it only delays the inevitable. In the end you have to do something that's much more to do with people's lifestyles. That means that unless Greenpeace starts dealing with the issues of consumption and population, we're just going to be skirting the issues, and we're never going to get to the heart of the problem. And Greenpeace is not going to raise money by campaigning for reduced consumption or telling the world to use condoms."

Greenpeace has done more than most environmental activist outfits to address huge ecological issues such as green economics and the North-South gap. But Affleck believes it has largely relinquished the opportunity to spread the word about these issues by failing to include them in its media representations. This is particularly true in rich countries, where questions of consumption are crucial.

In effect, Greenpeace inhabits two worlds. In recent years, it has deftly navigated its way through a complex world in which seemingly straightforward issues are complicated by a tangled web of social, cultural, economic, and historical factors and institutions. But Greenpeace also lives in the shadowland of the mass media: a one-dimensional world of phantom television images and raw emotion, a place of good versus evil, a place of simple stories and unambiguous endings. Sometimes, to the chagrin of organizers and organized alike, it is hard to tell where these two worlds intersect.

CHAPTER 5

BEHIND THE MASK

CONFLICT, CRISIS, AND CREATIVITY BEHIND THE MEDIA IMAGE

THE REPORTER'S JAUNDICED EYE CAN TURN YESTERDAY'S hero into today's villain about as fast as you can say O.J. Simpson. And that – to an extent – is what happened to Greenpeace in the two or three years after the Rio Summit.

As the media became bored with Greenpeace's headline-grabbing antics (as staged events and photo-ops largely replaced the voyages and actual campaigns as a media focal point) – and as previous waves of panic over environmental degradation subsided to make room in the public imagination for new crises (from the hot wars of Bosnia and Somalia to the cooling of Northern industrial economies) – media outlets became less likely to amplify Greenpeace's ecological siren calls and more inclined to hold the organization itself up to scrutiny. In the 1990s it seems you can confirm your own opinions on what Greenpeace is really about by simply selecting one of two prepackaged, polar-opposite images – angel or demon, faithful keeper of the covenant or betrayer of its own ideals – offered by an information industry that tends to like its villains sinful and its heroes unsullied.

Two recent hour-long film documentaries on Greenpeace illustrate the co-existence of these contradictory portraits. *The Greenpeace Years* and *The Man in the Rainbow* – made within three years of each other and with several key events and personalities in common – are as different from one another as *Scarface* is from *Ghandi*. If you watched both films in succession you couldn't be sure whether

Greenpeace was a criminal syndicate or a religious order avowed to personal poverty and selfless good works.

The basic message of the National Film Board of Canada's *The Greenpeace Years* – conveyed through the intermingling of scenes from the daily life of the affluent, highly organized Greenpeace of the early 1990s, with old footage and reminiscences of the campaigns of the 1970s – is that a new generation is now guarding the persistent flame of idealism, and that the renegade spirit of the sixties and seventies counterculture has survived within Greenpeace. The "tough questions" that the filmmakers ask their subjects do nothing to puncture that image. The answers are always cheerfully forthcoming and perfectly in sync with that persona of zealous commitment.

Like most films, *The Greenpeace Years*, conceived by veteran television journalist Michael Maclear to mark the twentieth anniversary of Greenpeace's 1971 founding, draws its power not from the content of the conversations, but from compelling moving pictures. We join young Greenpeace activists in a journey down the banks of the Mississippi River to a chemical town in Kentucky where grey-haired locals – radicalized by the epidemics of cancer that have ravaged their quiet communities – have called in the eco-cavalry; that is, the young freaks from Greenpeace. We travel as well to Halifax, Nova Scotia, where Greenpeacers buzz a nuclear-armed British warship from their positions in inflatable rubber rafts and unfurl a banner (manoeuvred into place by a Greenpeace crew of amateur human flies) on a suspension bridge overlooking the Halifax harbour. (The cost of staging these two attention-getters, a narrator tells us, is a cool $20,000 Canadian.) At the end of the sequence, a policeman on the scene bids the protesters "God Bless You" as he struggles to keep from bursting into tears.

We also visit Greenpeace's direct-action training camp in Florida, where young recruits are schooled in non-violent civil-disobedience techniques. The camp's program is run by a former journalist, who we are told has taken a pay cut from $40,000 to $5,000 per year. The young trainees, meanwhile, will move on to full-time Greenpeace jobs paying a subsistence wage of $300 a week.

But this film is not just a homage to the young, poor foot-soldiers but also a tribute to their mentors. Keeping alive the old spirit of heroism is retired chairman David McTaggart. We tag along with him as he wanders – with frantically screeching Geiger counter in hand – through the streets of an abandoned Ukrainian village, made uninhabitable by the meltdown at Chernobyl. McTaggart confides that the devastation here almost drove him to quit Greenpeace and renounce its commitment to non-violence. He is later seen escorting a team of Western doctors whom Greenpeace has brought to the Ukraine to treat children suffering from radiation sickness. The kicker in the film's section on McTaggart is the montage of Greenpeace officials agreeing that, although the ex-chairman could have been marketed as "Mr. Greenpeace, Superstar" – as a kind of green Lee Iacocca or Fidel Castro – the organization decided to forego a personality cult in favour of a strong group identity.

The Greenpeace Years was released in 1991, at the tail end of a funding boom that fuelled enormous expansion for the organization and buoyed the spirits of the faithful. Everyone was getting enough of the pie that no one would publicly break ranks and shatter this image of organizational tranquillity. But by the end of the Rio Summit in 1992, Greenpeace was starting to feel the full impact of a financial nosedive that had set an entirely different dynamic in motion: program cuts and job losses were leading to bitter personal clashes and to acrimonious debates over the organization's direction and future. As Greenpeace's own organizational imperatives moved to centre stage within the organization, the media were picking up on the sense of turmoil and looking at Greenpeace less as a source for news and more as a target for investigation and scandal-mongering.

During a run of generally bad press in the early 1990s, Danish TV-2 (through its production company, Nordiskfilm) released *The Man in the Rainbow*, a relentless trashing of Greenpeace and its retired leading light, McTaggart. While Michael Maclear and his Canadian colleagues had deemed it appropriate – after examining how Greenpeace was projecting itself into the public eye – to write a hymn of praise to the organization, Danish filmmaker Michael Klint focused on the internal politics of the organization and came up with something more like Canterbury Tales: a narrative of corruption, deceit, and ambition hiding beneath a veil of ecological righteousness.

Many of the allegations in Klint's film (which aired in several Scandinavian countries but, according to Klint, was kept off the air in Britain and Germany by court injunctions) relate to the question of how Greenpeace spends its money. Klint brings into the spotlight a number of disgruntled ex-employees, such as Franz Kotte, a former financial manager for Greenpeace International who was fired early in 1993 for alleged fiscal impropriety. Kotte had since launched a lawsuit against his former employer as a means of protesting his innocence, and he maintains that accurate financial figures for Greenpeace are shown only to a few select board members, who have diverted large packets of cash into secret bank accounts around the world. Allegedly included among those funds is a $20 million payment made to Greenpeace by the French government to compensate for its sinking of the *Rainbow Warrior* – a sum that Greenpeace told its members was used to buy and refurbish a replacement boat, but which was instead salted away in a Dutch bank account under the name of the dummy organization "Environmental Challenge." In the film Greenpeace spokesperson Uta Bellion says that this account exists as a "safety net," that its existence is openly acknowledged within Greenpeace, and that the funds are intended to be used to continue the environmental campaigns if some kind of financial disaster arises for Greenpeace.

Is this a credible explanation for secret bank accounts? I'm no forensic accountant, but it strikes me that it is only prudent for an organization with powerful enemies to have some kind of contingency plans in case the opponents try to shut it down. Bellion's answer casts Greenpeace as no different from a multitude of corporations that shift around their assets to protect themselves from seizure in the event of lawsuits. Her response is also consistent with internal Greenpeace communications – issued well before this film addressed the matter – dealing with long-term financial strategy. For instance, in an open e-mail to Greenpeace staff in August 1992, ex-chairman McTaggart urged the leadership that had replaced him to keep in mind the need "to be financially stable on an international basis, with money put away for emergencies." McTaggart reminded the new leadership that Greenpeace had historically aimed "to have enough money put away that we could make it through a cataclysmic loss in income – either as a result of an unpopular action by ourselves, a ghastly mistake, or the concerted attempt by a group of governments or industries to shut us down." In fact, the drastic shortfalls in revenue that face most environmental organizations in the mid-1990s support McTaggart's way of thinking.

Especially in areas where Greenpeace strives to have diplomatic influence, the organization does appear to spend its money in a high style that, in some minds at least, clashes with the image of a grassroots charity and activist organization. In Klint's film Bjorn Orkon, former leader of Greenpeace in Norway, says that although at first he bought into Greenpeace's Boy Scout image, after a year on the job he was "incredibly disillusioned." What particularly surprised him was the organization's jet-setting. "I've never travelled so much on business class and stayed so much in nice hotels as when I worked for Greenpeace," he tells the filmmakers. Orkon remembered a trip to Russia in which cases of beer, champagne, and whisky – intended for presentation as a Greenpeace calling card to make sure relations with the natives got off to a good start – made up a significant item on the budget. Klint's film suggests that this kind of luxury spending was not an anomaly.

Francisco Palacio, a Colombian marine biologist, tells about his role in the mid-1970s in Greenpeace's efforts to have the International Whaling Commission (IWC) ban commercial whaling. Palacio says it was his job to lobby Third World nations to join the IWC so that they could break the control of whaling nations over that body and vote against the continuation of commercial whaling. Apparently this kind of support did not come cheaply. Greenpeace was expected to pick up travel and accommodation costs and to follow diplomatic protocol by sending its governmental partners a few tokens of its affection. Over several years, Palacio says, the initiative cost "several million dollars, maybe four or five million dollars. I don't remember the exact figures but it was in that order of magnitude."

Unlike Orkon, Palacio was not offended by these expenditures. He accepted them as a normal part of doing a particular kind of business. "If I invite you first class I'm not going to take you to a fast-food place, but I'm going to take you to a fine restaurant. Maybe I'm going to send flowers to your hotel. And after a while that builds up."

The upshot of all these efforts was that a number of new countries joined the IWC, and some of them were represented at meetings by Greenpeace staff. At its 1982 meeting this expanded IWC voted to ban commercial whaling, which, for Palacio, justified the expenses. "You know the results," Palacio tells filmmaker Klint. "That's the only thing you look at. Did the new members support the cessation of commercial whaling? Yes. It's very simple."

The image of free-spending wheeler-dealers presented in Michael Klint's film forms a stark contrast to Michael Maclear's portrait of Greenpeace as a collection of young zealots with a propensity for hanging off high-suspension bridges for practically no pay. Yet considering that Greenpeace operates within a multitude of social spheres – and considering that its strategies are equally dependent upon grassroots theatrics and diplomatic arm-twisting – both films, taken in isolation, may have got it at least partly right. Organizations often do contain distinct subcultures with values that vary according to their job descriptions.

Where the two films seem almost irreconcilable is in their respective treatments of former chairman and enduring Greenpeace father-figure David McTaggart. To Maclear's vision of a Saint David, Klint offers a kind of Mephistopheles. Klint resurrects a number of skeletons in McTaggart's closet – ex-business partners, a former mother-in-law – who all cast doubt on the official version of McTaggart's life story. While Greenpeace advertises McTaggart as a former millionaire land developer who went broke and then took on the French nuclear weapons program as a way of finding spiritual fulfilment, his former business associates describe him more as a confidence man who never really developed anything. In the film one former associate, Wells Lange, tells Klint about successfully suing McTaggart (in absentia) for securities fraud. Lange and his brother had invested $1.5 million in McTaggart's plans to develop a ski resort in Colorado in the 1960s. Lange says McTaggart promised them that their money would be used to develop the sports complex, but it was actually funnelled into other projects, such as paying the mortgage on land in California and supporting a McTaggart-sponsored ski team. Before the misappropriations were discovered, Lange alleges, McTaggart was gone.

The film tells a similar story set in Bear Valley, California, where Gertrude Huberty, McTaggart's former mother-in-law, says that after McTaggart had quietly skipped town, leaving an avalanche of debt behind him, she was left on the hook for a $120,000 bank loan that her son-in-law had convinced her to co-sign. The film raises these distant episodes to suggest that Greenpeace International's business affairs were tainted by McTaggart's fast-and-loose approach to finances, a suggestion underscored by sinister music heard each time McTaggart's face comes onto the screen.

So what does one make of these allegations? Are they merely bits of trivia – as irrelevant to the story of Greenpeace as Roger Smith's parking tickets would be to the story of General Motors? Are they half-truths that have been pieced together to poison public good-will towards Greenpeace? Or are they meaningful clues into the organizational culture that developed in Greenpeace under McTaggart's leadership?

The context in which these allegations first appeared may help answer these questions. Klint's stories about McTaggart's past life in business and Greenpeace's lobbying before the IWC first surfaced in *Forbes* magazine, a U.S. business publication with a decided antagonism towards environmental protest groups. Of course, *Forbes*'s editorial bias doesn't mean that the stories it prints are factually wrong, but it does warrant a cautious reading of how the magazine links information with the conclusions it draws. The moral lesson of *Forbes*'s November 14, 1991, cover story, "The Not So Peaceful World of Greenpeace," can be summed up as follows: that Greenpeace's ability to play fast and loose with the rules – to issue creative financial statements and to influence cosy international committees by recruiting trouble-makers from the Third World – gives it a clear advantage over the beleaguered, shackled corporations that are strictly regulated by governments and accountable to their clamouring shareholders.

I suspect that this novel view of the power imbalance between environmental groups and big corporations would come as a surprise to anyone who has lived beside a toxic waste dump or an industrial smoke stack or drawn water from a poisoned river. Furthermore, the yardsticks that *Forbes* uses to condemn Greenpeace – that it may have employed questionable accounting techniques, that it may have sidestepped the ostensible norms of diplomatic politics – denotes a breathtaking lack of moral perspective. *Forbes* berates Greenpeace for its "ends-justifies-the-means" mentality – but itself constructs a ludicrously skewed moral hierarchy. Even if nuclear weapons manufacturers kept their books impeccably and followed the government's regulations to the letter, that wouldn't absolve them of their crimes of poisoning the atmosphere and casting a generations-long shadow of terror over the world, and it certainly wouldn't make them more virtuous than their environmental nemeses.

But that is the very point of the *Forbes* article: after attempting to discredit Greenpeace, the world's highest-profile eco-activist group, the authors pass the mantle of environmental responsibility to those conscientious, concerned folk in the corporate world. On the page directly following the anti-Greenpeace article is an advertising supplement, "The Profit in Preserving America." Taken together, the article and the ads form a seamless advertorial package: having read about the excesses of this environmental "vigilante" group, we are primed for the big-business pitch about how companies are using market forces to preserve the planet. The nuclear industry announces, "We need more nuclear plants" – in order to keep the air clean. (Forget about spent nuclear fuel that no one knows how to dispose of, or nuclear weapons proliferation, or the aftermath of the Cold War atomic arms race – it's got nothing to do with these guys.) Anheuser-Busch says we should buy more Budweiser in cans because it's ecologically friendly. The American Forest Council says it's not destroying wildlife habitat; it's really protecting it. And so it goes. Regardless of what those green cranks have told us, the real good guys are in the corporate boardrooms.

The same kind of vested interests are at work in Michael Klint's film. In several cases the people who criticize Greenpeace do so in order to advance their own, unstated political goals. By grasping at any hint of dirt – and by quoting any available "experts" regardless of whose payroll they've been dining on – Klint makes his own case that much easier to dismiss. By noting, for instance, that there is an overlap in the Western United States between the habitués of the offices of Greenpeace and Earth First! (an organization that condones tree-spiking and some forms of property destruction), the filmmaker arrives at the illogical conclusion that Greenpeace's commitment to non-violence is a sham. In reality, probably every organization from the Humane Society to the Republican party has members who also belong to organizations with philosophies that those groups do not endorse. To comment on the Greenpeace-Earth First! connection, Klint brings before the cameras a private investigator hired by timber, ranching, and mining interests to infiltrate the environmental movement in the American west. This particular gumshoe (shorn of the beard and long hair that he grew for his anti-green assignment) tells the filmmakers that he saw many of the same faces in the Greenpeace and Earth First! offices, and he offers the rather ridiculous assessment that Greenpeace would "just like to see the annihilation of man." In the same category of overheated non sequiturs is Ron Arnold's assertion that Greenpeace is an organization of "potential murderers" because some of its members also support Earth First![1] Arnold, who appears repeatedly in the film, is identified verbally by the narrator as "the American writer" and in print on the screen as an "author and publisher." There is no mention of the fact that Arnold (whose rather mangled précis of environmental ideology is that greens are "catastrophists" who believe the way to save the environment is to "stop humans") is also a hired gun and one of the chief ideologues of the so-called wise use movement, an anti-environmental lobby funded by the forestry and resource industries and closely linked to the Moonies and the U.S. religious right.[2]

Greenpeace obviously expects criticism from the likes of Ron Arnold and the wise use movement. Most of its members might even wear the criticism from *Forbes* magazine as a badge of honour – proof that the organization is enough of a threat to corporate polluters to warrant a counter-attack. But alongside these blasts from anti-environmental forces have come bitter denunciations from former friends – and these criticisms are sure to hurt.

A damaging blow was inflicted in Canada in mid-1993 after the firing of the two Greenpeace Canada star campaigners, Stan Gray and Gordon Perks, who had been involved in organizing a staff union. The pair decided not to go quietly. Instead, they released to the media an internal Greenpeace document that said only 5 per cent of revenues were being spent on actual campaigning. In the land of its founding, Greenpeace took a public relations pounding: *The Ottawa Citizen* broke the story on its front page under the banner "Greenpeace Canada at War with Itself."[3] *The Winnipeg Free Press* ran a cartoon showing a Greenpeace bureaucrat with a business suit and a briefcase, holding a sign saying "Save the Salaries."[4] Continued attempts by management to punish or expel Greenpeace's union organizers were met with headlines citing "union busting" and internal disarray. The left-wing magazine *Canadian Dimension* – "For People Who Want to Change the World" – ran a cover story on the "Green Giant" in the fall of 1994 that included bitter condemnations from former Greenpeace campaigners, board members, and Greenpeace Canada's legal advisor of sixteen years.[5]

From around the world came echoes of the same story: continued financial woe was unleashing a tide of discontent, directed largely at Greenpeace's growing bureaucracy. *The Australian* newspaper reported that Greenpeace in that country had only avoided a financial loss in 1992 and 1993 by reducing and then eliminating its contributions to Greenpeace International. The figures cited showed that – although the organization collected large amounts of money – it had also spent much of that revenue just supporting its own organizational structure. While Greenpeace Australia collected (Aust.) $3.5 million in fees from its members in 1992, in addition to $1 million in merchandise sales plus $778,000 in donations – it spent a huge chunk of that sum on administration: a full $3 million went towards "membership services and appeals."[6] Australia's *Independent Monthly* magazine commented, around the same time, that the corporate structure introduced to Greenpeace Australia in the late 1980s had raised the organization's profile and boosted its membership from 6,000 to 93,000, but also "made heavy cash demands for continued recruitment."[7]

This was not the first time that questions around the expense of Greenpeace's fundraising machine had been raised. For instance, the American National Charities Information Bureau (NCIB) calculated Greenpeace USA's 1985 fundraising costs at 63 per cent of contributions.[8] While the high cost of fundraising can be overlooked during good times, during a period of declining revenues its impact becomes magnified. The *Independent Monthly* noted that declining profit margins (resulting from falling revenues but continued high expenditures by the publicity and fundraising machines) had a direct impact on Greenpeace Australia's campaign strategies and labour relations. The magazine stated that financial worries "have curbed Greenpeace Australia's confrontational approach to industry because it could have led to expensive court actions." The cash-flow squeeze also led to the sacking of 30 of the organization's 70 full-time staff and about 100 of 140 casual workers.

The crisis was magnified at Greenpeace International, where managers turned their financial knives on Greenpeace's Latin America project, which had been subsidized during the fat years but now seemed a prime candidate for being cut adrift. A plan prepared by the executive committee for consideration at Greenpeace's 1994 annual general meeting would have concentrated extensive personnel cuts on the Latin American offices, effectively closing them down. When the volunteer board of directors flatly rejected this plan, the whiff of civil war was in the air. The infighting was so intense that the acting executive director of Greenpeace International, Steve D'Esposito, issued an e-mail cryptically threatening to fire anyone who spoke to the media.[9] The newspaper reports of the AGM read like obituaries. Britain's *Financial Times* asked, somewhat gloatingly, "Are environmentalists now in danger of extinction?"[10] Greenpeace International campaign co-ordinator Jim Puckett, quoted by the Reuters news agency, echoed the concerns of his fired Canadian compatriots that downsizing was keeping a self-concerned bureaucracy intact but destroying Greenpeace's work for the environment. Puckett, noting that 85 per cent of job losses were falling on the campaign side, asked, "Why are they cutting at the heart of what we do?" Others lamented that by maintaining budgets in the North at the expense of new Greenpeace offices in the Third World, the organization would be abandoning both its role as the first environmental lobby to bridge the North-South gap and its followers in places where environmental needs were the greatest.[11] The British papers hinted that Greenpeace's ailments were life-threatening. *The Guardian* characterized ex-chairman McTaggart's attempts to broker a deal amongst the combatants as "a bid to prevent internal wrangles [from] destroying the organization."[12]

Although the financial dimension of the crisis within Greenpeace was unprecedented – with greater cash flow came greater demands and larger problems when money got tight – the fact remains that Greenpeace has *always* lived in a state of explosive tension that has had the potential either to propel the organization to new heights or to tear it apart. Ideology and individuals' identities have often been the flashpoints.

"Greenpeace has always been an organization that's been crisis-ridden and perhaps crisis dependent," reflects former Canadian forestry campaigner and sociologist David Peerla. "But I think that's a healthy thing, because the organization is trying to internalize various standpoints. It's trying to internalize feminism within its organizational structure, so that it's not just boys in boats. It's been trying to incorporate people from the South, so its policies go beyond what's expected in OECD nations."

Dan McDermott, who co-founded the Toronto Greenpeace office in 1976 only to be purged about fifteen years later, has his own theory about why Greenpeace's history is stained with conspiracies and coups. "Greenpeace by its nature tends to attract the most aggressive people in the environmental movement," he says. "People who want something done quickly, dramatically and effectively . . . people who may be longer on some virtues than they are on patience. And putting all these aggressive people together in one organization is bound to create some turmoil on an ongoing basis."

I've spoken to numerous leading figures from Greenpeace's first decade – people who have long since left the organization and returned to "real life" – and most of them speak with the same confusing mix of emotions. They recall with fondness and pride the development of a movement that was so diverse that it couldn't help but challenge old assumptions and configurations of ideas. But they also speak of an experience of such intensity – invested with such massive emotional import and so rife with conflict – that its participants seemed constantly stretched to the breaking point. What is amazing – given the vast philosophical gulf between its factions – is not that Greenpeace would periodically erupt into civil war during times of transition or crisis, but that the organization came together as smoothly as it did and has lasted as long as it has.

★ ★ ★

In Greenpeace mythology – and in its promotional videos and brochures – the 1970s is Greenpeace's golden era. Over a period of seven, perhaps eight years, campaign after campaign added to the Greenpeace legend. Those projects – from Amchitka through the numerous anti-whaling campaigns and two Save the Seal campaigns, to the early drive against French nuclear testing – had enormous energy and were often vastly successful. But all of them also took place in an atmosphere of chaos and conflict.

Born of Vancouver's polyglot counterculture – a human goulash composed largely of draft dodgers fleeing the Vietnam war and ecological zealots seeking the counsel of mountains and forests and ocean – Greenpeace was from its inception a hybrid. What transformed the emerging Greenpeace into an apparently seamless and solid organizational alloy, says David Garrick, was the hostile political environment that surrounded it. During the decisive last years of the Vietnam War, the domestic struggle against the war – and against the Establishment in general – had turned white hot. These were times when riot police were routinely dispatched to recapture North America's city streets; when a whiff of cannabis or a glimpse of the counter-uniform of long hair and jeans was taken as a provocation in an undeclared war. It was the need to find creative means of counterattack, says Garrick – recalling those days with the quiet, composed intensity of a veteran remembering war stories – that gave the proto-Greenpeacers common cause.

Known at the time as "Walrus Oakenbough" – partly in reference to the imposing walrus moustache that he still sports – Garrick was a support worker on the Amchitka campaign who later moved into the entrusted positions of ship's cook and official record keeper during the Save the Whale voyages, and then into the role of co-organizer of the second anti-sealing campaign of 1977. When I met him in Ottawa, he was working in the dingy cloisters of Parliament Hill as assistant to the federal New Democratic Party's environment critic Jim Fulton (a post he would soon leave to do hands-on organizational work with an Aboriginal nation on Hansen Island, B.C.) Despite the surroundings, Garrick was clearly no bureaucrat: dressed in a T-shirt and jeans, his look was closer to that of a longshoreman, although his soft speech and deferential manner pegged him more as a writer of lyric poetry or, perhaps, a history professor. History, as a matter of fact, is one of Garrick's passions. As record keeper on the whale voyages and a scribe for *The Georgia Straight*, his main task was to witness the formation of this new movement and to pass the story on to future generations.

The historian's fondness for revealing overlooked fragments of fact is clearly on display as Garrick floats his revisionist version of Greenpeace's earliest days. The catalytic moment that brought this entity into being, he says, was not the formation of the Don't Make a Wave Committee, but rather a nearly concurrent series of events in All Seasons Park, dubbed "People's Park" by the counterculture types who occupied it from spring to fall of 1971. At issue was the city's plans to redevelop the park as offices and apartments – a scheme that would have created further environmental fallout in the form of a new crossing to North Vancouver and a superhighway cutting through Chinatown. To prevent this, an ad hoc citizen opposition moved into the space, putting their bodies on the line and opening up the park as a campground for U.S. war resisters who were pouring across the border and in need of a place to stay. It was a dangerous move given the tenor of the times and the verve with which the police approached their assigned tasks.

"The regime of Mayor Tom Campbell, in those days, had become notorious for hating hippies, the long-hairs from Ontario and Quebec, the draft dodgers from the U.S.," Garrick recalls. But although Campbell and the cops made sure that the occupation of All Seasons Park was no tea party, things could have turned out much worse. The spirit of non-violence prevailed, and the park's occupiers wrested a political victory from the jaws of a potential bloody pummelling. This, says Garrick, was the first experiment in the kind of confrontational yet steadfastly non-violent action that Greenpeace would become famous for, an episode that convinced future organizers that Ghandian resistance was a practical strategy, particularly if there were cameras on hand to amplify the political shock waves.

"The core group [behind Greenpeace] got to know each other under fire – people were being arrested and beaten up by the police," Garrick says. "But we defended the park all summer long, forced the city to have a referendum on it. They learned from the experiences of Berkeley People's Park in California – "where people were actually killed, where there was tear-gas and helicopters and it was a real confrontation. We avoided that, and I think it was working together in day-to-day strategic ways that made it possible for the people who were doing that to join the Quakers, join the Don't Make a Wave Committee of the Sierra Club, and to transform that into what became Greenpeace."

Garrick describes the personalities behind People's Park and the anti-Amchitka campaign as a "visionary motley crew" – a collection of war resisters and underground press types who had little basis for cohesion apart from a general commitment to social change. What kept them glued together, he says, was the imperative that they do something practical. This emerging movement didn't demand inspired speech-making or ideological fervour from its participants. It demanded some kind of action.

"From the beginning," Garrick recalls, "Greenpeace was self-sustaining. If people wanted something done they had to do it themselves or convince others to do it, and to do it well. Many of the people who forged Greenpeace had already taken on the establishment and learned that, to survive doing that, you had to be self-sufficient. These people acquired around themselves the skills and the people talent to pull off everything that came later."

Part of that "people talent" was the ability to accommodate different approaches to the same task. Garrick says that Greenpeace's Save the Whale campaigns – conceived of in 1973, but not launched on the high seas until two years later – provide the clearest example of how the "mystical" and "scientific" segments of Greenpeace could not only co-exist but also play complementary roles. Greenpeace initiated four anti-whaling campaigns in the 1970s, and in a sense the work was an outgrowth of the voyage against the Amchitka nuclear test. During the trip back along the Pacific coast many crew members were sickened at the sight of whale bones piled up onshore, and some of them had vowed to do something to stop the industrial harvest of wildlife that was pushing a multitude of species towards extinction. So while Greenpeace's anti-nuclear work shifted to diplomatic forums (such as the 1973 Stockholm Conference on the Environment) and to the South Pacific – where future Greenpeace chairman David McTaggart was recruited to take part in an Amchitka-style campaign against French atmospheric tests – the Greenpeace machine in Vancouver was gearing up to the wildlife campaign that would give the organization huge international exposure.

There were, however, special problems associated with the whale voyage. For a start, Greenpeace needed to raise funds for a faster, more seaworthy boat. The Russian whaling fleet that worked those waters – unlike the U.S. energy officials who had planned the Amchitka blast – were a moving target and had no intention of announcing their whereabouts beforehand. That's where, according to Garrick, Greenpeace's diversity worked to its advantage. The "mystics" and the "scientists" simply created their own roles: the mystics projected the kind of feel-good vibrations that could be the basis of a public relations and fundraising campaign, and the more mechanically inclined participants cogitated upon the daunting question of how to locate the whaling fleet.

The mystical people decided, Garrick says, "Well, we'll play music, we'll go do community benefits, and we'll sail our vessel up and down the coast for two months, and in the meantime give the other people a chance to fine-tune how they're going to find the whalers." Meanwhile the scientific people were "working on radio directional finding [RDF] equipment, trying to find maps that had earlier whaling data, and so on."

Despite the best efforts of the scientific squad, the Greenpeace crew remained hampered by their inability to "triangulate" their RDF – that is, to take directional bearings on a source of radio transmissions from three different locations. They could roughly locate the general source of a foreign radio signal but weren't able to determine how far away it was, so there was still plenty of room for improvisation. And so, as they drifted around the Pacific in search of an elusive target that could have been thousands of miles away, each faction of the Greenpeace crew continued to take its distinctive approaches to the tasks at hand.

"Because the crew took turns doing everything," Garrick explains, "you'd get the mystical types at the wheel and they'd see a dolphin heading off and say 'oh wow, there's sign from somewhere,' turn the wheel, and head off after the dolphin. Meanwhile, the scientific person comes in on the next shift, tries to follow the charts he's rigorously put together, finds they're way off course, and tries to get back on course. Then the next person comes on, sees the full moon and heads off in that direction. So we did this zigzagging, meandering course through this mystical ocean experience.

"Somehow," Garrick concludes, closing in on the moral of the story, "the two ways ended up with us heading straight smack-dab into the middle of the whaling fleet: dead centre. We couldn't have planned it better."

Any early Greenpeacer who wants to be taken seriously in this era of stiff rationality may have difficulty talking publicly about the flakier aspects of the early voyages. So it is with Bob Hunter, on the surface a jaded, wrinkled bloodhound of a reporter in his early fifties. I first met him on the street outside the television station where he works, just after he'd done his stand-up for a story on the searing summer heat and Toronto's pollution levels. Hunter has written about the mystical aura that permeated all of the campaigns of the 1970s. In person he remembers that aspect of Greenpeace's work with reticence and reserve at first, but then with the resigned sense that if he can risk death in front of whaling harpoons, he can certainly risk a little public embarrassment.

Hunter is a man of many facets who wears his contradictions well: a guy who, without a trace of incongruity, can navigate his propane-powered Japanese car across a tangle of streetcar tracks, raging about ozone depletion, chain-smoking cigarettes all the while. Somehow, by recognizing the dissonance, Hunter pulls it all off. He acknowledges the gap between ideals and real life with a reference to Herbert Marcuse's idea of the two-dimensional man, the citizen of the post-Hiroshima world who lives with the knowledge of impending doom but acts as if everything is normal. Recalling the mystical bent of the early Greenpeace voyages, Hunter seems – in a comic sort of way – irredeemably conflicted: it is in spite of himself that he rallies enormous enthusiasm for the notion that those early campaigns were being stage-managed by some spiritual force.

Hunter will admit to "many occasions" when mystical forces seemed to be at work. A classic case came in Newfoundland during an anti-sealing trip, when a huge storm moved in and a Greenpeace crew of about nine was trapped on an island, in tents, with the temperature dropping and the danger of overexposure mounting. "I threw the I'Ching," Hunter says, "and it said words to the effect of 'the prince goes to his throne,' which we interpreted as 'we should do something.' So we geared up our helicopters and then, lo and behold, the barometer changed and a little opening came in. We zoomed in with the helicopters, got everybody out, and then the worst storm in about fifty years hit. It stopped the whole sealing fleet, but we'd managed to pull our people out of it. Well, you know, in the old days, I suppose, you would just fall down on your knees and pray. In fact, there was a fair amount of that went on."

Was it just the tenor of the times (the budding of the New Age movement, a trendy interest in Eastern philosophy) that predisposed these eco-crusaders to interpret their experience in this otherworldly way? Or were real events so bizarre that they defied rational explanation?

"There were quite a number of us," Hunter says, "who had a feeling we were actually in harmony with some deep, primeval natural force trying to express itself. That sounds like pure gobbledygook, I know. But on the other hand, if you happen to be there and it's the middle of the night and you're out there in the Pacific and you're lost and you haven't been able to find the whalers and you're down to eating food that's soaked in motor oil – and you're almost out of food – and you see a rainbow in the middle of the night under a full moon and someone changes the course so they go straight for the rainbow, and then the next morning the Russian fleet is on the horizon – you're buzzed."

Other members of Greenpeace didn't buy all the New Age weirdness. Jim Bohlen, a former U.S. navy nuclear engineer who defected to Canada and the antiwar movement to eventually become a driving force behind the Amchitka campaign, told *Rolling Stone* magazine that he quit Greenpeace in 1974 largely because the "hippie-dippie element" had seized control.[13] But the struggle between Cartesian logic and divine inspiration was far from the most contentious dispute to be played out within the early Greenpeace. Today, in fact, the whole matter has a quaintly nostalgic ring to it.

A much more divisive issue – and one with much longer term ramifications – revolved around the organization's finances, and the question of whether it was right to exploit the commercial value of Greenpeace's emerging celebrity. Throughout its first decade of life the organization experienced pitched battles between those who wanted the organization to remain a purely grassroots movement –

poverty-stricken, perhaps, but in touch with its principles – and those who envisioned an ecological enterprise with the financial fortitude to doggedly pursue nefarious governments and corporations on the high seas, through the media, and at diplomatic conference tables around the globe. Because this debate was often accompanied by fierce personality conflicts, becoming engaged in these issues almost inevitably meant entering into a fight-to-the-finish: if you lost the argument, you left.

Such was the case with Ben Metcalfe, a principal architect of the Greenpeace media strategy and the first chair of the Greenpeace Foundation, set up in 1971. Although many of Metcalfe's personal traits appear to have been encoded into the collective DNA of Greenpeace, he has been all but banished from the official lore. After leaving Greenpeace in 1973, following a gruelling three-year tour of duty, he returned to journalism: writing a media column for *The Georgia Straight* and contributing sociopolitical commentaries for CBC radio.[14] Metcalfe's life, post-Greenpeace, also involved a number of pilgrimages and fact-finding missions both secular and spiritual, including a jaunt to Namibia to travel with the SWAPO guerillas in the late 1970s and a number of excursions to Zen monasteries.

Now in his mid-seventies, Metcalfe lives with his dogs in a small, sixteen-by-sixteen-foot cabin overlooking the idyllic Shawnigan Lake, British Columbia. A tall, almost Biblical sort of figure, with a well-trimmed white goatee peaking out from under a wide-brimmed straw hat, Metcalfe describes his existence as a "simple life, in tune with nature," consisting mostly of doing his chores, fishing, and writing in his journal. There are only a few remnants of his time with Greenpeace that affect his life today: one of them is the lifetime ban – imposed as punishment for his role in agitating against French nuclear tests – that prevents him from visiting his grandchildren in France.

There was a time, though, when Greenpeace was Ben Metcalfe's consuming passion. Most of the radio recordings chronicling Greenpeace's activities in Vancouver between late 1971 and 1973 feature Metcalfe's distinctive, fatherly voice – most often explaining the tenets of Greenpeace's anti-establishment anti-politics to one interviewer or another, and on other occasions presenting first-person accounts of the journey to the nuclear test site. Most often, Metcalfe used his platform to question the morality, the legitimacy, of the decisions that political leaders were making on behalf of the Earth's inhabitants. His speech is peppered with phrases like "hope is the religion of slaves" – a classic from his repertoire of anti-authoritarian incitements, recognizable as part of the Greenpeace literary tradition by virtue of their sloganistic brevity, but very different from today's buzz-phrases in the way it links personal conscience with political structure.

When I mention that phrase about hope and slavery to Metcalfe, he recognizes it immediately and begins to expound on its current-day significance. "I don't believe in hope," Metcalfe says, about a generation after the original utterance. "Governments hold out hope as some kind of panacea. You know, 'It's too early to tell' – until it's too late to do anything about it. Or: 'We'll just have to wait and see.' They try to offer us hope that everything will be alright, but I don't believe in hope. I believe that one is in control and one must do what one has to do, without expecting anything."

The sustained note of defiance in Metcalfe's words will be familiar to anyone who has seen footage of the standard Greenpeace stunts: dare-devils in rubber dinghies buzzing a nuclear warship, perhaps, or a high-altitude crew draping a banner from a smokestack or a suspension bridge. The basic message expressed in these actions – and carried through from the Amchitka days – might best be summed up in Peter Finch's memorable refrain from the film *Network*: "We're mad as hell and we're not going to take it anymore." Metcalfe confirms that, from the beginning, the public persona that Greenpeace crafted for itself was one of determined defiance: "We synthesized our stand in one word and that word was 'no,'" he says. "We did not involve ourselves, in the beginning, in the technical arguments about nuclear testing, which confused the people, confused everybody. A few years later Dr. [Edward] Teller would say to the world that we could have a hydrogen war and we'd be okay, we'd rebuild the planet from there. But those are insane arguments, and we clearly, openly, categorically refused to indulge in this debate about nuclear testing: there was enough evidence to show that it ain't a good thing. We decided to just say 'no.'"

Having staked out their own position, the early Greenpeace members then attempted to tell government leaders that they wouldn't accept their decisions. Although it is now commonplace for campaigning politicians to be dogged by protesters demanding answers to their questions, Metcalfe says that in 1971 Greenpeace clearly broke a taboo (one that existed in Canada, at least, where in

Metcalfe's view the social climate had long favoured politeness and obedience) by demanding that the prime minister personally explain why he was letting the Americans continue with the Amchitka test. Metcalfe's tape-recorded call to Prime Minister Pierre Trudeau's office, made over the Greenpeace boat's ship-to-shore radio, was a pointed piece of improvisational theatre that focused the controversy squarely on the man at the top: each time an embarrassed underling in Trudeau's office tried to deflect the caller's inquiries, Metcalfe demanded to know when Trudeau would return the call and tell Greenpeace – and the nation – why he hadn't told U.S. President Richard Nixon to call off the Amchitka test.

Metcalfe's insistent tone contained – in itself – a revolutionary statement: that an individual citizen has the right to demand answers from those in power. "We were responsible," Metcalfe says, "for showing the people that they could talk to government, that they could tell the Nixons and the Trudeaus to fuck off, to put it bluntly. We insisted that the game was far too urgent to touch the forelock and bend the knee and say, 'excuse me sir, please listen to me sir.'"

Like the idea of "bearing witness" that underlies Greenpeace's commitment to be present at the site of the nuclear test, Metcalfe's concept of, in his words, "the vernacular relationship" between the people and their government reflects another imperative of the Quaker faith – that of "speaking truth to power." Metcalfe says this principle provided the moral inspiration that made Greenpeace such "a force of intelligence" that politicians either had to confront it or ignore it altogether.

For Metcalfe, creeping commercialism was a threat to that approach. He took the position that financial success is poison to a social change movement, that once your eyes wander to the bottom line you begin to lose sight of your broader goals, that you risk becoming unable to speak uncomfortable truths for fear of alienating the people who send you money. Today Metcalfe's bitter assessment is that Greenpeace was "hijacked as a money-making machine." He says he got a hint of this possibility during his visit Down Under in the aftermath of Amchitka, when he was laying the foundations for Greenpeace's campaign against the French atmospheric nuclear tests in the South Pacific. In Australia he found people "begging" him to sell them the "Greenpeace franchise" for Australia. They would say, "How much do you want, Ben? We'll have the T-shirts, you'll have the mugs and the buttons." According to Metcalfe, "All they could see were dollar bills."

Although Greenpeace continued to specialize in spectacles of public defiance and disobedience well into the 1990s, for Metcalfe this long-lasting theatrical repertoire is not so much an indication of a grassroots strength as a sign of the resilience of corporate and governmental public relations. In the same way that the image-meisters of Madison Avenue tamed and controlled the rebellious posturing of the sixties youth culture (using rock 'n' roll to sell sneakers and cologne), Metcalfe says the defiant spectacles of eco-resistance pioneered by Greenpeace have been largely transformed into an advertising commodity that offers the synthetic sense of catharsis, but no genuine empowerment. The new crop of activists, he says, has turned that old strategy into "doing cheeky things, creating mischief and stuff like that." Meanwhile, the forces that direct world events "have learned to accommodate the protest. They'll do something and wait for the protest and just keep doing it. The protests are accommodated like Christmas or Easter . . . they're just part of the agenda. Greenpeace is now institutionalized, just like the World Court in the Hague – they do a few mischievous things, but they're getting their rocks off too, they're having fun. No, I think one of the big changes in world relationships is the way the "anti's" have been accommodated. Instead of being fought with truncheons and gas, they've been invited into the lower echelons for talks."

And so, in Metcalfe's view, the globalization of Greenpeace parallels the events in the movie *Network* (to return to an earlier cinematic allusion), in which the deranged TV anchorman inspires viewers across the country to poke their heads out of windows to yell out they are mad as hell and not going to take it anymore. In the film this public venting of emotion was not the starting point of a social movement but a last utterance of heartfelt sentiment, a final unrehearsed outburst of mass emotion before the network executives harmlessly – and lucratively – repackaged public discontent as just another entertainment product. The anchor gets his own program, a cross between a game show and a sermon, and at the beginning of it the studio audience gets to yell, on cue, "We're mad as hell and we're not going to take it anymore." Metcalfe thinks something similar happened to Greenpeace, and to much of the rest of the environmental and social protest movements.

The person Metcalfe blames for transforming Greenpeace into "a flourishing corporation . . . a highly successful money-making machine" (which projects images of defiance in order to solicit donations, not to challenge the status quo) is David McTaggart. "I know McTaggart very well," he says. "He is essentially an entrepreneur and I don't see him ever changing from that." Metcalfe recalls first meeting McTaggart after he put out the call for a yachtsman to open up the southern flank of Greenpeace's anti-nuclear work, focused on the French testing that was poisoning the tropical splendour of Moruroa, in the South Pacific. The whole enterprise, by Metcalfe's recollection, came about essentially as the result of a dare.

A few days after Metcalfe was chosen to head the Greenpeace foundation, he says, "a columnist in the Vancouver *Province* called Lorne Parton – who didn't like me particularly – put a snide little item in his column one day, pointing out that the French were about to explode one of their Moruroa atmospheric devices, and he said, 'Of course Greenpeace won't be there, because they're just after the Americans.' That was just a lot of people trying to tag us with the anti-American thing, and missing the point altogether. So he said, 'They've got my dollar if they go after the French the way they went after the Americans.' Well, I read that and I sat up for a long time that night and I decided, 'By God, we're going to go after the French.' We had already sort of been talking about it in any case."

When Metcalfe phoned Jim Bohlen to discuss the idea, Bohlen reminded him that Greenpeace had no boat and that the $9,000 in the treasury wouldn't go far. The way around this was to recruit someone who already had a boat in the South Pacific. "What I did was write a longish cable and send it overnight to the major newspapers of Australia and New Zealand – knowing that there would be Reuters and AP offices down there, and those correspondents would bounce it back into their European and North American headquarters. In other words, I didn't announce this in Canada; I announced it in Australia knowing that it would come back with the authority of the news line." The effect of this manoeuvre was twofold: a new sensation about Greenpeace's international plans, which notched up its profile back in Canada; and an attraction of interest from potential participants Down Under.

"The next day," Metcalfe says, "my telephone was crowded with offers of boats from all kinds of people; freaks and madmen, it was really quite exciting." One of the callers was David McTaggart, who was in New Zealand at the time and had a boat. McTaggart "was a Vancouver boy . . . his brother was a well-known child psychiatrist in Vancouver." Metcalfe picked him.

The two talked over the telephone, and Metcalfe says he wired McTaggart some money to outfit his small sailing vessel – the *Vega* – for the voyage into the French test zone. Metcalfe then travelled to New Zealand to meet the new recruit. "I met him at the airport – a bright young guy, he was fortyish at the time, and a bit rascally look-ing," Metcalfe says. "He was barefoot – that's because he was playing the beachcomber role with the girls down there – and he was a good-looking young man." The two assembled a crew and set sail in the *Vega*.

Shortly afterwards their relationship began to sour. According to Metcalfe, McTaggart got worried about Metcalfe usurping his authority on the boat. Metcalfe also alleges that McTaggart began to undermine him by badmouthing him to the rest of the crew and by sabotaging the shortwave radio that Metcalfe used to maintain con-tact between Greenpeace and the outside world. Beyond the per-sonal rivalry, Metcalfe says, they had vastly different attitudes towards their mission. "One of the things he talked about on the boat," Metcalfe says, "was how we could make a lot of money out of it: *Life* magazine and Hollywood and things like that. His whole atti-tude was so grossly different from the one we had on the Amchitka thing. It was offensive to me, although I bit my tongue, because my attitude was, 'here we are at sea, we are doing something, and we have to make it work.'"

It also became apparent to Metcalfe, during that voyage and later, that the two embraced radically different social ideas. While Met-calfe's words bristle with a working-class disdain for the privileged and the powerful, McTaggart is much more at home – so his nemesis maintains – in the company of high-fliers. "I know that McTaggart would be pleased to dine with Trudeau," Metcalfe says. "He might go out to sea and do brilliant things, but he still retained the culture in which he was bred: that is to be respectful of the politicians."

It's impossible to determine how much of Ben Metcalfe's com-mentary is dispassionate, analytical assessment and how much is simply an outgrowth of his deep-seated personal conflict with McTaggart. It's easy to see how Metcalfe's view of Greenpeace his-tory, post-1973, could be coloured by a sense of loss and betrayal: being in his situation – leaving Greenpeace after helping to shape it

and breathe life into it, only to see it go on to achieve world prominence under the leadership of his rival – is a bit like being the fifth
Beatle, a person that history passed by.

McTaggart's remembrances of this period of time appear in his
book *Outrage! The Ordeal of the Greenpeace III*, in which he portrays
Ben Metcalfe as a man of questionable competence and ethics and a
burden on the first voyage against the French tests.[15] McTaggart
depicts his former colleague in a negative light from the moment
Metcalfe arrives in New Zealand: "My first sight of Ben Metcalfe
shook me," McTaggart writes. "He was about six feet tall and must
have been a good 225 pounds. Beyond the fact that he certainly did
not appear in the condition of a thirty-five year old, his size was an
obvious drawback, for we would have to spend about 60 days ahead
of us in a very confined space."

McTaggart compiles a list of grievances against Metcalfe: that he
didn't know how to operate the ship's radio, that he couldn't navigate the boat, that his boisterous manner upset the crew, that he fed
misinformation to the press. Later McTaggart describes with some
delight how French nuclear testing had been put on the agenda of
the Stockholm conference, but fails to mention Metcalfe's leading
role in lobbying to achieve this goal.

Metcalfe believes he was deliberately scapegoated by McTaggart,
and two decades later he is still sensitive about how he was portrayed. He refers to "that book in which actual lies were told about
me. Silly little lies, like that I was over six feet and 250 pounds, when
in fact I was a nice neat 170. And while I'm not a great yachtsman, I
am able. He [McTaggart] also sabotaged my radio, so that I couldn't
be in touch, as I had been on Greenpeace's first voyage, when I acted
as propaganda minister and operated the radio." Metcalfe believes
McTaggart undermined his status among the crew in an effort to
solidify his role as unchallenged kingpin of Greenpeace Down
Under.

Patrick Moore, another veteran of the Amchitka campaign,
believes that personality rather than ideological differences played
the largest role in their squabbles. Moore, who became president of
Greenpeace in the late 1970s and remained a major player in the
organization until the late 1980s, says that with both players sharing a
flamboyantly patriarchal style, it was inevitable that one of them
would be forced to leave. "They're both pretty serious egos. They
have that kind of male ego problem, as to who's in charge and stuff."

Metcalfe and McTaggart were not the only early Greenpeacers to differ over the role of finances in the organization. Perhaps the most ferocious and consistent critic of the commercial vein within Greenpeace is Paul Watson, a high-profile player in the anti-whaling and anti-sealing campaigns of the 1970s. Watson is known for his swashbuckling, swaggering style and his apparent immunity to fear of physical harm. Following his expulsion from Greenpeace in 1979, Watson reinvented himself as the head of the Sea Shepherd Conservation Society, an organization he built on the same kind of "biocentric" nature-worshipping ideology as Earth First!, which embraced Watson as a kind of kindred spirit and patron saint during the second surge of grassroots environmentalism in the United States in the 1980s.

Watson speaks without reservation about the greed that he insists destroyed Greenpeace; it seems, in fact, that he gets more ink by denouncing Greenpeace than by explaining the campaigns of Sea Shepherd. On a lecture stop in Ottawa, the greying, stocky sailor reiterates his belief that, for environmental groups, the quest for money has become primary: the object is to meet an ever-expanding payroll rather than to win environmental battles. He says the tendency took root in Greenpeace during the first decade, when the organization "allowed fundraisers, lawyers and bureaucrats to control their board."

"Greenpeace," Watson tells me, "has become the Avon ladies and the Fuller Brush men of the environmental movement; you know, knocking on everybody's door asking for a handout. They don't do a hell of a lot with it. They hang a few banners here and there and take credit for everything every grassroots organization is doing. But it's become a major corporation. It employs a lot of people, and those people's primary concern is their jobs."

Watson clashed with Bob Hunter over the question of finances – although Hunter has since become a regular guest on Watson's boat, and often endorses his campaigns. Unlike Watson, Hunter doesn't believe that Greenpeace does nothing with the money it raises. Its sizable cash flow gives Greenpeace its clout in the diplomatic arena, he says. And that's exactly the place where Hunter became convinced of the need to get the organization on a solid financial footing.

"By the time we got to sending members to the International Whaling Commission," Hunter says, "our first discovery was, 'My

God, there are these entrenched bureaucrats working for the whaling industry, who'd been here since day one and who will always be here trying to make things happen their way.' Basically, it's a military thing: we had to put our bureaucrat battalions into place to constantly fight theirs in a trench war that's going to go on forever." To make his point Hunter loosely adapts an old psalm: "He who guards Earth neither rests nor sleeps."

Another reason that Greenpeace began its fundraising and merchandising drives, Hunter says, was to be able to resist the lure of the government grant programs that were being offered, for better or worse, to countercultural organizations in Canada at the time. For Greenpeace, taking government money would clearly have made it dependent upon its enemy: consider, for instance, the Canadian government's deliberately inept handling of McTaggart's complaint against the French government, whose sailors had boarded the Canadian's boat in 1975 and beaten him to a pulp. Canada's motive for torpedoing McTaggart's case later became clear when it was revealed that France and Canada were price-fixing uranium – making Canada a de facto partner in the French nuclear test program that McTaggart sought to undermine.[16]

In Hunter's view, voluntarism provided no real alternative to getting hooked on government grants. He had become convinced of this after quitting his job at *The Vancouver Sun* to work full-time as the (unpaid) president of Greenpeace, taking over the office from Ben Metcalfe. Long-term strategy, he decided, should not rest on the shoulders of unpaid activists: eventually the people carrying out campaigns wind up burnt-out and in the poorhouse. "Ad hoc is only good for a while," he says. "I mean, there were some of us who thought, 'If we work hard at this for ten weekends we'll have saved the world, and we can go back to lying in our hot-tubs,' or whatever the fantasy might have been at the time. The fact is you've got to have people who can stay in month after month, year after year, and can sustain a long-term commitment that way. Sooner or later you've got to get some money to finance it."

CHAPTER 6

CIVIL WARS AND SEAL HUNTS

IN THE GREENPEACE OF THE 1970S NOT ALL OF THE squabbles centred on internal, organizational questions. Greenpeace's decision to campaign against the seal hunt in 1976 and 1977 created divisions over policy. With the anti-nuclear and anti-whaling campaigns there had been unanimity: everyone was firm in their commitment that preparing for nuclear war is evil; that using enormous, high-tech killer ships to hunt whales into extinction is obscene. The seal hunt raised more nuanced political questions. There were different groups of sealers – the Norwegian fleet, the Newfoundlanders, the Inuit – who used different methods to hunt seals and whose activities, arguably, had different impacts on the seal population.

While hard-liners like Paul Watson still stick to the blanket commitment that "sealing is despicable, and it has no economic foundation for even existing – it's a glorified welfare scheme," others like Bob Hunter were prepared to view some types of sealing as relatively benign ecologically and to concede to the Newfoundlanders and the Inuit a limited right to hunt seals. An often-forgotten footnote to the campaign is that during the first trek to Newfoundland in 1976 Hunter had brokered a tentative deal with the Newfoundland Fishermen, Food and Allied Workers' Union whereby the Newfoundland sealers would support Greenpeace's call for a 200-mile fishing limit in exchange for Greenpeace directing all of its anti-sealing efforts against the Norwegians. According to David Garrick, the deal was partly an attempt by Hunter to perform "a very delicate balancing act in front of a room full of very irate people," so as to be able to leave St. Anthony, Newfoundland, without being lynched.

Hunter maintains that this tentative alliance was not so much a hasty bid for self-preservation as it was a reasoned political manoeuvre based on the analysis that "the problem was not the little guys that go out in their boat with their kids, and it certainly wasn't the Inuit in Labrador or anything like that." The problem, according to Hunter, was "the large icebreakers, mainly from Norway, that were going into the berthing grounds. These were the real threat to the viability of the seal herds."

There is a continuing dispute over whether the Newfoundland sealers were as blameless in threatening the existence of the seals as Hunter now suggests. In any case, the alliance between Greenpeace and the fishermen's union was abandoned for tactical reasons the next year. Greenpeace and its partners (notably the International Fund for Animal Welfare, which had campaigned against sealing for some time) returned to the ice floes in 1977 with a campaign that centred around the visit of French actress Bridget Bardot to the sealing grounds as well as the dissemination of more images of baby seals being bloodily bludgeoned to death. The pictures became a powerful tool that would soon secure a European ban on the importation of seal pelts, killing virtually the whole market for seal products. So much for a focused campaign targeting the Norwegian fleet.

John Amagualuk, an official with the Tungavik Federation of Nunavut, says the Inuit were "innocent bystanders" hit by the flying shrapnel of a propaganda war that really shouldn't have involved them: the Inuit hunted adult seals rather than baby seals, he says, using high-power rifles that would kill the animals instantly, rather than the bludgeons that so sickened television viewers across the world. Yet by being associated with the techniques of the commercial hunt, Amagualuk says, the Inuit were deprived of their link to the cash economy and abandoned in a no-man's land somewhere between their traditional past and the modern world. "The collapse of the sealskin market," he says, "meant that many of our communities lost an important part of their economy, because people need cash to maintain their snowmobiles, to keep up their hunting equipment, and for things like gasoline and ammunition and everything else. That resulted in an increase in the social problems that we have. There was a marked increase in the rate of suicide among our young people, especially in communities that depended heavily upon the sealskin industry."

That Greenpeace's anti-sealing campaign would have this effect upon northern Native communities was a source of grief for a number of Greenpeace members who identified strongly with Native culture and had embraced traditional Aboriginal teachings as a cornerstone of their own emerging philosophies. Aboriginal lore figures prominently in the first few years of Greenpeace mythmaking: the organization had adopted a book of Aboriginal prophesy called *Warriors of the Rainbow* as one of its sacred texts. As well, the crew of the first Amchitka voyage had been made honorary brothers of the Kwakiutl nation during their homeward journey down the coast of British Columbia.

For some Greenpeacers, this aspect of the group identity was bolstered by personal experience. David Garrick took part in a sweat-lodge ceremony in Wounded Knee, South Dakota, in 1973, where he and Paul Watson had journeyed as part of a "quasi-official Greenpeace expedition – I think Greenpeace kicked in $70" when Wounded Knee was under siege by U.S. federal authorities. As FBI bullets whizzed by the participants in the sweat lodge, Garrick committed himself to work on Native issues, to use his skills as a reporter to bring Native American social justice and environmental struggles as far into public view as possible. The next year he followed through on that commitment by attaching himself to an Indian caravan engaged in a historic pilgrimage across Canada: protesting for fishing rights in British Columbia, occupying Anishinabe Park in Kenora, and finally setting up camp on Parliament Hill, where the RCMP special riot squad was called in to beat up the protesters and clear the grounds.

Given his clear and heartfelt commitment to working *with* Aboriginal peoples on environmental issues, it is understandably the source of some remorse for Garrick that the Save the Seal campaign – which he helped organize – had such a devastating effect upon the Inuit. Garrick and some of his colleagues had foreseen that the anti-sealing campaign might rebound against Inuit sealers as far back as 1974, he says. They tried to avert that possibility by attempting to assemble a Native crew whose presence on the ice might draw the attention of the media, thereby making the distinction in the public mind between Native sealing and the commercial kill. (This account is disputed by Patrick Moore, Greenpeace president during the second anti-sealing campaign, who told me that the idea was proposed only in passing and never seriously considered.) Garrick also recalls that Greenpeace sought to immunize the anti-sealing campaign against unintended side-effects by seeking help on the spiritual plane.

"I personally tried very hard," he says, "to approach this in a systematic and alternative way. One thing I did do, in a traditional way, was to offer tobacco to some medicine people for ceremonial connection with the seals. I was told during the ceremony – which was quite an experience in itself – that the spirits of the seals were very far away. This was in British Columbia. I was told I would have to do something further. So we did another preparatory expedition. The idea was to take our intention, to encapsule our intentions symbolically, to the point where we could announce it to the world on the mystical or spiritual plain. So a number of us went into the Rocky Mountains, this was in February, and climbed one of the peaks in the Jasper/Banff area, and had a little ceremony on top of the mountains where we affixed a Greenpeace button and said some prayers. The idea was that when the sun came up from the east it would reflect on this little Greenpeace button and it would know that we were coming from the west to the east because of the seals. And we had a number of ceremonies, including sweat lodges, purification ceremonies, to try and make that work. We wrote to the Inuit Tapirisat to try and announce our intentions. It wasn't enough. Out of ignorance or improper timing, or relying too much on assumptions, it didn't work. And unfortunately, anybody who took any seals were painted in the same way by the media."

As Garrick remembers it, the Save the Seals campaign brought into sharp relief two key but inherently contradictory aspects of Greenpeace's nature: the intense spiritual commitment of many of its members, and the organization's alliance with the mass media – that fickle, superficial, unforgiving appendage of the consumer society that we all know and sometimes hate. This contest between the inner eye of the campaign's participants and the public eye of the television lens, Garrick says, turned out to be no contest at all. While some Greenpeacers had envisioned a precisely targeted anti-sealing campaign that would exempt the traditional Inuit sealers, once the issue hit the airwaves the campaign had the indiscriminate impact of a neutron bomb.

"Our attempts to differentiate between the commercial slaughter and other types of sealing didn't make it into the media," he says. "And we did have that analysis."

The experience of the two anti-sealing campaigns of 1976 and 1977 reveals a widening chasm between the understanding of the participants (campaigners and their opponents alike), who see the issues from ground level, and the perception of the "audience," which watches events unfold in a condensed form from a distance. The seal-hunt campaigns reveal an unfortunate quality in media-based activism: while television can sway public opinion to the extent that policy-makers *must* respond – and while it can deliver a mass following for environmental groups – that new following will most likely be based upon a narrow understanding of the issues. The danger, ultimately, is that environmentalists will start pandering to an underinformed public in order to keep their support.

Bob Hunter says the perceptual schism between Greenpeace's leadership and its constituents in the major urban centres became unmistakably clear to him in 1976. While he insists that most of the leadership had factored social and economic elements into their analysis of the seal hunt, this was definitely not true of the organization's supporters. Several thousand of them sent Hunter a mountain of crushed Greenpeace buttons to protest his proposed deal with the Newfoundland fisherman's union, a move widely perceived as a sell-out of the seals. John Amagualuk adds that urban environmentalists – both supporters and some of the leadership – made their decision about the Inuit seal hunt without any knowledge of the Inuit way of life, presumably on the basis of television reports on sealing. "I remember one particular incident," Amagualuk says, "when we were having a large meeting in one of our communities, and we invited a spokesman from the Greenpeace organization. One particular Inuk asked the Greenpeacer, 'If we can't hunt seals, what are we going to do? How are we going to feed our families?' And the guy from Greenpeace suggested we should all build greenhouses and grow vegetables. I mean, this was a real insult to our people."

This gap between reality and image became even more pronounced outside of Canada. While the social and economic impact of the seal hunt (on both Newfoundlanders and the Inuit) eventually came to dominate discussion of the seal hunt in Canada, in Europe that side of the debate was invisible.

The seal hunt is an issue that frames Dan McDermott's career with Greenpeace like a pair of bookends: he came on board to cofound the Toronto office just as the seal campaign was taking off in 1976, and his final project before leaving in 1991 was to prepare an internal research paper summing up the impact of the anti-sealing campaign. One of McDermott's conclusions in that report was that Inuit communities had always been at the mercy of cyclical trends in the fur industry, and that – regardless of what Greenpeace would have done – local Inuit economies would have crashed because the fur industry had already decided to close the market for seal pelts.

McDermott says the anti-sealing campaign had two totally different impacts down on the field and out in the stands: in Canada the campaign produced a levelling-off and probably a decline in support for Greenpeace, but in Europe it helped lay the foundations for Greenpeace's exponential expansion in the 1980s. "I took a holiday in the Netherlands in 1990," McDermott says, "and I would see in rural communities a save the seals window sticker still on people's windows years after the campaign, so it wasn't too difficult to get some visual idea about what campaigns had helped spark that growth. To everyone else in the world except the Canadians [the seal hunt] was an open and shut case. You know, the sole question was 'how could this be allowed to continue?'"

★ ★ ★

The internal disputes that had been simmering within the organization throughout the 1970s finally reached a boiling point in 1978 and 1979, when Greenpeace was compelled to make a final, convulsive surge out of Vancouver and onto the world stage. Continuing disagreements over finances, over the tone of Greenpeace campaigns, and over subsidiary policy questions – which had led to the departures of leading dissidents such as Metcalfe in 1973 and Watson in 1977 – remained the source of discord and division for a Vancouver office that divided its time between bitter infighting and the creation of brilliant, magnetic media campaigns.

Meanwhile the Greenpeace mystique had begun to spread. Small, self-actualizing bands of eco-freaks around the globe had been so impressed by the images of high-seas bravado projected by the original Vancouver gang that they began to open up shop under the Greenpeace banner in their own neighbourhoods – with varying degrees of approval and support from the principals in British Columbia. While this was clearly a testament to Greenpeace's success, it was also the source of more conflict. Without any central authority or control, disparate cells flying the Greenpeace pennant began to issue contradictory policy statements and to invite cameras to follow them on their own private missions.

Garrick remembers being caught in the struggle over "ownership" of the Greenpeace moniker while taking part in the occupation of the Trident nuclear submarine base in Bangor, Washington. "At one point," he says, "I had a courier run down from Vancouver saying 'this is not an official Greenpeace campaign; you have to stop using the name.' Well, this kind of thing was going on right across the planet." The other source of conflict between old and new outposts was, to quote Ben Metcalfe's litany of euphemisms, "money, the filthy lucre, the root of all evil." Vancouver wanted a cut from the donations collected offshore; the upstart branches said "no way."

In 1978 the final showdown began, aimed at resolving the fundamental, knock-down, drag-out questions of "What is Greenpeace?" and "Who, if anyone, will control this transnational activist outfit and dictate its policy?" At the centre of this melodrama was Patrick Moore, a bearded, tousle-haired veteran of the Amchitka campaign, who held a PhD in ecology and had been president of Greenpeace since succeeding Bob Hunter in 1976. Moore recalls how the principal actors in Greenpeace's Vancouver office had seeded the international expansion of Greenpeace: after the 1975 Save the Whale campaign (which propelled Greenpeace to stardom in the United States) Moore, Hunter, and Paul Spong enlisted the help of a San Francisco lawyer to establish an office in that city with its charitable status secured under U.S. law but with trademark and copyright controlled by Vancouver. A similar story unfolded in Europe, says Moore: in 1977 Bob Hunter helped David McTaggart launch a campaign against Icelandic whaling that led to the establishment of a European flank of Greenpeace, with offices in several countries.

Despite the helping hand from the home office, some of the new branches started clamouring for their freedom. In 1978, Moore says, "the board of directors of Greenpeace USA – including the lawyer who had volunteered to protect us in the first place – announced their intention to be autonomous and to break away from the originating group. And, of course, to take all the money and all our photographs and everything we had done before they existed. So in about June of 1979, in an effort to bring the situation to a resolution, my board of directors sued Greenpeace USA for infringement of copyright and trademark." (San Francisco responded to the $1 million suit by launching a $2 million countersuit for slander.) By taking legal action, Moore cast himself into the role of Public Enemy Number One and guaranteed that all the regional Greenpeace offices (which, according to Hunter, had numbered about fifty by 1976, including chapters in U.S. centres such as Portland, Boston, and Seattle, and as far afield as New Zealand and Japan) would rally against the heavy hand of imperialism in Vancouver. Even the new office in Toronto, Moore says, did not want to submit to the tyranny of the West Coast control freaks.

Moore says he had two reasons for challenging the branches' independence. The first was money: while the new Greenpeace cells could raise funds largely on the strength of previous campaigns devised and executed by Vancouver, he relates, "Back in Vancouver we were about $180,000 in debt from renting the ships and doing all the things we'd done over the years. And of course, they didn't have any debts; they were riding on the now fairly popular movement that had been established."

The other factor behind the lawsuit was a desire to maintain Greenpeace's international scope. What distinguished Greenpeace from other environmental outfits, Moore says, was the idea that it could operate across national boundaries, chasing down international polluters as easily as multinational corporations could drift from country to country. This capability would be threatened if Greenpeace broke down into autonomous regional and national offices.

"From my perspective, the issue was whether Greenpeace would remain a single organization, or whether Greenpeace would become a word like Kleenex, that everybody uses to describe everybody else – a generic term," Moore says. "In fact, Greenpeace is still the only true international activist organization, that has an international constitution and where all the money's on one table during international meetings."

Although Moore takes some credit for preserving the global scope of Greenpeace, his role in that process was certainly not what he would have liked. Having cast himself as the bad guy – the overambitious Canadian kingpin against whom all the new offices had rallied – Moore set the stage for David McTaggart ("who had been operating kind of independently in France during this period," Moore says) to ride in with a proposal that everyone could accept. "McTaggart's role was to play the white knight," Moore says. "He

successfully rallied the others against me. So he succeeded in unify-
ing them – which had been the problem in the first place, that they
hadn't been unified. To that extent he played a valuable role,
although it was at my expense."

In the home office in Vancouver, Moore says, Bob Hunter
"resented the fact that I took over from him, and resented the fact
that after that I didn't seek his counsel on a regular basis." A number
of Hunter's followers in Vancouver withdrew their support from
Moore. Standing alone against the upstart Greenpeace colonies and
without the backing of his peers, Moore was forced to negotiate on
his rival's terms. McTaggart's timing was impeccable: he brought all
the belligerents to the table the day before the Vancouver-San Francisco lawsuits were to proceed to court, averting a legal battle that
most insiders thought could only lead to disaster. They negotiated a
settlement whereby Greenpeace USA recognized the Greenpeace
Foundation's worldwide legal right to the "Greenpeace" copyright and
trademark. In turn the Greenpeace Foundation agreed to the formation of the Greenpeace International Council. Europe got two votes on
the council, Canada and the United States one each, and McTaggart –
the chairman, who represented no country – another vote. Canada
agreed to all of this in return for having its entire debt paid off by the
other countries. "That was the deal," Moore says. The international
headquarters were lodged in Washington, D.C., London, and Lewes,
England, before settling permanently in Amsterdam.

By Moore's recounting, the structure of the new board reflected
McTaggart's particular genius for promoting his own political interests. Having formed close links with the European offices, chairman
McTaggart could count on the two European votes to support his
position, and his own vote would give him a clear majority of three
votes out of five. In addition, the lingering bitterness between the
Canadian and U.S. Greenpeace offices made it unlikely that the
North Americans could mount a challenge; while other members,
such as Australia and New Zealand, which could potentially upset
the balance, were neutralized by being denied voting status. In this
way McTaggart assumed firm control over the newly corporatized
Greenpeace, an overhauled organization that he would lead through
the following decade of frantic expansion.

For his part, Patrick Moore took control of Greenpeace Canada,
now just a national branch plant rather than head office. He had a
seat on the international board but was left in charge of an office that

had drastically shrunk in status and power. While many of the original Greenpeace players such as Hunter and Garrick had by the end of the 1970s decided that it was time to drift off to other things, Moore stayed on with Greenpeace Canada until 1986. "I was a survivor," he says. "I don't think anyone but McTaggart has had a longer stint."

Most of Patrick Moore's account of the Greenpeace civil war – and of the formation of the new international structure – is consistent with the stories told by his contemporaries. The differences are largely a question of tone. The commissioned history of Greenpeace, Michael Brown and John May's *The Greenpeace Story*, portrays the fight more as a mechanical reorganization than an emotional struggle, as a move necessary for reconciling an outdated organizational structure with the enormous growth that was shifting the organization's influence away from its original geographic base. "Such international co-ordination was becoming increasingly necessary," the authors write. "By early 1980 there were 25,000 paying supporters in the Boston area alone. In the Netherlands, new members were being signed up at a rate of 1,100 per month."

Bob Hunter sees the conflict more as a case of egos and tempers getting out of hand, and he lays much of the blame on Patrick Moore. In an October 1980 *Saturday Night* magazine article, "The War within Greenpeace," Hunter wrote that Moore's announced intention to set up an international board – with Moore in charge and with control over international fundraising – drove McTaggart to set up Greenpeace Europe as a separate legal entity and alienated Greenpeace offices throughout the world. According to Hunter, the idea of letting all the new offices go their own way appealed to his "anarchist instinct."

Although McTaggart and Moore both agreed that an international structure and centralized control were imperative for an organization that had grown so much and so widely, Hunter saw in the new model the death of a noble and innocent experiment, the passing of a countercultural organization whose meetings "were like conclaves of some polyglot religious order." For his part, Moore today is saddened that the re-engineering of Greenpeace was driven so much by resentment and personal bitterness. "I didn't find that it was carried out in a particularly civilized fashion," he says. "There was a certain amount of vilification and demonization in the thing which I thought was quite juvenile."

Being vilified by his peers is an experience that, evidently, Patrick Moore was fated to return to. Ironically, in the 1990s Moore has become, once again, an arch-villain for many environmentalists. After departing Greenpeace in 1986, Moore resurfaced as a partner in a B.C. fish-farming operation, a type of enterprise blamed by some environmental scientists for ecological ills ranging from the contamination of the oceans with antibiotics (used in large quantities to keep the penned-in fish disease-free) to creating havoc in the ecological order of things by introducing foreign species of fish into new marine surroundings. Some environmentalists – especially former colleagues – see this work as a defection to the side of darkness, a sell-out of his former environmental principles. Moore defended himself in a CBC television interview by saying that it's "a form of fascism" to expect that the natural environment will remain static and constant.[1]

But the fallout from Moore's resurrection as piscatorial entrepreneur was nothing compared to the loud wails of "traitor" that greeted his appointment as director of the B.C. Forest Alliance, an industry-sponsored group that critics associate with the notorious wise use movement, the loose amalgam of anti-environmental citizen front-groups. The B.C. Forest Alliance was founded at the suggestion of a company with extensive links to wise use groups in the United States: Burston-Marsteller, the world's largest PR firm, perhaps best known as the outfit that dreamed up the story of the Chad babies who, in some well-publicized but entirely fictitious accounts, were ripped out of their non-existent hospital incubators by Iraqi troops just prior to the Gulf War.

According to writer Joyce Nelson, B-M has honed its spin-doctoring on forest issues through extensive work for international forestry firms, including thirty-six of the main corporate sponsors of wise use groups in the United States, as well as the Brazilian company Aracruz Celulose, implicated in the destruction of the Amazon rainforest. B-M counted as a client, for example, the U.S. forestry firm Louisiana-Pacific, during the time that the company successfully broke the union and reorganized workers into anti-environmental groups fighting against the ecologists who were accused of campaigning against their jobs. Nelson says the environmentalist "threat" was such an effective red herring that it allowed Louisiana-Pacific to quietly shift its pulping jobs to Mexico, where workers would be paid one-tenth the wages of the U.S. workforce.[2]

A Burston-Marsteller subsidiary, Cohn & Wolfe, has also worked for a group called "Sharenet" – a consortium of wise use organizations in Washington and Oregon states. Not surprisingly, having secured such positive results with this strategy in the United States, B-M advised British Columbia's forest companies to take a similar tack. The result was the B.C. Forest Alliance – a group funded by the forestry industry but positioned in the public debate as a "broad-based, grassroots" voice for the "rational middle-ground."

By accepting a job offer from the B.C. Forest Alliance, Patrick Moore found himself on the same payroll as such notables as Jack Munro, former head of the B.C. division of the International Woodworkers of America (IWA) and one of the most dedicated anti-environmentalists in Canadian history. Moore is also working directly at odds with the environmental organization he helped found: for while Greenpeace had been vigorously campaigning for a ban on clear-cutting in B.C., Moore's job was now to provide the press and public with elaborate justifications explaining why clear-cut logging is ecologically and economically sound.

The fact that Moore is now toiling in the Other Side's trenches can be interpreted either as a statement about the ideological splintering of the environmental movement or as a reflection of the personal impact of the battles that remain endemic in the movement, a group dynamic that has left its mark in the bitter, battered tone underlying many of Moore's recollections. The idea that Moore's differences with his ex-colleagues are a result of the ideological fault-lines that have opened up in the movement makes sense if you accept at face value Moore's explanation of why he decided to work for the Forest Alliance. "The reason that I'm on this path," he says, "is that I grew up in the rainforest in the north end of Vancouver Island, in a logging and fishing community. So it was natural for me to go back to B.C. and try to help the forest industry, which is our biggest economic base, is operating in our most important environment, and has the most environmental impact of everything we do. I'm taking my knowledge and trying to apply it to helping the forest industry to get out in front; to adopt more progressive thinking, to accept things that it should accept, but to fight misinformation on the other hand, and to not accept things that it shouldn't accept, like a ban on clear-cutting, which would be stupid."

Moore criticizes his ex-comrades on the environmental front lines on two grounds: first, that they don't acknowledge the forests' ability to recover from clear-cutting after being replanted; and second, that by making forestry one of the major focuses of their activities, they have abdicated the responsibility to set priorities. In Patrick Moore's personal hierarchy of environmental ills, the impact of logging comes well down the list. Forests, he says, are a renewable resource; as long as forest companies are committed to replanting the forests, there's no problem. Far more of a threat, in Moore's worldview, is the impact of using non-renewable resources that both contaminate the environment and promote the poisonous touch of an industrialized human society.

According to Moore, fossil fuels "are the underpinning of unsustainability," and "we wouldn't be able to abuse the forests as badly as we do if we didn't have the damn things." The fossil fuels lead to "the chain-saws and the bulldozers and automobiles and asphalts and every other bloody thing that we're using to chop the planet up." He argues: "Long after the fossil fuels are completely gone, and minerals have become scarce, trees will be the wealth of Canada and of many other countries in the world. They will be the giver of wealth, and they will still be here as they have been through successive ice ages. The fact is that it is pavement that is the first most important aspect destroying biodiversity. Agriculture is second. Managed forestry is the next best thing to wilderness. People are not seeing the spectrum clearly."

Why then, do people get so upset about clear-cut logging? In Patrick Moore's unconventional view, it's because the images lie. The dramatic use of photographs to illustrate ecological destruction – a technique perfected by Greenpeace – deflects public attention away from the larger picture. To support his position Moore lifts a quote from Garrett Hardin's *Tragedy of the Commons*: "The morality of an act cannot be judged from a photograph." For Moore the key question is, "To what extent are dramatic images appropriate in terms of shaping public policy and public opinion?" You can ignore the aerial shots of acres of barren land, shorn of trees, and forget what you've heard about clear-cut forests destroying species. According to Moore, it's not like that at all. Clear-cutting can result in the loss of biodiversity, at least temporarily, he admits. But "So does a fire." The state of biodiversity is lowered if all the plants in one place are killed, but this is a temporary phenomenon. "It's different from an oil refinery, which for all intents and purposes is a permanent phenomenon. This myth about how forest fires don't kill biodiversity whereas clear-cuts do – that's all bull-shit."

The alternatives to clear-cutting proposed by environmentalists are ultimately more destructive, Moore says. Selective logging, or thinning of forests, requires the construction of large numbers of roads, and roads encourage the things that lead to permanent loss of wilderness: human settlement and agriculture, to name two. So, Moore argues, the environmental movement should give the forest companies a break and start tackling the larger issues of population and petro-chemical use that threaten to turn the globe into one large industrial park-cum-shanty town.

For those who choose to discard his intricate rationale, as most environmentalists do, Moore also presents a more visceral, emotional explanation for his decision to part company with his environmental colleagues and join the opposing team. In the course of several lengthy conversations, Moore confides that – despite a decade and a half of dedicated service and ingenious campaigning – he left Greenpeace feeling bruised, embittered, and underappreciated. He left like a shell-shocked soldier trying to find his way in an unfamiliar world.

"We used to have a saying that 'you can't get off the boat,' meaning that it's difficult to get out of campaign mode and back into civilian life," Moore says. For him and others, working with Greenpeace was very much like being in the military or in a big-time election campaign. You have to make sacrifices in terms of having a normal life. "It's like going on the crusades, and you come back from the crusades and everything has changed, and you're ten years or fifteen years behind in a number of things. And you have no sort of defined career, you have no pension plan, you have no savings . . . those sorts of things that seem like they're not important at the time you're fighting the war. For fifteen years, it's full-time, real-time."

Reviled by his former friends after switching sides (particularly after "a vitriolic series of columns by Bob Hunter, in which he targeted me as the eco-Judas," Moore says), he nonetheless feels confident enough to turn the tables and question his accusers' motives. Moore says they have no right to be critical of what he has done, after all the time he spent mounting the barricades.[3]

Moore's impression is that after fifteen years of being the head of Greenpeace Canada he had become a symbol for his friends' concern for the environment. "They could stay in their cushy lawyer and

doctor jobs and volunteer once in a while, but I volunteered for fifteen years. And here they all are with this expectation that I'm going
to continue to provide them with this role, that I am doing the job
for them. So when I started doing things that they did not perceive
to be what they wanted their 'environmental leader' to do, that really
affected them. So I can understand it in that sense. Not at a personal
level but at a larger, social level. I failed them, I disappointed them,
and I was no longer on a pedestal where they had me before."

Moore says that the distance between him and his old friends has
started to shrink. He is now back on speaking terms with some people who had once avoided him like the plague. When he mentions
this in my conversation with him, his tone mellows. He steps back a
bit. He looks at the disagreements and puzzles over what they say
about environmental philosophy. The environmental movement is
prone to schisms, he concludes, because its members come from different intellectual traditions. There is "the biology angle" and "the
social science angle," he says. "The life science environmentalists
like myself either discount the class analysis, or in my case, just can't
deal with it intellectually. The black hole in ecological philosophy is
that there's no comparative philosophical approach to synthesizing
ecology and political science. There was the term 'human ecology,'
but it never did catch on and it was always soft and fuzzy. It was not
really a hard approach." So it's no wonder that the movement is rife
with disagreement, since few environmentalists speak the same language to begin with.

Still, even amongst the divergent collection of interests represented on the first Greenpeace voyage, the participants had that all-
important "common cause." For that first mission, Moore says,
"Our common cause was to stop five-megaton hydrogen bombs
from being detonated under an island in the Aleutians. Our enemy
was the Atomic Energy Commission of the United States – the
Darth Vadar of all Darth Vadars."

That sense of common cause, of camaraderie, of mission, would
dissipate as the 1970s wore on. While the first generation of Greenpeacers emptied their hearts and souls into the Grand Battles of that
era – fighting against atomic testing, against the slaughter of the
whales and seals – they also turned their rage against one another. By
1979 Greenpeace looked like a spent force: divided, disorganized,
fixated on petty interpersonal and pecuniary disputes. But that was
all backstage politics. When David McTaggart brokered the deal that

rescued Greenpeace from itself, he transplanted onto European soil an organization that had lost little of its shimmer in the public eye. Greenpeace could still capture headlines, could still stir public passions.

The Greenpeace strategy for campaigning through the media was a golden, inspired notion that would need little fine-tuning as it left Canada. The name itself – with that swashbuckling spirit now embedded within it – had become a precious commodity. Using the mythology of that first, romantic era as its launching pad, Greenpeace would in the 1980s move on to new issues such as toxic waste disposal and industrial pollution, which became defining concerns for the environmental movement of that decade. The 1985 sinking of the Greenpeace flagship, *Rainbow Warrior*, was a tragedy that cast an even more intense public spotlight on the organization and ensured its continued growth into the early 1990s. The 1992 Earth Summit in Rio de Janeiro would symbolize the spread of environmental concern across the planet, a process to which Greenpeace had made a significant contribution.

All of these landmarks can be attributed, to some extent, to Greenpeace's willingness to embrace diversity and to adopt an expansive, multidimensional vision of its target-world. Those characteristics would always create conflict and crisis as seasons changed; as an altered political landscape presented new and more problematic challenges; and as issues evolved and traditions collided.

CHAPTER 7

THE QUEST FOR COVERAGE

IN TECHNOLOGY WE TRUST

WITHIN THE SPRAWLING ORGANIZATIONAL ANATOMY OF Greenpeace there is a spot where the frequently conflicting imperatives of environmental campaigner and media spin-doctor intersect. In a partly gentrified section of the City of London, just outside Britain's famous financial district, the scrubbed offices of film production companies reside a few paces away from an old fish market. Here is a neighbourhood where the happy wanderer can either preen on the outdoor terrace of a trendy bistro or soak in the more traditional ambience of a dim-lit public house where the plat de jour is egg and chips but the real attractions are the draught beer and gambling machine.

Down a sidestreet in this maze of urban ambivalence is a building you'd probably miss if you didn't know what to look for: a drab yet respectable-looking concrete rectangle, a renovated warehouse with a fortified front door, an intercom system, and no name plate. This is the headquarters of Greenpeace International's Communications Department – known as "Coms" to the people who work there. It is separated from the campaign offices of Greenpeace UK (about one tube stop away) and of Greenpeace International (in Amsterdam) by both physical space and a certain state of mind. Although the campaigners and planners in those other places may perform the heroics, capture the spotlight, map out the strategies, and plot the diplomatic manoeuvres, in many ways Coms is the most important facet of Greenpeace and also its most privileged.

106

"That's where the money goes to," Andy Booth tells me. Booth, a former grassroots campaigner who had become Greenpeace UK's campaign director and then served as head of international communications from 1990 to 1992, pegged Coms' basic operating costs (not including specific campaign-related media expenses) during his tenure at about U.S.$1.2 million per year. The communications department single-mindedly applies those funds to the task of pumping the environmental message out through the international airwaves (and to a lesser extent, through the print newswires). "That's how Greenpeace built its profile as an organization," Booth explains.

"By focusing, without exception, all its communications resources on the mass media. There's absolutely no money that goes into educational material within Greenpeace as an international organization. It doesn't target softer outlets for stories: it targets news outlets with hard news stories, and that's it."

So now we're clear on the psychology of the place. This is no think tank, no ivory tower, no shrine to the glory of nature or pulpit for activist rage. It is a well-oiled machine running in sync with the great communications mills that pump out info-product daily, by the hour, by the minute. "Here we think news-like," says Blair Palese, who since our meeting in New York in 1993 has advanced in the corporate hierarchy and crossed the ocean, where she is now filling in for GPI's current communications chief, Richard Tichen. "We think about what do broadcasters need, what do news desks need to tell these stories." The staff walks "the middle ground between the real media world and Greenpeace's campaigns." According to Palese, when campaigners come in and say, "We'd like to send a crew to cover this," the Coms staff can answer, "That's not going to fly."

Using this communications department Greenpeace has been able to ford the massive cultural divide that separates news people from the rest of humankind. It has entered the psyches of those deadline-driven, Rolaids-popping automatons who propel the international news machine, and it has talked to them in their own language.

Such is the role of Elaine Adams, head of GPI's video department. Adams rides the electronic tide from the top floor of the Coms building. From there – under the skylights cut into a metal roof, with the exposed brick walls, corporate grey carpets, and the muted strains of big band jazz drifting around her desk, along with the residual aroma of coffee – she makes her frequent pitches to the all-powerful international brokers of television news footage: Reuters TV, Associated Press Television (APTV), World Television News (WTN) – and to the regional outfits like Eurovision, a satellite consortium of European broadcasters.

All of these agencies are headquartered in London, which is why GPI based its communications department here rather than in Amsterdam. On any given day, with a local phone call Adams can reach a media gatekeeper who just might be solely responsible for determining what millions upon millions of watchers will see on their television news at dinner time: it's not uncommon for a lone desk editor to decide what footage makes it onto an agency's satellite news package, the feed from which most G-7 broadcasters extract their international news, and which many broadcasters in the Third World and Eastern Europe will run unedited, translated into the local language.

Elaine Adams is in rare position of power: one faxed press release, followed by one phone call, and – potentially, at least – she's got a global audience. In exchange for this extraordinary access, for being allowed to pass through the eye of the needle, the deal is that Adams speaks to the agency people on their terms. She pitches stories according to their criteria and delivers the product with the technical demands of television foremost in mind. There is no point, it seems, in social crusaders flogging their cause on the basis of moral imperatives or intellectual import, because the hyper-competitive business of TV news is increasingly driven by purely technical and technological questions. How quick can you deliver it? Are the pictures exciting? Is the quality up to broadcast standards? Adams knows that her first function is to act as a kind of translator and psychic medium: bridging the gap between dimensions, channelling information from one realm to another without any nasty poltergeists getting loose.

"We don't let the campaigners talk to the agencies," says this engaging and energetic woman with short, straight-cropped brown hair and a surprising sense of calm. "Because the campaigners will say, 'it's a wonderful, fantastic, amazing action,' and of course it isn't – it's a banner hanging on a tree or something. So we're a filtering system, and the agencies really appreciate that. Otherwise they just have mad people talking to them all the time. It's really crucial that they have someone to talk television language: have you got all the right shots, cutaways, what's on there, where are you shooting from? You know, a proper conversation. But a campaigner doesn't know the difference between a high-8 and a Beta, so it's hopeless."

Another quality that will win a person the fleeting attention of an editor at Reuters, WTN, or APTV, Adams says, is the solemn recognition that agency staff are constantly under deadline pressure and only have enough time and interest to fast-forward to a story's point of impact. "We made a video on land mines," she recalls. "It was eight minutes, which is far too long for the agencies. They phoned me up and said, 'for God's sake, it's eight minutes Elaine.' And I said, 'Yeah, but I'll tell you where the juicy bits are. Man with leg being blown off at time code so-and-so. Bomb: time code so-and-so. Soldier diffuses bomb: time code so-and-so.' So they said, 'Thanks, those are the three shots we'll need.' So their job is done. You have to tell them where the juicy shots are so they don't get bored. And sell it well: it has to have a good press release with a good hook, so the story is already written for them. They have no time to think, these people."

This level of involvement in the production of news reports represents a quantum shift in the degree to which campaigning organizations are willing, in their quest for coverage, to bow to the bureaucratic and technical imperatives of the news media. Most environmental and social change groups accept the premise – driven home by the wildly successful Greenpeace media antics in the 1970s – that the television age requires them to offer the media some kind of spectacle to hang their story on. But the current-day Greenpeace goes further than that. Not only will Greenpeace create a media event by sailing a ship out to the site of a nuclear test or a toxic waste dumping, but it will also hire the film crew to record what happens.

This aspect of Adams's job demands all the character-reading skills of a Hollywood casting director. "It's quite hard to find someone who can stay on a boat for two months and not go mad on us," she says. Once the cameras are in place, the action either has to be beamed live to the networks for direct, CNN-style coverage or finely edited into clips for news reports – both of which Greenpeace Coms undertakes as a matter of course.

The standard format that Greenpeace uses to get its message out to the electronic media is a Video News Release (VNR) – delivered in the afternoon, in advance of most daily journalists' deadlines – containing two reels of video: the "a" reel is a finished report giving Greenpeace's version of things; the "b" reel is the package of video clips that the news peddlers can cut into their own reports alongside the denials and dissent from the bad guys. The possibility that someone might want to air a five-second or ten-second slice of video some time in the future also requires that shots be meticulously filed and catalogued after being first used. Two full-time employees view every video report and index them, shot-by-shot, on a computer data base – a desperately slow process ensuring that every tiny sequence of video can be located with a few computer keystrokes. "Actually, this is the only way we feel we could ever find the material again," says Greenpeace's video library manager, Jane Freedman. "It's very time-consuming but otherwise we could never respond to requests quickly enough."

In a better world – one in which rich global broadcasting outfits undertook their own investigative reporting for the benefit of their viewing audiences – it might be redundant for an advocacy group to apply its donors' contributions to the expensive business of generating raw material for the news agencies. But in the real world the only way to get the TV news people's attention is to do the legwork for them. The Russian dumping of nuclear waste in the Sea of Japan only became an international news sensation because Greenpeace managed – in October 1993 – to track down the polluters and catch them in the act; beaming back live pictures using the sophisticated digital compression equipment on board its ship, the *M.V. Greenpeace*.

It's almost unthinkable that a news agency itself would have followed up on a lead from an environmental group and sent a film crew out to the middle of a remote body of water to get the story. In an earlier era, when print was dominant and muckraking and public interest crusading sold papers, that might have happened. In fact, Greenpeace has worked with publications such as the British tabloids *Today* and *The Daily Mirror* on precisely that basis: the advocacy group provides the lead and some research, and the reporters go out and find the environmental culprits, verify the story, snap the pictures, and claim the scoop as their own. But advances in television technology – and the resultant changes in the nature of the medium itself – have made that kind of digging far too time-consuming and costly for television news. The switch from film to video and then the introduction of satellites and live microwave feeds have dramatically increased the speed at which news can travel to viewers and altered the process of newsgathering: it is now *immediacy* – who can get to the story first – that has become the measure of a newscast's worth and the primary ground for competition between broadcasters.[1]

The increased pace of newsgathering brought about by the latest generation of technology has had a direct impact upon content by fortifying the medium's reliance upon official sources. In an age of almost instant reporting, broadcasters are much less inclined to invest precious time wandering down the avenues of real life in search of a story that may or may not come together within the required time frame and with the requisite visual punch, lest they be upstaged by a competitor with a breaking, real-time story and be put into the embarrassing position of having to report stale news. It's much safer for broadcasters to plant themselves someplace where they are guaranteed of getting what they need, when they need it: in most cases, that turns out to be those conveniently wired press galleries attached or adjacent to government buildings, where important people deliver professionally scripted sound bites in just enough time for the news reporters to patch together their nightly reports, and with the retention of that all-important breathless sense of urgency.

In Britain that facility is 4 Millbank, an ex-prison a few steps away from the Houses of Parliament, a place Charles Dickens once described as "a melancholy waste." In his article "Agenda Benders," writer and television reporter Roger Bolton examines how Millbank has irrevocably changed the practice of journalism in Britain, clearly for the worse.[2] By investing heavily in a high-tech media centre where politicians' words and images can be chopped up and spit out instantly, media managers have created an institutional preference for the sound bites of politicians and other official sources, to the exclusion of real people dealing with concrete concerns outside the confines of this self-contained media Disneyland.

"The argument," Bolton writes, goes "something like this: if you put resources in, you have to get stories out, regardless of whether they are news or not. As a programme editor myself, I was well aware that if you sent a crew abroad on an expensive filming trip, you would have to transmit the results whatever happened. If the story they went to shoot didn't stand up, we'd just have to find another one. I'd notice that the 'overkill' on some news stories was due to the fact that if you put all your very expensive eggs in one basket, you have little left over for anything else."

Pouring money into Millbank as a means of ensuring instant access to the musings of policy-makers, Bolton concludes, guaranteed the political elite disproportionate exposure and wiped a

multitude of other issues off the agenda. "So great was the invest-
ment in the building, equipment and people, and so vital the need to
demonstrate efficiency and productivity, that more Westminster programs had to be made and more Westminster news carried."

The spin-off effects of this are familiar to anyone who lives in a
country where the government's press corps gets top billing on the
nightly news. As the words of politicians become more newsworthy
than events in real life, the media find controversy more in the mis-
spoken phrases and intemperate responses of leaders in the firing-
line than in the actual effects of those leaders' statements or policies.
The official with the best coverage is the one who is best-rehearsed
and least prone to the slip-ups that lead to embarrassing headlines.
This, Bolton argues, leads to the diminution of openness in the public debate and to the replacement of critical argument with a compelling but ultimately meaningless new form of political blood sport.

The process, Bolton continues, feeds off itself: the more frenetic
things become within this Roman Circus, the less time already har-
ried reporters will have to cast about for stories that might have a
tangible impact on their viewers. "Despite the sound and fury and
intense excitement," Bolton writes, "it has often seemed to me that
news was strangely passive. There used to be an old joke at the BBC
that the one instrument in the newsroom that was never used was
the telephone. Everyone was too busy dealing with incoming material to initiate their own inquiries."

Greenpeace's success at inserting its own bottom-up environmental message into the global flow of TV news is not only testament to
the organization's practical cunning, but a validation of McLuhan's
view (which is clearly supported by the evidence presented by journalist Roger Bolton) that electric media are driven so much by their
technological characteristics that content-selection becomes an
almost unconscious process.

Many activists believe that the reason their concerns are not
expressed on television is either that TV programmers and their
audiences are too dim to deal with social criticism, or that there is a
conspiracy by the powerful corporate interests and their executive
managers to control the medium to keep dissenting views off the airwaves as much as possible. But such interpretations are probably
only half the story: the idea that the technology itself is in the
driver's seat – exerting influence on format, style, and therefore on
content – seems to be borne out by the experience of Greenpeace,

which placed its bets on McLuhan's more mechanistic, less ideological interpretation of the medium, and seems to have come up a winner.

When McLuhan wrote that "the medium is the message," he meant partly that television (among other electronic media) is not so much a vehicle for conveying information or expressing particular thoughts as it is a self-contained and dominating entity whose intrinsic characteristics rearrange how we process information, realign old relationships, and totally skew our view of the social landscape. That may have seemed an abstract and obscure idea when McLuhan first presented it, but Greenpeace has built a concrete and common-sense strategy around that notion by addressing the purely technical barriers that shut opposition movements out of the TV universe; by assuming that it is process – not prejudice – that makes television blind to most of the world's most pressing issues.

If the increased pace of television newsgathering (induced by technological advancement) has shortened the public attention span and shut out items that have complicated story lines; if it has focused the gaze of the television camera lens on places where stories are readily available and can be delivered to deadline (thereby casting the rest of the world into a kind of obscurity bordering on non-being), well, the people at Greenpeace Coms believe there are technical ways to overcome these barriers. If the technological constraints and economic logic of newsgathering prevent the agencies from tracking down environmental plunderers, the solution is to do it for them.

Certainly, ideological consequences do flow from the process of making TV news, but Greenpeacers will tell you that process is not ideologically driven. Deliver good pictures in a convenient package, to deadline, and the agencies will run them. Says Blair Palese: "If an action is big enough – and if it's relevant – anyone will take our footage. This notion that 'We don't take advocacy groups' footage' is bullshit."

★ ★ ★

McLuhan's insights into the nature of electronic media have guided Greenpeace from the very beginning. As founding member Paul Watson told me: "The reason that Greenpeace rose from a grassroots organization to one of the largest environmental groups in the world is simple: it was the first organization to understand the nature of the media. It took a Marshall McLuhanesque approach to environmental campaigns. Very few organizations, even now, have learned to do that."

Still, the shape of the industry has evolved over time – and so has Greenpeace's adaptation to it. Tony Mariner was a key figure in the formation of Greenpeace Communications and an architect of the strategy that targeted the international television news brokers. A South African cameraman who first hooked up with Greenpeace during the 1977 Save the Whales voyage, Mariner recalls that a number of organizational and attitudinal shifts led to the replacement of the old Greenpeace Films with the new Greenpeace Communications. "Originally, it wasn't actually seen as a news thing," says Mariner, a grey-bearded freelancer (and occasional employee of Greenpeace) who smiles wistfully when he's asked about the past.

The founding Greenpeace media experts were radio and print people who, when they thought visually, gravitated towards the more contemplative medium of documentary film. Television news, Mariner says, was a minor offshoot of their work until the very end of the 1970s, when Mariner began to forge a relationship with Viznews, the market leader among international news brokers of the time. Viznews was then co-owned by NBC, the BBC, and several smaller national broadcasters but was later sold to Reuters and transformed into Reuters TV. After Greenpeace discovered Viznews, "We started targeting and coming up with specific programs to hit the news, and to shoot it in a way that was right for them," Mariner says, taking a break from his current project in the techno-dungeon that is the basement of the Greenpeace Coms building, where he's been toying with the image of a spinning globe on the computer screen in front of him. The Viznews needs meant constructing Greenpeace campaign events into short, snappy items.

Sending footage out through agencies like Viznews gave Greenpeace an instant international impact. "Our idea was to reach the global audience through the agencies," Mariner says. "And the direct action gave us, if you like, a product to sell, in terms of a news event. That's one reason why direct action works. One of its effects is to create an impact. The other is to create a platform."

Mariner is part hard-nosed, seasoned professional, and part unreconstructed idealist who speaks of his enduring commitment to the spiritual exercise of "bearing witness" – the practice of which, he says, invariably underlies a good Greenpeace action and the absence of which explains the bad ones. In short, Tony Mariner is a practical zealot. That goes a long way towards explaining his casual acceptance of the fact that Greenpeace – in order to deal with the news agencies – would have to sign away any notion of editorial control; to surrender its grasp over the material to that great god of Journalistic Objectivity.

"We never editorialized the material as such, although the structure of the visual material might have meant that the editorial was implied," Mariner argues. "My approach to this was always that the organization and the campaign could dictate the editorial as much as they like within their action. So you set the thing up – in terms of what you do, how you contrive it – but then the recording of that event is not editorialized."

This approach gives a nod to the networks' golden rule of being "objective" – a concept that is applied in the strictly formal sense that reporters are obliged to seek rebuttals or "both sides of the argument" and write their own scripts. But much like government agencies and corporations that orchestrate press conferences and media events, the Greenpeace media crew knew that creating the "context" for reporting can provide a much more compelling influence over content than controlling the whole process yourself. So while other activist groups born at the same time might have aimed at pure propaganda promoting a party line, Greenpeace considered it an adequate victory just to get its issues into the media spotlight, to force a degree of public debate in which an issue could not be ignored. This brings forth the danger, of course, that your own footage can be used against you. Video library manager Jane Freedman says this is taken as a more serious threat in the context of documentaries, and that the standard way of dealing with an unintended use of footage is to grant only limited rights and then to sue for breach of copyright if the program is negative.

Mariner has also reconciled his social conscience with the media mind-set that treats Greenpeace footage like any other kind of commodity. While he'll put his life in danger to retrieve some pictures he believes the world *needs* to see, he accepts that news editors will be searching for that "gotcha" value, not moral lessons. "That's the reality of the job," he says. "I remember going into Viznews with a 400-foot role of film and waiting while it was being processed. It represented a week of my life, and it was given to this editor who watched everything in fast-forward, and then kind of pulled the film off in yards rather than looking at the pictures. But that's the reality of it. The best kind of reward you can get from this is when these jaded news editors who see all kinds of pictures actually stop and say, 'oh, gosh' – because they've never seen this stuff before."

The success of Greenpeace's collaboration with Viznews – combined with the internal, organizational shift that saw Greenpeace International take more responsibility from the national offices – helped boost the profile of the Communications Department and confirmed the news agencies as the preferred vehicle for reaching the public. Until the mid-1980s, Mariner says, Greenpeace's international wing had been little more than the communications department and the marine services division – the two "service units" that ensured the co-ordination of different national efforts on actions that were international in scope. Yet Mariner says that, since there was "usually only one thing happening at any given time" the need for such co-ordination was minimal. John May, former Greenpeace archivist and the author of several Greenpeace-sponsored books (including *The Greenpeace Story*, with co-author Michael Brown), says that the current communications strategy really gelled after the 1985 sinking of the *Rainbow Warrior*. Inundated with requests for information from the international media, Greenpeace found itself "in terms of brand recognition" an even more valuable commodity than before. It began organizing its film, photo, and text libraries within one facility so that it could service the news media's requests at a moment's notice. The story of *Rainbow Warrior*'s sinking took several weeks to build, via the front pages of the world's newspapers, to the damning conclusion that French secret agents had sunk the Greenpeace ship and killed one of its crew members. The process launched a public relations juggernaut for Greenpeace that continued to gain momentum throughout the rest of the 1980s and into the early 1990s.

Andy Booth says that when he became head of Greenpeace Communications in 1990 (where he would stay until after the Rio Summit in 1992), Greenpeace had a 70 per cent success rate in pitching its material to the agencies. Elaine Adams says that figure, for European-based Greenpeace campaigns, is now down to about 40 per cent, but that's still probably much higher than the rate of international acceptance for stories generated by state broadcasters. According to Tony Naetes, news director for the European Broadcast Union (EBU), only a tiny fraction of the 20,000 stories EBU members distribute among themselves each year are picked up by world agencies.[3] The agencies were keen to run with Greenpeace's stories for several reasons: they had hard-news pegs, were released to deadline, came with exciting pictures, and were given to the agencies without editorial restriction. Greenpeace's "brand recognition" didn't hurt either; nor did the fact that environmental issues in general had risen to the top of the political agenda by the late 1980s.

In Booth's mind the foremost factor in Greenpeace's success was that "the strategy plays into the economics of the system. If an agency gets a story free, it makes more money on that feed." The agencies are already one of the most lucrative aspects of the television business, a success that Booth attributes to the fact that they have the laws of supply and demand on their side: a vast number of national broadcasters are willing to pay for an international news package, and since comparatively few contributors are gathering news information with cameras there is very little competition for the patronage of those national broadcasters. And the agencies apparently welcome any means of increasing their profits.

What Greenpeace gets in return for adding more black ink to the agencies' balance sheets is a rare means of making politicians accountable in the court of public opinion. Television may not do a good job of explaining complex issues, Booth says, but it is an effective tool for embarrassing decision-makers when the issues are straightforward enough and carry a certain emotional charge. That threat of embarrassment can change policy. "During my time at Greenpeace it became increasingly apparent that political attention was focused by media attention, by and large," the soft-spoken Booth tells me in his new office in Bristol. "If the media were asking targeted questions over a period of time, then policy decisions would often be made on the hoof by ministers. They would often make party political decisions and change their approach on certain issues instantaneously. The ability to have access to senior decision-makers, to ask them pointed questions when the world is watching, can have an impact."

One of the most profound cases in which television reporting had an instantaneous impact upon policy, Booth says, was during the first reporting of the Ethiopian famine in 1984. In the same week that committees of both the United Nations and the European Community (EC) had defeated motions to provide additional famine relief for Ethiopia, a BBC news crew flying over Africa en route to another destination decided to stop in Ethiopia to check out rumours that something major was happening on the ground. The BBC's subsequent report of the famine was picked up on an agency feed and aired worldwide, triggering a political tremor of historic proportions. The EC convened an emergency session of its food council the day after the report was broadcast, and by two o'clock that afternoon the council had rescinded its previous decision and allocated resources for Ethiopian famine relief.

This ability to expose political nerve-endings in order to activate the policy-making reflex makes access to the nightly news a particularly useful thing for campaigning groups that target the diplomatic process of international treaty-writing. Andy Booth remembers several occasions during his tenure at Greenpeace when the blinding glare of media scrutiny forced positive action on an issue that had previously been a dark secret in some bureaucrat's briefcase. One example was the ban on the ocean incineration of waste by the London Dumping Convention. "To generate enough interest in something that was happening in the middle of the ocean, and to have it banned within three years of starting the campaign, was one of our greatest successes," Booth says. The reason for the banning came down to the television pictures of the burning waste and the Greenpeace confrontation. "We were able to hold the media's attention for three days and develop a running story around a tanker that was sitting in the middle of the North Sea burning waste."

Booth has since taken the media sorcerer's skills he learned at Greenpeace and launched out on his own. Joining forces with former Viznews/Reuters TV employee Peter Sibley, he is co-proprietor of a specialized global news distribution agency called World Environment News (WEN). Home base is Bristol, an old industrial centre in southwest England. The city's bombed-out core was rebuilt in the decades after the Second World War as an angular pastiche of gleaming glass and concrete. Nurtured by the presence of a BBC regional production centre, the city has also become home to a number of independent film and TV companies.

The WEN office is close to the city core in an old printing shop, where an idle behemoth of a printing press sits – in an uncannily symbolic juxtaposition – on the same floor where Booth and his co-workers edit video images at PC terminals. With this enterprise Booth is hoping to replicate the logic and primary functions of the Greenpeace Communications department, though with a few significant differences – including being a for-profit business. "Our role is essentially to provide agency-type material to broadcasters on issues that they wouldn't normally cover, or that the big agencies wouldn't normally offer them," he says, sitting back on a couch in a temperature controlled editing suite, a cup of instant coffee in hand. "So we provide ten to fifteen minutes of packaged news a week on environment and development, or human rights stories in different parts of the world."

The scale of Booth's expectations is lower than when he directed Greenpeace's international media efforts: he can't beam stories out by satellite, timed and targeted to hit the headlines in sync with a major political event, but instead must deliver a cassette of softer, less newsy reports to broadcasters by courier. But the overall goals are similar. By providing a regular flow of environmental features for broadcasters to use on their magazine programs, Booth hopes to send a message to the big boys – to remind the agencies that supply footage for flagship national newscasts that the environment hasn't dropped off the public agenda since Rio, and that they should continue to carry environmental stories in their nightly feeds.

Booth believes that it is a good time for enterprises such as his, since there is now a greater opportunity to influence the mainstream from the margins – to establish a foothold in the lower-rent regions of the television universe, with the idea that the issues will migrate upward to programs with greater influence, prestige, and budgets. This concept, he says, is a product of the ongoing fragmentation of the broadcast market. WEN's major clients include the new satellite news channels such as CNN, StarTV in Asia, and Euronews (which translates its material into every European language) – challengers that have created a voracious appetite for slick, cheaply produced programming. The existence of these outlets is not just a boon to suppliers like WEN, but also to campaigning organizations. Booth advises that those groups now have a better chance of getting their issues on TV if they target the right market niches within this highly stratified industry.

As for his own work, Booth has no problem reconciling his role as a news producer with his personal desire to place certain types of issues on the newsroom blotter. He carries with him the lesson from Greenpeace that news organizations will allow outsiders to help shape their agendas, so long as the content stays within the strictures of mainstream journalism about "accurate," "fair," and "balanced" coverage. Of course, it also has to "tell a good story" – which means a story that falls within a certain restricted "range" of stories that the media are willing to cover at a particular time.

A second facet of WEN's business says a lot about how Greenpeace's early vision of a media-centred strategy has become the conventional wisdom. In addition to supplying material for broadcasters, WEN contracts out to non-governmental organizations (NGOs) and international agencies such as Amnesty International, the Red Cross, the World Wildlife Fund, and the United Nations High Commission for Refugees, to create the same kind of video release packages that Greenpeace produces in-house. Increasingly, those organizations feel that their ability to act depends upon having the means to influence the policies of governments (and of international bodies), which set the context for their work.

Speaking about the new challenges facing NGOs caught up in so-called "complex emergencies" – that is, the kind of multiple military and humanitarian crises that have emerged in the post-Cold War period in places like Bosnia, Rwanda, and Somalia – Oxfam UK-Ireland director David Bryer notes that the first challenge facing NGOs is to break through the barrier of bureaucratic inertia that prevents governmental and international agencies from doing their part. Media attention, Bryer says, is essential to achieving this goal. In Bosnia, for instance, military intervention by more powerful countries was essential both to ensuring that relief agencies were physically able to move supplies to endangered populations and to convincing feuding warlords that genocide carries political consequence.

"Media pressure has now pushed the rich world to make Sarajevo a safer haven," Bryer says. "Western, and indeed we now realize Russian, public opinion and the media played a significant role in prompting this albeit minimalist containment strategy." Wealthy nations were forced to provide aid and militarily protect aid convoys in the former Yugoslavia, "because of media-driven pressure and the need to be seen to be doing something." Echoing Andy Booth's sentiments on the role of media coverage in forcing politicians to make snap decisions to do the right thing, Bryer concludes that "NGOs have a practical role in assembling information" and "in trying to raise media, public and political attention on gathering darkness." Part of that strategy, said Bryer, would be for NGOs to directly fund TV crews and journalists to bring important stories into public light

– which is precisely what Greenpeace has been doing since the 1970s.[4]

★ ★ ★

And so you have it: it's now an almost universally acknowledged fact that political power in today's world comes not so much from the barrel of a gun as through the lens of a camera. Television is the means to recapture the democratic accountability that can no longer be exercised at the ballot box or in the town hall.

But wait, maybe that's too sweeping an endorsement.

Andy Booth has been in the news game – both as a Greenpeace flack and as an independent producer – long enough that his astonishment at the political clout of television has been tempered by a jaded recognition of the medium's many faults. In many ways, the performance of the electronic media (both television and the print wire services) at the 1992 Rio Summit simultaneously revealed the promise and the pitfalls for NGOs that seek to use the media as a central campaign tool. In general Booth is enthusiastic about the degree to which Greenpeace could cash in on Rio, where the convergence of an army of international correspondents cast an enormous spotlight onto the environmental cause. (Then again, Booth might well be expected to portray Greenpeace's performance positively, given that he was in charge of Greenpeace Communications at the time and had devoted a year of his life to preparing for the event.)

Most international gatherings are, in media terms, little more than photo-ops for powerful government leaders. They are celebrations of the status quo, choreographed by slick bureaucrats with the resources and the sophistication to control the flow of news and manipulate its presentation. But Greenpeace, Booth says, showed that the other side could steal the show by being just as well organized and technologically tuned-in. "We were able to monitor, in real time, what governments were saying to the agencies, and what stories they were picking up," he says. "So if George Bush made a statement on the environment, two minutes later we had a response on the wire, which means that our name and our tag runs alongside Bush's tag. That's a tremendous tool."

In other cases, as events unfolded at the Summit Greenpeace was releasing news features that had either been preproduced or shot on the run in Rio and beamed back to the Coms office in London for overnight packaging. "We were delivering a ninety-minute package every day to the agencies on our view," Booth says. "And they used it because it was saving them a shitload of time and money. A lot of times the agencies were feeding our stories direct – they weren't even cutting them."

Behind this apparent triumph, however, there were signs that a big chunk of the news media missed the whole point at Rio. Most of the NGO delegates may remember the Earth Summit as the place where Northern and Southern perspectives – where the sometimes conflicting priorities of development and environment – achieved a kind of reconciliation. But all of that was at best a faint murmur in most of the mass media of the North. While Greenpeace, like other groups, issued statements endorsing and amplifying the Southern view of environmental destruction as driven by factors such as debt, economic hardship, and colonial models of resource exploitation, media outlets outside of the South rarely picked up on this message. This blindness to the concerns and ideas of people outside of the club of rich nations is something that Booth continues to deal with day to day, regardless of how the new paradigm that emerged at Rio may have recast many environmentalists' perception of the issues. This cultural blindness is caused, he believes, partly by structural, economic considerations: the simple truth is that the agencies tailor their product to fit the expectations of the wealthy, G-7 broadcasters from which they earn most of their money.

"What you are seeing," he says, "is that the agencies are trying to maximize their profits. They've identified trends in terms of what broadcasters are buying. G-7 broadcasters pay cash to follow their political or business leaders around, or by following disasters. So that's where the resources are being focused. The decision to follow a story in Africa has to be balanced against a possible story in London where a company is announcing its share results. If it's an important company, the decision is usually to go with London."

The second factor that cements the Northern bias in place is more personal and psychological. It's hard to think of changing the assumptions of news, Booth says, when the agencies are staffed by people from Northern backgrounds, with very rigid views on what is newsworthy, who are confined by a top-down form of decision-making. He illustrates his point with a reference to a hypothetical desk editor preparing a feed for Africa. "I don't think there is any way she could package the news to make it culturally sensitive to people in Mozambique," Booth says. "The most she could expect to do is package the news from a Western point of view, and deliver it in the exact same way as to a Western audience."

If she didn't do it that way, Booth tells me, her boss would come along and say, "What the fuck is this? What do you mean you ran a piece on racial unrest in Northern England, because you thought it would be interesting for people to see that racial unrest exists in Northern countries as well as Mozambique? Why didn't you run this story on Bill Clinton or John Major?"

Nick Bell, writing in the magazine *Television Business International*, confirms that the cultural mind-set of international news distributors – even those such as CNN, which strives to appear cosmopolitan – is determined by the location of the majority of its audience. "Newsroom editors," Bell argues, "tend to adhere to the principle that there is only one kind of news – there's domestic news happening at home and domestic news happening abroad. Viewers watching CNN or any other U.S. network during the policing of Somalia would be ignorant of the fact that there were just as many Italian and Pakistani troops involved as Americans."[5]

Despite his optimism that the monolithic mind-set of the news giants will be offset by the effects of fragmentation – by the creation of new spaces for public debate as the upstart services desperately search for programming – Booth is aware that the process of fragmentation also poses dangers. In an environment of more intense competition, he says, every broadcaster is searching for the greatest market share at the least possible cost. Under these conditions, the serious, investigative TV documentary – the program form most likely to piece together the big picture for the viewer, and most likely to uncover what powerful polluters and sundry corporate conspirators don't want the public to know – is being pushed towards the brink of extinction. In Britain broadcasters are attempting to salvage both money and market share by pushing documentaries out of the prime-time slots, where the greatest potential audiences are, and by chopping documentary budgets.

"*World in Action* is the program that people remember as being half an hour, investigative, as getting inside of corruption," Andy Booth says. "Each half-hour program costs £100,000 to make. Compare that with an entertainment program that's half an hour long, say, clips from home videos presented in a funny and charming way, one presenter in a studio, no reporters; price per hour: maybe £50,000?

You go further downhill and watch the Discovery Channel, which is one of the few organizations showing documentaries, they pay $3,000 an hour. Nowhere near £100,000. So even the specialist niche satellite organizations which say 'we present serious documentaries' aren't willing to pay the money you need to have a strong investigative program on television. The type of documentary will change, and become more adventure-based: looking at people who are trying to skydive from the highest mountain in the world, things that are more entertainment. The perception of the broadcasters is that the masses don't understand much and can just about cope with game shows. And game shows will get more viewers, and make a hell of a lot more money."

So Booth is gloomily looking towards a "dumbing down" of international television to match that much-lamented process in the United States, where exploitative talk-shows – tabloid TV – have become the defining genre of an era that's seen television channels sprouting as prolifically as Burger Kings. With his sunny prognosis for the future of television becoming decidedly overcast, Booth turns his attention to the project under way in his office today in order to illustrate the limited narrative range of the medium. A three-person crew – having just completed the gruelling journey back from a week in Australia – ambles jet-lagged and giddy into the offices where WEN reports are made. Their task had been to shoot material for a feature on the destruction of the Tasmanian rainforest. Although they have gathered enough tape to produce a half-hour documentary, the extended news feature that will be distributed worldwide will probably clock in at about four minutes. Andy Booth admits that this is really not enough time to explain the problems in Tasmania.

"If you watch the development of a script for a television news story," he says, "even one of ours here, they tend to be standard format script." The Tasmania script would be set up very simply as an issue: "These animals are in danger. These people are chopping trees down. They think it's a good idea to chop trees down. These people here are demonstrating about it. Time is running out." This story, he says, would take the crew five days to shoot. "You have to present very simple story lines that are very black and white."

For Booth this process is part of a negative historical trend: the bastardization of television's ostensible role as a deliverer of detailed information that ideally keeps the public involved in the democratic process. When television presents issues in black and white terms, in oversimplified terms, the public often ends up not engaging with those issues. "Often the images are clichés that are projected onto the viewer, which after a while don't generate any response whatsoever."

But while the economic demands of the information industry may be partly responsible for restricting the level of debate in environmental reporting, green organizations themselves have similar financial interests that make them complicit in the process. In the April 10, 1995, issue of *The New Yorker*, writer Gregg Easterbrook chastised environmentalists for presenting their message in a way that may help maintain a certain public profile and donor base, but that ultimately undercuts other vital arguments that the public needs to hear.[6] Many observers have remarked to me that environmental organizations that built their stature and influence by feeding the public perception of ecological crisis are now unwilling to retreat from their established role as the bearer of bad news, for fear of diminishing their own support base. Easterbrook believes that this is ultimately a destructive stance, because U.S. greens (and the progressive political community that supports them) have denied themselves the ability to trumpet their own successes. "The left is afraid of environmental good news because it undercuts stylish pessimism," he writes.

Although acknowledging that the worst of the environmental crisis has shifted to the Third World (where calamity does loom just over the horizon), Easterbrook contends that within the United States the basic problems of water and air pollution have improved significantly since the 1970s, while advances in environmental technology have made U.S. industry more efficient and competitive. This is a huge victory for political liberals who believe the state has a clear and legitimate role in protecting the public interest. It could also be a major political weapon in the fight against the advance of the radical right in the United States (and elsewhere), which has managed to demonize Big Government to the point where most legislative milestones of the progressive movement are in danger of falling to the conservative axe of deregulation.

"Liberalism is on the defensive today," Easterbrook asserts, "because, as a philosophy, it concentrates almost entirely on what has failed – about America, about public policy, about daily life. Obviously, there are failures aplenty, but there are successes as well. In the

West, environmental protection is the leading postwar triumph of progressive government."

So when environmentalists and their political allies talk up the doom and ignore the successes, they may indeed be stoking that sense of urgency that keeps supporters writing cheques. But, in Easterbrook's eyes, they are also ceding a far more important argument to the right-wing forces that have based their campaign to dismantle environmental protection legislation on the mistaken – and deceitful – statements that such efforts are ineffective and economically burdensome.

I get a similar sense of short-term gain overriding a larger opportunity when I sit down to watch a series of fundraising videos in the Greenpeace Communications office. Video library manager Freedman informs me about two classes of fundraising tapes: the standard ones are mostly a collection of "A-reel" news releases that Greenpeace had sent out to the media; the more specialized missive directed at "high donors" is technically more ambitious, featuring an impressive split-screen introduction to Greenpeace UK chairman Lord Peter Melchett, who brought subscribers up to date on what the organization had been doing. A capsule Greenpeace history called *Warriors of the Rainbow*, intended for the general audience, proves that much of what Greenpeace has to sell today is the mythology and mystique of the past: the rehashing of the early campaigns against Amchitka, whaling, and sealing takes up a lot of screen time and packs more punch than the subsequent discussion of Greenpeace triumphs at treaty conferences. There is an obligatory reference to whaling in all of the videos I see, even though Greenpeace today has only a token involvement in the issue. There is very little on Southern issues; with the exception of a report showing Greenpeacers and locals reloading a boat with barrels of toxic waste at a Philippines dockyard, a cargo sent back to its owners in Geneva.

The only disturbing thing about these tapes is the sense created of something missing. They leave viewers with a passive role – "send money" would probably sum it up. Otherwise there doesn't seem to be any meaningful way for people watching the video to plug in. And that's what seems to me like the lost opportunity: while most of the Southern NGOs at the Rio conference had targeted the vast overconsumption of resources by the populations of the North as a prime cause of the global environmental crisis – and Greenpeace enthusiastically endorsed this view at the time – there is no mention

of this issue in Greenpeace's communication to its supporters a scant
three years later.

When I suggest to Blair Palese that Greenpeace might be censor-
ing itself so as not to offend the people who send it money, she
responds that Greenpeace refrains from targeting the Northern cult
of consumerism not for fear of alienating donors, but simply because
the organization has set its sights further up the food chain. "Our
focus is not to pick on individuals and the consumer and say, 'It's
your fault,'" she says. "In fact, by and large, the research we've done
shows that it's *not* actually your fault – it's the people making money
off the products you buy who don't give you environmental
options." Instead of working to make people feel guilty, she says,
Greenpeace tries to focus on alternatives. "Because a lot of people
would much rather buy a solar car, but let's face it, they're not given
that option."

To illustrate this emphasis on the producer rather than the consumer – on supply rather than demand – Palese broaches the subject
of the celebrated "Greenfreeze" refrigerator, the CFC-free icebox
that runs on the energy from a butane lighter. In its quest to halt the
destruction of the ozone layer Greenpeace funded the development
of a technology that is ozone-benign; then it waived the rights on the
patent so that any manufacturer could use it. All German fridge
manufacturers now use Greenfreeze technology; so too will new
fridge-manufacturing plants in China, potentially the world's largest
market for refrigerators.

It's interesting to note, however, that although Greenpeace's international ozone co-ordinator Mike Affleck considers the introduction
of Greenfreeze to be one of the most significant steps towards halt-
ing ozone destruction, he also believes that technological solutions
will only forestall disasters that would be better addressed by lifestyle
changes.

"The answers," he says, "are actually relatively simple, and the
alternatives are there: riding bicycles, public transportation, solar
energy, reduced use of certain products. These kind of things are not
big, flashy solutions, but they're the kind of solutions that have to be
adopted if we are going to resolve the problem. You know, raising the
number of miles per gallon on a car is a good thing to do, but it only
delays the inevitable, and that is that you have to do something about
changing people's lifestyle."

Palese insists that Greenpeace is not afraid to get that kind of message out – it's just that, with such a wide range of environmental work to be done, it has decided to leave the attack on consumerism to other groups. She is adamant that Greenpeace would never back away from publicly stating its principles, even if it rubbed the donating public the wrong way. "Our campaign strategy is not run by fundraising, by any means," she says. "We'll campaign on issues that don't have any sex appeal for fundraising, and have done for years and years."

But Andy Booth remembers one campaign that was called off precisely because it was considered too threatening to those average folks who might otherwise have bought Greenpeace's message. "Greenpeace toyed for six or seven years with the idea of launching an anti-car campaign," he says. "But it could never reach agreement internationally." According to him, when the issue came up the U.S. office would respond by arguing, "There's no way we're going to let you run an anti-car campaign. It's the lifeblood of the American way of life. The implications for us financially would be disastrous." Or "What's the point of launching a campaign against cars when you have no chance of winning?" Booth says that an organization campaigning for a cause has "tremendous trouble" attacking mainstream products that enjoy public support. "A car, as far as the public is concerned, represents freedom. So a campaign against the car risks playing into the hands of industry and government by fulfilling their prophesy, which is that all environmentalists are dedicated to bringing us back to the stone age."

Although Booth is sympathetic to the idea of campaigning against cars, he concedes that the issue was so complex and problematic that it would have been difficult to convey a clear message. For example, although it would have been possible to publicize the broader impact of automobile use (that is, the assault on the Earth's atmosphere arising from the mass burning of fossil fuels), Greenpeace would inevitably find itself on the losing side of the argument when specific, more personal scenarios were introduced. To advance its argument that cars are essential to human health and happiness, the auto industry would only need to turn to a hypothetical family that lives in the country and needs fast access to a hospital. And then, what angle would Greenpeace use to show the public what's in it for them, to personalize the issue? Mass carnage on the highways is already well-known to the public and has done nothing to diminish private automobile use. Alternately, an appeal based on the issue of technical standards (such as unacceptable carbon monoxide levels inside the passenger cabin) might prompt manufacturers to address specific engineering issues, but if the manufacturers did fix those technical problems, that kind of focused campaign could wind up *enhancing* the image of the automobile rather than diminishing it.

Then there are the subsidiary policy questions that threatened to embroil anti-car campaigners in some broader political fights that they'd probably prefer to avoid. Booth says that – at the same time that Greenpeace was contemplating its anti-car campaign – the British government of Margaret Thatcher was pushing a broad program of deregulation and privatization; one facet of which involved the dismantling of existing transport systems, the building of new motorways, and the restructuring of the tax system to favour private auto use. Campaigning against the car would therefore compel Greenpeace to take stands on some contentious, partisan political issues – such as the obligation of the state to raise taxes to pay for revitalized public transport, as an alternative to the private car.

Ultimately, though, questions about the psychological and political approach of an anti-car campaign remained minor issues. The real problem was that a campaign against cars would have required an attack on a personal behaviour pattern that is deeply entrenched in our culture. "I think running an anti-car campaign would require a lot of guts, really," he says. "You've got to attack individuals, to change their attitudes."

Evidently, the prospect of taking on the average consumer was too scary for Greenpeace. It wound up running a campaign that focused on the technical shortcomings of cars, as a compromise solution. Ultimately, Greenpeace was afraid of the philosophical implications of an anti-car campaign. The campaign was dropped, Booth says, because it would have "imposed upon the whole American dream, which is that anyone can make it, and the end point is megawealth status, where you as an individual can live a tremendously enriched life and are able to have these massive options about how you want to live. And the American view has actually become the dominant worldview: cars provide access, the car is freedom of choice."

One might think, though, that environmentalists need to challenge that very mythology – that wealth is endless, that our lives will get better the more stuff we get – if all the speeches and reports on environmental issues over the past decade are to be more than hollow utterances. Seen in that light, what was perceived as threatening in the anti-car campaign could also be seen as a great opportunity: a chance to force the profligate Northern middle classes to take a good, hard look in the mirror – to challenge the orthodoxies and assumptions that our societies are built upon.

CHAPTER 8

MASS MEDIA AND MASS ACTION

THE CHALLENGE OF A NEW
ENVIRONMENTALISM

JOHN MAY BELIEVES THAT THE TIME MAY SOON COME WHEN people will welcome a message that challenges the current order; a message that suggests there is a better way for us to live our lives.

The 1992 meetings in Rio "represented the marriage of the environment and development movement, and the realization that you can't save the trees without saving the people," May says, competing with the strains of Miles Davis music that fill his top-floor studio in Lewes, East Sussex. "Now, these concerns as a whole remain to be translated into a powerful new form of politics and action and lifestyle that will address the problems on a sufficient scale and in a sufficient way."

Discontent with old ideas is widespread, he believes, and much of the public – even in Northern countries – has a sense that the interlocking problems of environmental decay and economic imbalance are at the root of the current global malaise. The Rio conference made that much clear. What's needed now are some popular manifestos to turn that sentiment into action.

"My feeling is that the awareness is there, in people's heads, and the world is changing because of this. I believe that there are new industrial revolutions under way and that new forms of politics will emerge. Since politics begins with language, you have to find the form of the language first, and that language is both verbal and increasingly multimedia. There are people who specialize in language; they are called writers, and they have an important role."

This is the kind of thing May had been telling the leadership of Greenpeace for some time: that their public communications have to evolve to incorporate the complexities, the nuances, and the revolutionary possibilities of the new environmentalism, post-Rio. But it's a message he thinks has fallen on deaf ears. May spent eight years "inside" Greenpeace – some of that time when the organization was headquartered in his beloved home town of Lewes – first as the outfit's archivist and the author of four Greenpeace-sponsored books, and then as a "creative consultant" whose job it was to come up with new ideas for reaching the public. He has high praise for the organization's effectiveness and robustness in the early years.

"During the first days over here there was a feeding frenzy among journalists to get on board because it was very romantic and swashbuckling and fresh and different," he remembers. But May speaks with clear disappointment – even a sense of personal hurt – when he recalls how the glory days dissolved into confusion. "I feel that Greenpeace fulfilled its first historic purpose, to alert the world to the problems of the environment, around 1989-90," he says. "And like many other campaigning organizations, it failed to make the shift into a new position."

What was fundamentally to blame for this, May believes, is the decision to stick with modes of communication that had proved successful – in pragmatic terms – in the past. Europeans craved the kind of images that came out of the anti-whaling and anti-sealing campaigns, but by continuing to communicate to the public using this kind of imagery, Greenpeace was no longer using its public profile to change the public consciousness but was simply responding to consumer demand. May feels that Greenpeace has abdicated its role as a prophetic voice, and precisely at the wrong time: at the very point when a new language – a new environmental lexicon and a new set of images – is needed to galvanize the strongly felt and well documented environmental concerns of the 1990s into a new political and social agenda. He cites the Greenpeace direct-mail campaigns as an example of how the organization is wasting its potential to communicate meaningfully to large numbers of people.

May criticizes direct-mail fundraising as a simple "call/response" mechanism: "Here's a picture of a seal being bashed on the head, isn't this awful, send us some money and we'll stop it." The organization becomes geared towards issues and events that suit that kind of purpose. Its practical, institutional concerns – "keep the show on the road, pay for the headquarters, pay for the staff, pay for the pension scheme" – come to dominate, and its campaigns become less capable both of articulating unconventional wisdom and of "reinventing" the organization itself as circumstances change.

May believes that organizational security may not be worth the price. "For people of my generation," he says, "the idea of being paid to do this type of thing – let alone making a career out of it – was completely absurd. And the growing professionalization of campaigning organizations is, I suppose, an inevitable process, but a lot is lost in the meantime."

May's own career (as both a writer and social activist) has been something of an odyssey. He started out as a journalist in the British underground press of the 1960s before moving on to find a home in the music press and then becoming a Fleet Street freelancer. He says he's seen a whole constellation of issues that were once relegated to the underground ghetto become topics of discussion in the mainstream press. Living in Lewes must also contribute to his long view of the issues. His top-floor studio in a house on a hilltop – looking down onto aged slate roofs and postage-stamp gardens – provides a historic panorama of a town that has been on the leading edge of change through the centuries.

May marvels at how appropriate it was that Lewes was a temporary home to Greenpeace, given the town's historic links with various groups and individuals involved in the quest for democracy and enlightenment. The Battle of Lewes, he points out, was a major event leading to the formation of the British Parliament. Over the centuries this immaculate, hilly town of cobblestones and trees has also been home to various waves of religious dissidents, whose presence here is recalled, for instance, by an ancient Quaker meeting hall and a Unitarian Church dating from the eighteenth century. The church can be found just down the road from the old jousting grounds, near the town's castle.

To top it all off, Lewes is also the birthplace of Thomas Paine, political philosopher and intellectual architect of the American Revolution. The townsfolk have honoured Paine's memory by planting a tree in his name – a social event on a par with the various bonfire celebrations and burnings-in-effigy that occur here routinely. Not that Paine lives only in history: in a few hours, on the day of our meeting, John May will be boarding a train to London to attend the launch party for the British edition of *Wired* magazine, and who should be adorning the front cover of the first issue but Thomas Paine.

This is the delightfully synchronistic backdrop to our conversation, as May talks about old dreams of democracy, new technological promise, and the possible connections of Greenpeace's experience to both of those things. One thing May feels strongly about is that today's new technologies are not the new technologies of thirty years ago. Television may have been just about the only game in town in the 1960s and 1970s, he says, but its position has been eroded by the vast fragmentation of information flow and by TV's own inability to convey the multidimensionality of issues.

So May is critical of Greenpeace for tying almost all of its fortunes to television news and the print wire services. His criticism, though, does not so much centre on the choice of medium as revolve around his own observation that by working so closely with hard news agencies, Greenpeace has absorbed their production-line ethos and lost sight of the early concept, promulgated by Bob Hunter, that the mass media should be used as a conduit for "mind bombs": influential, sometimes archetypal images that can cut through the hypnotic drone of the day-to-day babbling to reach people at a deeper emotional level. May remains convinced that it is the force of impact that counts, not the number of media hits an organization scores.

"Often I would go into Greenpeace Communications and say something about this," he recalls, "and they would pull out a wad of clippings and say 'we've had mentions in forty-five newspapers,' or something like this. But as far as I'm concerned, that doesn't do it. If you have something important to say, you have to have images that are powerful enough to register. I mean, how many images do you see in a day? How many adverts? How many TV programs? You can go through a newspaper, flicking through page after page, and then you stop because there's an image that grabs you – occasionally it's so strong that you cut it out and stick it on the wall."

The key to it all, May says, is the search for that kind of intensity. Without images – and verbal messages – that resonate, environmental issues will stand no chance against competing concerns. He believes this is especially true as ecological matters get more complex. "Greenpeace elevated climate to the number one issue and were then unable to communicate it in a meaningful way, apart from demonstrations and having people wear white suits and sunglasses." The problem is, when people are having a hard time economically, just trying to survive, the message that "over the next fifty years the weather might deteriorate" just doesn't strike home. This means that you have to "find new forms to communicate these ideas to' provide context."

May says Greenpeace showed very little interest in his suggestion that multimedia, digital technology (such as CD-Rom) was an important key to the future. But that hasn't dampened his enthusiasm for the idea that multimedia and environmental issues are an almost perfect match. "The thing about multimedia is that you're receiving information on a number of levels at the same time, so it's image, symbols, text, in a very dense sort of multilayered picture," he says. "You only have to see children watching adverts on TV to recognize how sophisticated our pattern recognition and our sensibilities have become. We have no problem understanding a fifteen-second advert which may have sixty-four scenes in it and all this stuff happening. Our brains are designed to handle it. That kind of multimedia, multilevel thing is actually perfect for communicating environmental information, since environmental information is also complex and multilevel."

Not that John May is fixated on new and flashy technologies. Like other journalists I spoke with in Britain, he applauds Greenpeace's tradition of prompting and often playing a role in investigative print journalism – and he wonders what has happened to this practice. Old ways of communicating, in fact, may be coming back into the fore as television loses some of its lustre. Among the suggestions that May was hired to work on for Greenpeace (none of them were acted upon, he laments) was the founding of a film and television production company "that has a relationship with the body politic but is distanced from it" to produce documentaries, dramas, animated features, and children's shows – the kind of material that can register on the levels that the news headlines do not reach, and that can take a more integrated, complex approach to the issues.

May also worked for eighteen months with the photo agency Magnum, trying to co-ordinate a book on life across the planet "based on a year's worth of original Magnum photography." The idea was that "there are uses for images that convey what's going on in the rest of the world." The book was never produced.

★ ★ ★

I spent considerable time testing the theories of John May against the opinions of other people whose business, similarly, has been to communicate on environmental issues. For a start, I wanted to know if there was any kind of consensus that the news agencies (both in television and print) might be the wrong place for environmental organizations to invest all their time and money.

I found a general agreement with that proposition from two of the principals at Media Natura, a communications consultancy set up to provide British environmental groups with the guidance and technical aid of media professionals in various disciplines. Located in a high-security office in Covent Garden (they'd just had their computers ripped off a few weeks earlier, prompting the installation of metal gates and buzzers to protect the Apple Macs that replaced them), Media Natura has as its neighbours an old marketplace that clings to life in the face of a threatened redevelopment, as well as the live theatre where Agatha Christie's *The Mousetrap* ("the longest-running rubbish in the West End," as projects manager Chris Bligh tags it) continues to lure new waves of American tourists.

Inside the fortifications and up a flight of stairs are the offices where Media Natura will diagnose its clients' communications condition, prescribe a remedial strategy, and start assembling the talent to produce the posters, advertisements, documentaries, press packages, newsletters, whatever is needed to get the message out. Examples of the agency's past work hang on the walls. (Probably the most attention-grabbing is a broadsheet newspaper ad for a human rights campaign. The ad is dominated by block letters commanding "Read This, You Piece of Shit." Although it was agreed that the ad did catch the reader's eye, it never made it into the newspapers.)

Media Natura begins its campaigns by looking into what specific media an organization should focus on. "One of the starting points of this organization is that environmental groups do not necessarily have to rely upon television," says Media Natura's director, Michael Keating, whose résumé includes both television work and service to United Nations organizations. "When you are thinking about communicating something, you should think about who are we going to reach? And what are the ways of reaching people that do not necessarily include television? It can include television, but relying on television exclusively is a very foolhardy thing to do."

As Keating implies, one of the reasons that the currency of television has been devalued is that the mass audience is now of lesser importance to social activist groups. The question "who are we going to reach?" does not mean "how many?" but "who are these people and what is their level of commitment?" A mass audience that does nothing is not worth as much as a smaller audience that buys green, pressures politicians, or does something concrete. So the strategy has become more focused: "It's narrowcasting rather than broadcasting," comments Keating's colleague Chris Bligh. Television has also lost appeal, Keating says, because the idea that politicians can be forced to change policies if they are embarrassed on TV has become less applicable as the government and business spin-doctors have refined their craft.

"Politicians are now able to absorb the shock that television creates," Keating says. "They can look as if they are reacting and are very worried, and do absolutely nothing about it and get away with it."

The other problem is that most environmental issues are not big enough to provoke mass outrage; a lot of ecological work is being undertaken by small groups of people trying to chip away at their own corners of the larger concern. And feeding those groups' activities – providing them with knowledge and motivation they need to affect change on a more limited, day-to-day basis – is something that probably doesn't require a mass media hit.

"We try to steer our clients away from saying, 'We want to get a message to the general public' or 'Let's get this commissioned by Media Natura because we want a cinema commercial,'" Bligh says. "With us, they need to get into 'Right, let's get into the heads of metal-bashing industries that use CFCs on a regular basis for treating metal,' or something of that sort."

The idea of finding your target market is, of course, standard practice in the advertising industry and something that is especially applicable to consumer-based campaigns. Bligh cites Media Natura's campaign to promote an ethically produced coffee, the primary goal of which was to expand the market beyond a small circuit of church basements, to get the product into the major supermarkets. Its strategy to achieve this was to zero in on a group of consumers likely to travel on Britain's InterCity rail line and striking a discount deal to have posters placed on the main platforms. Meanwhile, in the case of a lobbying campaign, the intended target group won't be people who are willing to alter their consumer habits, but rather people with the specific knowledge needed to pressure for a change in government or corporate policies.

Electronic-mail has made it possible to disseminate detailed information widely and quickly, so that an informed constituency can lobby around precise policy objectives at the same time that public bodies are dealing with them. "You are now able to get a message out of the climate change conference, for instance, saying, 'The real problem is that the Kuwaitis, or whoever, are screwing up on carbon dioxide emissions. Would five thousand of you please fax the Kuwaiti embassy addressing these specific points?'"

Bligh believes this type of informed response is more effective than traditional forms of mass protest – that is, the demonstration – since there is a widespread belief that "there are groupies for these sorts of events, who will march against the Poll Tax or for Rock Against Racism and who think of it all as a party."

At its worst, Bligh's call for a finely targeted type of environmental activism can be seen as an elitist form of politics built on the realization, as he proposes, "that there are probably only two thousand people in London who actually affect the opinion-forming agenda or the decision-making agenda" and the rest of society is superfluous. Democracy, he argues, is virtually irrelevant in the struggle for environmental protection. For one, despite a vast growth in ecological consciousness over the past decade, environmentalism has practically no sway over the most obvious implement of democratic politics: the ballot box.

"The problem," Bligh says, "is that we are not voting people in on an election manifesto about quality of life. Electoral politics is fought over economic issues." But Bligh does not feel that it is inherently more democratic to conduct a mass media campaign. Television reports may ignite the outrage of large numbers of people, but they won't provide them with the context, the outlets, or anything else they need to engage that outrage as practical, political action, apart from, of course, writing a cheque for their favourite environmental organization. The response to a mass media hit "would be fundraising or maybe membership," he says. "Which is fine; you get support for the issue. But it doesn't actually get you support for solutions to the issue."

Not that Bligh and Keating want to beat up on Greenpeace for continuing to use television as its medium of choice. They don't question that Greenpeace puts its supporters' contributions to good use by attempting to influence the international, diplomatic forums that citizen groups are normally shut out of. It's simply that, as the issues have changed, Greenpeace's work and its media representation have become an increasingly awkward fit. "Greenpeace has gone upstream in terms of the issues," Keating says. "Whereas in the past you could have accused them of focusing on the consequences of the problems, they are now focusing on the causes of the problems and on solutions. And that is much more difficult to do through television."

Bernadette Vallely is another environmentalist who is wise in the ways of television but increasingly prefers to ignore the electronic cyclops. A former Friends of the Earth campaigner, Vallely has combined her career as social activist with that of best-selling author: in addition to founding the Women's Environmental Network (another WEN, not to be confused with Andy Booth's World Environment News), she has also penned several environmental books, including the influential green manual *1,000 Ways to Help Save the Planet*. While she continues to cater to the mass audience, at the same time Vallely has been drawn into the world of desktop publishing. She produces a small, inexpensive information lifeline that's mailed out to green adherents throughout the world. She believes the gap between the influence of mass media and of more target-specific vehicles, the products of media fragmentation, is becoming more and more narrow.

"You've got to ask who the mass media actually influence in the end," Vallely says, tending to a sick three-year old in her flat in the London suburb of Hackney. "It sometimes surprises me that I've done things with three people and had the same effect, campaigning-wise, as when I've been on the mass media. I've been on *News at Ten*. I've been on every TV station in the country. I've been on every chat show. My books have been serialized in the *Daily Mirror* and the *Daily Express* – huge circulation, millions of people, absolutely no feedback whatsoever. And I can write a little article in a nondescript magazine and have a hundred letters. It depends on what people are turning on to, what's happening. Just because you get mass media doesn't mean you get mass action. It's not the same thing."

Operating from what she terms a "practical feminist" view of environmental issues, Vallely offers an intricate feminist reading of environmental crisis that is at once highly radical in its implications but eminently workable. Her attack on consumerism focuses on the role that women have been enlisted to play: she returns to the dismantling of the rural economy that took place when the industrial model of production took root in the North. Women, who were once equal partners with men within an integrated household economy, were recast as consumers whose job it was to purchase the products that their husbands produced. Because consuming products became the primary social and economic function of women, women's identities and self-image became tightly bound up in the culture of consumerism – a process that became more entrenched as the influence of the advertising industry grew.

Disengaging women from this destructive consumerist cult requires an understanding of its psychological underpinnings: it is necessary for women to find a new, positive sense of identity in order for them not to define themselves by the products – and the quantity of products – that they buy. It is easier to campaign on this theme in Europe than in North America, Vallely says, because the memory of war has left a whole generation with the idea that it is possible, desirable, and morally right to live frugally. But faced with the bombardment of the advertising industry, and the spiritual vacuity that often marks life in wealthy Northern countries, it is still an uphill struggle to resist the deification of "things." So her WEN likes to focus on individual products, to draw the larger political implications out of the objects of everyday life.

"We don't want to make the issue so big it is uncontrollable to people," she says. The problem is that, no matter how sensible, her analysis is still too complex for television. And it is also likely to get lost in the ocean of advertising propaganda that is telling people precisely the opposite.

"In the women's movement, we have another strategy to deal with that, and that's personal contact," she says. "I prefer any time to go to a meeting and to switch the lightbulbs on in people's heads. Once the lightbulb is on people say, 'Ah, I never thought of that.' You can see them thinking, and that turns me on. If you can influence one person at that level, they'll go and tell somebody else. So I'd rather go to a public meeting every week than go on mass media. Talking to people is really the most superb form of communication. You can really get your message across; you can communicate spiritually, emotionally, in every single way. And you can't do that in print or television. You can produce an image that will stick in their minds, but they still won't get it exactly."

So is mass media campaigning obsolete? "Oh, I still think you need both," Vallely says. "It keeps the energy high. It gets your name around. If it's on television, somebody, somewhere will see it." Pausing briefly, she adds that – since WEN's messages have considerable content attached – "It's the more considered, carefully written pieces that have had most impact for us." Those kind of stories are found in publications that don't fit the definition of mass media (in the Murdoch or Turner sense of commanding audiences of millions of people), yet which are a considerable step above the audience reach of the desktop publications that environmentalists circulate within the activist milieu.

It's in that middle ground between mass media and marginal media that you'll find the weekly environmental section of Britain's *The Guardian* newspaper. With a daily circulation hovering around 300,000, *The Guardian* is considered the most progressive of Britain's slate of quality broadsheet papers favoured by policy wonks and professionals. Each Wednesday it publishes a tabloid section called "Society." The back half of that section contains classified ads for positions in government and the non-profit sector, and the front half is devoted to articles on broad societal shifts that may or may not have a current news peg. The paper allots four pages of this section to environment. One issue I saw, for instance, had articles on a permaculture agricultural project in Zimbabwe (permaculture is the opposite of monoculture, where one crop dominates a large tract of land); the environmental ramifications of British electoral reform; the movement to change land-zoning laws so that urban and agricultural functions are not treated as distinct; and Local Economic Trading Systems (LETS), where local currencies, sometimes known as Green Dollars, are used as the basis for a barter economy functioning outside the established financial system. All of these articles illustrated a commitment to the idea that environmental issues intersect with economic and political questions and are, in a practical sense, inseparable from them.

Sitting in the basement cafeteria at *The Guardian*'s concrete box of a headquarters in the City of London, a short walk away from the Greenpeace Communications department, environment editor John Vidal confirms that the meaning of environmentalism has indeed changed since the Rio conference. "We're trying to deconstruct the word environment, which is one of the worst things standing in the way of people understanding what's going on," he says in the precise tones of a British public school graduate.

"The word itself doesn't allow for the broader social debate. And the environment debate is moving into many other areas, cross-cutting with other agendas: social justice, economics, and culture generally throughout the world. It's taken a long time for news organs to appreciate that. What I'm trying to do is throw the net extremely broadly."

It's not only a question of environmentalists looking towards political and economic reform to help them save the planet, Vidal says. The traffic moves the other way too: as economic crisis and the resulting social breakdown intensify across Europe and throughout the world, people are looking towards environmental ideas as potential solutions to social and economic calamities. "It's a very interesting phenomenon that environmentalism isn't being seen as a middle class thing here. It's rooted in the deprived, marginalized groups. In that sense, it's the same as what is happening in South America and Asia." As an example Vidal cites the popularity of LETS schemes in Britain, which not only follow through on the green movement's promise of local-scale economies, but also deal with the inescapable reality that the traditional economy is no longer able to absorb the labour or meet the needs of huge numbers of people within society. Green visions of the city are also being taken seriously, as local authorities struggle not only with environmental contamination but also urban rot, economic decline, and social unrest.

The convergence of a multitude of problems, Vidal believes, is now allowing for a radical reassessment of our values. "The new debate is: let's start rethinking money," he says. "Let's start debating cash and economies in a different way. The debate about land – you can say that land is being degraded, but what is land, what is our relationship to that land? It's a question of looking at the fundamentals: what kind of a society do you want?"

Vidal stresses that this type of environmental coverage is far from the norm; *The Times* or the *Daily Telegraph* wouldn't give a second look to the stories *The Guardian* runs. That means that while other newspapers may still seek out Greenpeace-type media stunts to hang their environmental coverage on, Vidal would argue that there's a growing constituency (among his newspapers' readers at least) with a deeper interest in the issues, people who can learn nothing from such theatrics. I ask the editor what his general reaction is to the material that's sent by Greenpeace. "It's quite simple, really," he says. "They send me their stuff and I dump it in the bin."

A few days later I encounter another illustration of how this particular organ of the press has jumped ahead of Greenpeace on its own turf. At the Greenpeace office I speak to Tony Mariner about what seems to me an irony in the organization's operations: while Greenpeace works in a multitude of countries around the world, the images it uses fail to bring home the reality of those places to the majority of Greenpeace supporters in Northern countries. This is presumably what John May had wanted to accomplish with his ill-fated collaboration with the Magnum photo agency. Mariner candidly admits that Greenpeace, having been absorbed in its own internal turmoil, hadn't attempted to find any new visual language to convey the complexities of North-South environmental issues. He says that finding such a new approach would be difficult: "What you have to guard against is portraying developing countries as dusty, disease-ridden places – it's just not true. I think the new language is going to have to understand some underlying cultural issues – which is why breezing into a place in a Safari suit and covering things from a certain perspective doesn't really work."

Mariner argues that as difficult as it might be to part with the visual clichés of the past, doing so is entirely possible and highly desirable. Then, within a week of our conversation comes evidence that at least one outlet of the "mainstream" media had taken on that very goal. Inside *The Guardian*'s weekend magazine is a photo supplement called "Small World – Life Is in the Details." Of all things, it is part *advertisement*, co-produced by the eco-friendly detergent company Down to Earth, whose logo appears at the bottom of each page.

The twenty-four-page, glossy booklet is basically a scrapbook of images and related factoids detailing how people live their lives in different countries of the world; each couple of pages takes on one small detail of the broader picture: how do people travel from one place to another, what do they do in school, what do they buy for dinner, what are their sleeping arrangements, how much water do they use when they wash? What emerges is a fascinating, colourful composite portrait of life on Earth that makes the major environmental issues of the time tangible and understandable, and which challenges the readers' understanding both of their own culture and of cultures in the South.

We get a nuanced portrait of life in the Third World: far from a picture of abject misery, we peer into the lives of families (whose consumption represents the statistical average in their country), see their joys, their struggles, understand that they are poorer than us in obvious ways but wealthier in others. It's a captivating collection of images that brings the big picture back home and challenges our own assumptions about life at home and abroad. It subtly juxtaposes material advantage against the more intangible qualities of family, community, and culture. It is, in short, a mind bomb.

★ ★ ★

With major environmental organizations like Greenpeace now much more timid about presenting their public messages than grassroots organizations and even some mass media outlets, one has to take seriously a question posed by the *Utne Reader*: "Is the Mainstream Environmental Movement Sustainable?"[1] The magazine's proposition is essentially that a number of well-established ecological groups have become so dependent upon a middle-of-the-road public image for continued public support that they are now unable to take the lead on controversial policy issues.

"It's a deeply relevant question," John Vidal says. "There's a new generation of environmentalists coming along, and the old ones are going to have to change the debate or go out of business." Vidal points to two vast and spontaneous campaigns in Britain – one against the building of more roads in the English countryside, the other against the exportation of veal calves to Europe – to show how the environmental agenda was, at that point, once again being set at the grassroots. (Keep in mind, though, that Vidal made his remarks before Greenpeace's massively successful campaigns later in 1995 against the Brent-Spar oil platform and renewed French nuclear tests.)

At his desk adjoining Vidal's, *Guardian* environment correspondent Paul Brown, a close acquaintance of David McTaggart and the author of a children's book on Greenpeace, offers that Greenpeace has lost much of its ability to influence the public discussion on the environment, partly because its actions are now seen as being more showbiz than an expression of heartfelt commitment. He refers to an action in Britain where a convoy of nuclear materials was blocked: "I would have called it more of a photo-call than an action," Brown says. "They didn't really hold it up any longer than it took people to take a picture, whereas before they would have talked about blocking the motorway for three days to call attention to the issue. They would have been arrested and injunctions would have been served."

Brown believes that the same attitude affects Greenpeace's work at sea. "I think it's because they've got too much to lose in terms of economic hardware. Before they couldn't give a sod because the economic hardware was a crappy old ship. Now it's stuffed with electronic gear and expensive survival suits and rubber boats and things which cost a few million dollars to put together."

Several months later Brown would write a story for *The Guardian* reporting that the crew members of a Greenpeace ship impounded by French commandos in the South Pacific were to be punished by the Greenpeace brass (despite the success of their mission) precisely because they took too great a risk with the fate of their ship.[2] Brown reported that the crew of the *MV Greenpeace* were to face "the equivalent of court martial" for disobeying orders and sailing the ship into French territory, thereby losing control over several months' worth of supplies and endangering other crews involved in the protest against nuclear tests.

Bernadette Vallely disagrees with this analysis that pits new grassroots groups against that old dinosaur, Greenpeace. While those grassroots organizations may indeed be as vital, spontaneous, and fresh in their thinking as Vidal and Brown portray them, does this mean that Greenpeace wants to crush the new competition? Quite the opposite, Vallely says. In Britain, at least, Greenpeace has used its established profile and fundraising skills to become the sugar daddy of the grassroots movement. "Greenpeace will give start-up funding, and they'll never ask for any credit for it," she says. "They'll see amazing people at the local level – people who would have to give up their jobs to do it properly, who need some source of funds – and they'll just give them the money, without asking for it back. I know. They gave WEN money when we started, and they never wanted any publicity."

Back in Lewes, John May is contemplating whether Greenpeace is headed towards extinction – or whether there are early signs of atrophy, at least – and true to form he declares that the problem lies in the technology. In the spirit of McLuhan, he proposes that the mechanical adjuncts of Greenpeace do not just influence its message, but are also the primary formative force over how the organization itself is constructed. How to fix Greenpeace? How to make it more spontaneous and flexible? How to avoid the incessant infighting that has damaged Greenpeace's good name and impeded its mission? "They need to be radically re-engineered using digital technology as the backbone of their global structures," May says. "That was the task that Greenpeace should have done. Because the wired organization has completely different characteristics; it is able to do things in completely different ways, it thinks in a different way and has a completely different culture."

May's ideas are out of sync with those of many veterans who have seen technologies create monstrous problems. According to Andy Booth, electronic-mail "tied the organization up enormously – screwed it right up. It increased the organization's ability to communicate amongst itself, but it made one person's business everybody else's business. You couldn't do anything or say anything without getting a e-mail back from the director of Greenpeace Germany, or someone, saying 'What the fuck are you doing? You don't have the authority to do that or say that.'" Booth believes that a "devolution" of power and authority – returning to the scale of small, independent cells – is the only way for Greenpeace to regain its former glory. "But it's probably too far gone, he says."

In his basement study in Syracuse, New York, Mike Affleck characterizes his disembodied working life – he is in contact with his co-workers only through e-mail, fax, and telephone – as "totally bizarre." Affleck says, "I haven't seen my assistant, who works in Chicago, in over two years. I haven't been to my office once in that time." Rather than having flattened the hierarchies, Affleck says that the type of wiring that runs through Greenpeace now has merely become an extension – the electronic tentacles – of a frightening, confusing, and incoherent establishment of control and command. "Every time the phone rings, you have no idea whether it's your boss calling to fire you, or someone calling to praise you," he says.

But May is adamant about the benefits of digital technology. For one, he believes that physically sending staff to conferences is an unecological, overly costly exercise that most often serves to demoralize a lot of people. "It's a horrendous calculation to think of the amount of time spent on planes by Greenpeace campaigners – and it was never questioned," he says. "It's the 'what's today – it must be Kiev,' syndrome. So the first thing you do is build your global video conferencing network to replace it. I wanted to create this virtual Greenpeace. You know, here's this messy organization called Greenpeace, let's start conceptualizing the virtual one that doesn't have these problems. We take the good things over, but leave behind what doesn't work."

May is convinced there are multiple benefits to the wired organization. Firstly, he says, it "flattens hierarchies," giving individuals more autonomy to take initiative themselves. It also allows an organization to break apart and reform as the issues change, because the technology can hook up pieces of the organization in a "modular" fashion. Finally, it would reduce some of the crushing demands on personnel, which routinely result in personal crises and premature burn-out of staff. The technology alone won't solve this problem, he says. The "virtual" activist organization of the future also needs to incorporate a fundamental shift of attitude, to recognize that people are its most precious asset.

"All radical organizations of this kind are very, very damaging to people's personalities. That's been my general experience," he says. "They're very hard on people's personal lives and on them as individuals. I mean, Greenpeace had absolutely no support mechanism for people who spent all day grappling with nuclear proliferation or any other difficult, depressing subject. At the end of the day you go back to your flat and sit there and think 'my God' – so you get drunk a lot. You're constantly moving around the world so your marriage breaks up as well. The majority of people who have been through it have suffered a lot. That's not just Greenpeace, it goes with the territory. New forms of organizations have to emerge in the twenty-first century that take this into account."

CHAPTER 9

MANUFACTURING EVENTS

SWASHBUCKLERS, SCIENTISTS, AND DOLPHIN-TUNA TURF WARS

A whale ship was my Yale College and my Harvard.
— Herman Neville, *Moby Dick*

PAUL WATSON IS SITTING IN A NONDESCRIPT, OVERHEATED hotel room, a few hours before he's scheduled to deliver a speech to an Ottawa university. He is dressed in a captain's uniform, fielding questions about whales, forests, and what it takes to get your message on TV. As soon as I press "record" on my tape recorder, Watson's casual, friendly speaking voice (a surprise when you first meet him) falls away; in its place emerges a stern, rapid-fire cadence, full of Biblical invective and apocalyptic wrath.

Watson, the former Greenpeacer who became the skipper of the Sea Shepherd Conservation Society, has many times sailed off to interfere with whaling and fishing fleets, and Sea Shepherd takes credit for sinking half of Norway's whalers while they were in port. Indeed, the Sea Shepherd Conservation Society has specialized in creating the kind of high seas dramas that replicate and in some cases exceed the swashbuckle-quotient of the early Greenpeace campaigns. In an ironic twist, Watson scored a huge media hit in 1993 when he was arrested off the coast of Newfoundland for cutting the nets of foreign trawlers. While Watson was once reviled by Newfoundlanders for his prominent role in the Greenpeace anti-sealing campaign, his 1993 arrest prompted the locals in St. John's to don placards and chant "Free Paul Watson."[1]

Watson says his gift for getting media coverage is based on a clear appreciation of the mass media's appetites. "The mass media," he recites, "is not too concerned about facts and figures and statistics and science. Basically, it's only interested in three things: sex, scandal, and violence. And if you can get any of that into your story, you've got yourself a story, and maybe then you can tag your message to it." So there's the formula: find an alluring, archetypical setting (life on the high seas, the menace and the beauty of the rolling deep), then add some blood or sex as an additional attention-grabber.

It's ironic that, in the case of Greenpeace – an organization avowed to non-violence – the most memorable campaigns have essentially been about blood. Greenpeace's anti-whaling and anti-sealing campaigns catapulted the organization to international prominence and, in retrospect, have clearly had the greatest shelf-life in the public imagination. The images of confrontation and death on the high seas and later on the ice floes off Newfoundland secured their place in history long after the memory of Amchitka had faded. What put them there was the simmering sense of conflict, the smell of blood.

In these campaigns Greenpeace was attempting to end the massive slaughter of wildlife, a bloody and unpleasant business, using the most obvious means at its disposal: by relaying graphic images of the slaughter to the public and by interposing the members' own, unarmed bodies between the hunters and the hunted. In New-foundland, supporters of the seal hunt would argue that such images blinded the larger public to the economic and social issues behind the hunt; that they overpowered rational argument and obscured complex social and scientific considerations. But to environmentalists these pictures were the greatest possible educational tool. They brought the public face-to-face with an indisputable, unpleasant reality, an indelible representation of truth that was impossible to rationalize away.

However one might pass judgement on these campaigns, it is undeniable that the images of blood and conflict were a highly effective means of capturing public attention. In *The Greenpeace Chronicle*, Bob Hunter recalls a television newscast that signalled Greenpeace's arrival as an international presence. In November 1975 the Green-peace boat, which had set off to intercept the Russians' Pacific whaling fleet, finally encountered its adversary about sixty miles off the coast of Mendocino, California. With cameras rolling, Hunter and his colleague George Kortova set off in a rubber raft to disrupt the whale kill. The two placed their own bodies in the line of fire between the whaling boats and the whales, assuming that their own presence and the possibility of humans being killed or injured would dissuade the Russians from firing at the whales.

This assumption proved incorrect: the Russians, undaunted, fired a harpoon that missed the two environmentalists by about five feet. The harpoon travelled on to land in the side of a whale, sending a shower of blood into the air. Greenpeace's cameraman, Fred Easton, filmed the harpoon hurtling past Hunter and Kortova's heads, and then spun around to catch its entry into the whale in the water behind them. *Voilà!* – Greenpeace's mission statement to the world. Along with photographs taken by Rex Weyler, those few seconds of film communicated more than Greenpeace could ever hope to convey with words: a graphic illustration of Greenpeace's message about the cruelty of the whale kill, at the same time cementing the image of Greenpeace as a noble and brave group of crusaders up against a heartless and barbaric band of murderers.

According to Hunter's account: "With the single act of filming ourselves in front of the harpoon, we had entered the mass consciousness of modern America – something that none of our previous expeditions had achieved. It was Walter Cronkite himself who introduced our footage to the mass TV audience, footage that was then run on every single television channel in the U.S. and Canada, spilling over in Europe and even Japan. Weyler's photographs went out to every country in the world that had a wire service."[2]

Not all of Greenpeace's anti-whaling voyages would generate spectacular images. Hunter wrote of two later anti-whaling journeys in the summer of 1977, during which Greenpeace was once again successful in tracking down the Russian whaling fleet and nipping at its heels. By this time, however, the Russians had changed their strategy. To avoid a confrontation that would bring more bad publicity, they chose not to hunt down whales while the Greenpeace boat and its cameras were in the vicinity. As a result the encounters were less confrontational and bereft of blood. Hunter believes that the mere presence of the Greenpeace boat achieved part of its purpose by stopping the Russians from killing whales during that period of time, and members of the Greenpeace crew twice boarded the Russian whaling vessels, attempting to propagandize and fraternize with the Russian crew. But none of this was considered newsworthy, and the images were of no interest to the television networks. Ironically, Greenpeace did not make the news when it achieved its goals; only when its efforts led to failure, to the continued slaughter of whales that television audiences could witness, would the media coverage take hold.

"If there was any lesson to be learned – or relearned – it was that the mass media, by and large, was not interested in diplomatic exchanges between adversaries," Hunter commented. "The only thing, besides sex, politics and sports that grabbed its attention, excited it, made its juices run, was violence. A harpoon fired in the vicinity of human flesh was news. Dialogue was not news. . . . Without confrontation – the risk of life and limb – the mass media could not have cared less what we did."[3]

But while these remarks suggest that the Greenpeace crusaders were innocents who had to learn the ways of the media through bitter, disappointing experience, quite the opposite is true. From the beginning, Greenpeace's media-managers were hardened, seasoned professionals who orchestrated the flow of news using the kind of street-fighting tactics that would be familiar to any hard-bitten newshound fighting for a scoop or a sensational headline. As the first anti-whaling campaign was set for launch in 1975, organizers were well aware that their job of stoking the fires of press interest would not always be a noble undertaking. Bob Hunter writes candidly about how "news" was massaged, manipulated, or manufactured, and how his own dual role as a journalist and a Greenpeace organizer had somewhat corroded his professional standards:

> As chief propagandist for the voyage, I was now fully committed to being a "flack" for the whales. In order to sustain our global media presence, I was going to have to use every trick I ever learned from Ben Metcalfe and be ready to invent quite a few on top of that. In preparation for the trip, I had resigned as a columnist for the *Sun* in order to be on board as a reporter. The advantage of that was simple. The subjective stuff written by columnists is never picked up by the wire services. But the "objective" stuff from reporters is picked up as legitimate news. Thus, I could file an "objective" report from the *Phyllis Cormack* one day, and flush a reaction out of Tokyo via the Associated Press wire service within less than twenty-four hours. All I had to do was to make sure never to quote myself. Instead, I invented quotes, placed them in the mouths of various agreeable crew members, then "reported" to the outside world what

they had said. As a journalist, I was, of course, a traitor to my profession. As a "news manager" for the expedition, I could censor any unflattering realities, control the shaping of our public image, and when things got slack, I could arrange for events to be staged that could then be reported as news. Instead of reporting the news, I was in fact in the position of inventing the news – *then* reporting it.[4]

One quite spectacular news invention arising from the first anti-whaling voyage was a story that Hunter had concocted about the possibility of the Greenpeace crew encountering giant squids and sperm whales doing battle. Hunter quoted crew member and future Greenpeace president Patrick Moore, who held a doctorate in ecology, speculating about the chain of events that can occur during full moons, when giant squids can rise from the ocean floor in pursuit of the tiny organisms that they feed on. Those organisms rise to the surface in order to soak up extra lunar light. The squids may in turn come into contact with sperm whales, which normally reside closer to the ocean surface and feed off squids. The story concluded that the Greenpeace crew was hopeful that it could observe and film an encounter between an eighty-foot sperm whale and a fifty-foot giant squid, locked in a dance of death.

As Hunter acknowledges in his book, the possibility of anyone on board the Greenpeace boat actually witnessing such an encounter was so remote that it was barely worth mentioning. Even though the story did not contain any scientific errors, it was wildly speculative. Nonetheless, this near-science-fiction story achieved its goal of reviving flagging press interest in the Greenpeace voyage. By concocting another exciting episode in Greenpeace's serialized drama on the high seas, Hunter hoped to build momentum towards the 1975 meeting of the International Whaling Commission. The tactic worked. The press latched onto this invented tale of exotic ocean life and submarine passions. *The Vancouver Sun* ran the story under an eight-column banner headline: "Greenpeace Ships Sail to See 'Awesome' Battle of Pacific Giants." The wire services also picked up the story. One Australian paper ran it under the headline "Man Lands on Giant Squid-Whale Ground."[5]

Stories like these may make members of the present-day Greenpeace squirm with embarrassment. Paul Hohnen, Greenpeace International's political director in Amsterdam, insists that nowadays before any scientific data is released to the public, the information undergoes a peer-review process as rigorous as in any academic institution. "Because we're so dependent on information, what we say *has* to be right," Hohnen says. The appointment of new staff such as Jeremy Leggett, former reader in Earth Sciences at Imperial College in London, who became director of science, was a key to shoring up Greenpeace's scientific credibility.[6] But the move towards paying more meticulous attention to detail – and the desire for a finer grasp of both the scientific and political/diplomatic dimensions of an issue – opened up a generational rift within Greenpeace, with some of the oldtimers feeling that this precision has come at the expense of panache.

Greenpeace's ex-chairman David McTaggart seemed to be driving at that in a memo he sent, in August 1992, to air his unease about the current direction of the organization to Greenpeace staff around the world. Having been beaten so badly by French commandos in the 1970s that he nearly lost sight in one eye, having organized the campaign that led to the sinking of the *Rainbow Warrior* in 1985, McTaggart felt he knew what would stir public passion and create sympathy. He pushed for the return of a type of campaigning that flirts with danger, the where campaigners' skins are on the line and there is a genuine possibility of harm hanging in the air.

"There is a grey area between violence and non-violence," McTaggart wrote in his 1992 memo. "Years ago, once we decided on a specific campaign goal, the most intense debate usually centred on how far we could take our actions and still remain non-violent. We need to reopen this discussion, I believe, and investigate ways of making our activist campaigns heavier. Don't misunderstand, I'm not suggesting we go violent, but we need to look at new ways to spur action and concern."

Meanwhile, close to two decades after that unlikely story about giant squids and sperm whales, Bob Hunter expresses similar disenchantment with Greenpeace's approach to the media. "Quite frankly, I think they've lost their handle on the media work," Hunter says. What the current crop of Greenpeace activists may have forgotten, he says, is that – while the issues may be more complex today – the news media are essentially the same. "The sad fact is that we had to go out and do those kinds of stunts because that was the only way to get the attention of the media," Hunter says. "I believe the hard-news line is still 'If it bleeds, it leads.' If you get a shot of a guy on a bungee cord that doesn't work, that's your lead item on the news."

No Greenpeace campaign was more blood-soaked – and more controversial – than the anti-sealing campaigns of 1975 and 1976. Working in concert with a number of other animal rights groups opposed to sealing (notably the International Fund for Animal Welfare), Greenpeace brought its media expertise to bear on the issue by staging a confrontation with sealers on the ice floes, a skirmish intended primarily for the television cameras, and eventually the importation of Canadian seal pelts into Europe was banned – virtually destroying the Newfoundland and Canadian Inuit sealing industries and devastating Aboriginal communities in the Canadian north.

An obscure footnote to this famous episode was the decision of the premier of Newfoundland, Frank Moores, to fight back against the environmentalists using what he believed were their own tactics. Moores, deciding to appeal to the U.S. media, held a series of press conferences in Boston, New York, and Washington to *explain* Newfoundland's position on the seal hunt to the wider world. What followed was a classic exposition of the relative powers of television versus print cultures – indisputable proof of McLuhan's assertion that in a battle between the direct, visual assault of television, and the cerebral, expository processes of print, television would win every time.

The U.S. media covered Moores's addresses, but from the beginning his campaign was doomed to failure. Whether one found his arguments about how economic, historical, and scientific issues affect sealing to be insightful or spurious, the fact remains that complex and nuanced discussion of this sort could never cut it on television. When asked by a reporter to comment on Premier Moores's speech, the London *Times*' Washington correspondent Pat Brogan rated him high for content but gave him no chance of success in the living rooms of America.

"When it's shown on television," Brogan said, "however good a case he has, it can't stand up against the films of the seals being slaughtered. As they all admit, the slaughter of seals is a nasty business. Baby seals are very appealing little creatures, and the sight of them being clubbed to death is very disagreeable. However lucid and however clear Mr. Moores and his colleagues are in explaining that this is, in fact, a humane way of killing them; that a cull of seals is necessary to protect the fishermen, to protect the fish; and that the people of Newfoundland depend to some extent upon the seal hunt – nonetheless, when people see a film, they forget all about the arguments, and their sympathy is entirely with the animals."[7]

Many politicians, like Frank Moores, still had to learn that mere words have no chance against strong TV pictures; and you'd probably do better to keep quiet than to give the networks another opportunity to beat you up with stock footage. Brian Davies of the International Fund for Animal Welfare had by 1976 learned that lesson. And Davies was overjoyed that Premier Moores was still living in the pre-TV age. Davies called Moores's press conferences "the best thing that could possibly have happened" for the forces opposed to the seal hunt. In terms of TV language the scenes from the press conferences were "a crushing bore" and the television networks would show footage of baby seals being killed to back up the conference activity. "You're not going to turn off public antagonism to the seal hunt by this type of activity," Davies said. "In fact, I don't think there is any way of doing that."[8]

Bob Hunter finds it surprising that even public relations types were slow to realize that visual images had changed the rules for communicating in the television age. He cites Greenpeace's 1976 campaign to shut down Australia's last whaling station, at a place called Cheyne's Beach near Albany in Western Australia. Like Frank Moores, whaling officials believed they could explain their position on why whaling should continue, and again the results were predictable.

"The whaling station hired a public relations man," Hunter recalls, "whose first brilliant public relations move was to fly all the media from the big cities in Australia over to Albany and put them on a boat, so they could go out and take pictures to show how *humanitarian* the whale kill was. Well, most Australians didn't even know they had a whaling industry. The next thing they know, they're being besieged with these images of giant whales, thrashing and dying on the ends of cold harpoons, and blood all over the place. Our job was done."

★ ★ ★

The early Greenpeacers – who gave birth to their movement in the midst of a cultural revolution that aimed to cast off much of the old baggage of Western culture – don't seem to have lost much sleep worrying about how the media strategy at the centre of their campaigns was helping to erode our society's capacity for rational argument. This parallels the attitude of their mentor, McLuhan, who often noted the electronic media's capacity for breaking down the tradition of Western logical thinking but who, once again, refrained from passing judgement on that trend.

The Global Village: Transformations in World Life and Media in the 21st Century (adapted and compiled by Bruce Powers, using McLuhan's notes and conversations, but published nine years after McLuhan's death) contains extensive ruminations on how electronic media have changed the way people think – but the language used to describe the shift is neutral and ambivalent, rather than lamenting.[9] McLuhan postulated a complex theory explaining why the argumentative approach (which Frank Moores had used to defend sealing) does not translate well into the visceral language of television.

According to McLuhan, written language operates within the sphere of "visual space," while the electronic media inhabit an "acoustic space," which has traditionally been overlooked in Western culture. Visual space is linear – arranging information, one piece at a time, in a straight line that leads to a conclusion – while acoustic space can accommodate overlapping impressions and simultaneous sensory inputs. McLuhan believed that Western society was falling back into an acoustic space as it was being bombarded with random information and impressions, transported through the electronic media simultaneously and in no particular sequence. This sensory deluge, McLuhan believed, was re-creating in Western society a mode of perception that had existed in preliterate times – in a time when tribal people received information from nature using all of their senses and perceptual faculties; in a time before humanity came to favour intellect and the visual sense that drew information up off the page, to the exclusion of other senses.

While people like Frank Moores and the Australian PR man might have cursed the resurrection of "acoustic space" – a hierarchy of understanding that values sensory impressions above the kind of logical, sequential arguments they sought to communicate – McLuhan believed the change was not necessarily negative. Falling back into acoustic space, McLuhan felt, could potentially temper the rigidity of Western thinking that had historically led to conflict and war: within acoustic space, apparently contradictory points of view can co-exist; there is no need for them to be placed either inside or outside of a particular logical continuum in order to have their own place.

For Greenpeace – a group that was, initially, as committed to opening up new doors of perception as it was to stopping atomic tests and saving whales – the idea of replacing the rigid, linear systems of thought upon which our industrial society had been built with something more holistic and in tune with nature would have in itself been a reason for embracing the electronic media. McLuhan's description of the new media as a force that was returning the world to its "tribal" origins holds a particular resonance for a group committed to opposing the blinkered logic behind the industrial state; a logic that cannot see beyond the next quarter's profit or the hollow victory at the end of a nuclear war. Greenpeace, in its earliest incarnation at least, was bent on shattering the self-contained logical loops that would not permit change. As Ben Metcalfe, credited by Bob Hunter as being the brains behind Greenpeace's media strategy, declared during a 1973 CBC radio interview: "We are so fluid, we are so flexible, we are so non-linear in our thinking, so silly, so pathetic and so bloody hopeless, that we can do anything. And we are totally unpredictable in that way. We don't have to play the game according to their rules, because we've already rejected their rules. It's their rules that killed Lake Erie."[10]

It's a bit odd to look back on an era when the illogical, fragmented nature of electronic media could be seen as a weapon working in favour of radical causes. As corporate control of media has solidified; as MTV and CNN have abbreviated already short audience attention spans; as the disquieting television images of the Vietnam war were replaced in the public imagination by the controlled and choreographed coverage of the Gulf War – television has been tagged, more and more, as a tool of indoctrination by the establishment. Greenpeace now finds itself in a more problematic relationship with TV: its increasing concern with how questions of trade, economics, and political structures affect the environment has been virtually shut out of a medium that abhors complexity and rational debate.

But there are two sides to this issue, and Greenpeace has found itself on both: while visual presentation can pre-empt crucial discussion, it can also cut through obfuscation, spurious assertion, and hollow propaganda. A good thing about television images is that they can be tough to bullshit around. Arguments can be twisted, the truth can get lost in the ambiguities of debate. Pictures can be an antidote to that – bringing the public face to face with bedrock reality that lodges itself in the human gut. Greenpeace's campaigns to save the whales are a good case in point.

Whaling, says Bob Hunter, had survived into the 1970s because it was protected by a layer of old mythology and irrelevant debate that sheltered the general public from the knowledge of what was actually happening on the high seas. In the public's view, whalers remained the brave underdogs in an uneven fight with a maritime Titan. The whales were fierce beasts, the whalers their potential prey. "Everyone was still believing in the mythology of Herman Melville and of everyone who drew those wonderful wood engravings back in the fourteenth century of giant sea-monsters pulling ships down," Hunter says. "We all had picked up on that image, and thought of the whale as this incredible, fierce embodiment of blind, pitiless nature. Melville, in fact, when he wrote *Moby Dick*, created Moby Dick as this embodiment of the power that man could not control, and that forever was its enemy."

The Greenpeacers who went out in the 1975 encounter with the Russian whaling fleet off California discovered differently. For one thing, the whales that the Russians were hunting down were little more than babies. Greenpeace photographed whales being killed that were just 17 feet long – far below the limit set by the International Whaling Commission for the whale kill, and no comparison to Moby Dick, which was supposed to have been 120 feet long. All of the adult whales had apparently been killed; the Russian fleet was now going after the few remaining infants.

If the whales off California didn't measure up to the myth of Moby Dick, neither did the whalers live up to their mythological image. What Greenpeace found in the Pacific was not valiant sailors staring down death on the high seas, but a whaling "factory ship" that doubled as an instrument of the Cold War. A fleet of killer boats would harpoon whales and tow them to this factory ship, which was decked out with an array of satellite dishes designed for eavesdropping on U.S. military communications. In fact, the whaling was not being carried out for its own sake, but merely as a cover for military operations. Still, the whale killing that took place was as efficient and mechanical as one might expect from a Cold War appendage created to serve a vision of mass destruction. Hunter says the Greenpeace crew had no idea of what they would find as they closed in on the Russian factory ship. Following the killer ships, the Greenpeace boat steamed towards a "huge grey shadow on the horizon."

"It was so huge, it was the biggest ship I had ever seen," Hunter says. "It was somewhere around 700 feet long. I would describe it as

being about ten stories tall. It was just immense. It was a whole floating city: there were probably a thousand people on board, playing
volleyball on the upper decks while, on the lower decks, the whales
that they winched in through this hole in the stern of the ship were
being chopped up. Blood was pouring out of the scuppers. A foun-
tain of blood was coming out of there. It was like a sewage discharge
the whole time, non-stop.

"It was a giant, floating slaughterhouse, probably amounting to
the largest predator that had ever been loosed, in all of evolution, on
the ocean. It was just sucking up the last of the whales. And they
were so small by now that they were like minnows being dragged
into the anus of this giant machine, that was eating from its wrong
end."

This was the new image of whaling in the industrial era; a mirror
image of the myth of Moby Dick, the whale Melville described as
"one grand hooded phantom, like a snow hill in the air." And
nobody knew about it until they saw the evidence. The circulation of
this new picture of industrial whaling led to a quantum leap in popular thinking about whaling. The whale was no longer the monster,
Hunter says. "We, in fact, were the monster by far, and these creatures had become something that had no chance whatsoever against
us. It was like running down rabbits with bulldozers."

That realization caused a political sea-change to take place. The
film shot was pivotal in placing pressure on the International Whaling Commission (which until then had functioned as an agency of a
cartel of whaling nations) and in soon leading to the moratorium on
whaling. Hunter says the pictures jump-started a stagnant debate.

Says Hunter: "People who had been active trying to save whales,
because they knew of the problem for years – we're talking up to
1975 – up until that point had not been able to get the attention of
the media, because it seemed like some sort of arcane debate about
wildlife management, off somewhere, that no one ever saw. I think it
then became connected with public emotions and it was no longer
an academic resource-use debate. I think that was the strength of it,
because we don't necessarily vote on the basis of statistics or projec-
tions, we vote on the basis of our feelings."

★ ★ ★

Arousing strong feelings in the public often leads to political victory, as it did with the anti-whaling issue into the late 1970s. Now fast-forward two decades: there is still drama on the high seas, a fight to keep an age-old species from falling into oblivion. But in the meantime there has been a costume change, with a few new characters coming on stage. Instead of whales and seals, the main object of anxiety is now the dolphins. Cast as the villains opposite the environmental crusaders are not Newfoundland or Inuit sealers, or the mechanized, militarized descendants of Melville's brave whalers, but a few new tuna-fishing fleets from the Southern Hemisphere.

Greenpeace is still a big player in this drama over the survival of ocean life, but it's playing a much different role than it used to. While an earlier generation of Greenpeace activists generally used to let the pictures do the talking, the new breed have a lot more lines to remember, and it is complicated stuff. Many current-day Greenpeacers actually find themselves wishing – ironically enough – that they could turn off some of the pictures in people's heads, that public emotions would cool down long enough for some serious thinking to take place. Environmentalists may once have laughed at Frank Moores for trying to explain the economic and historical factors that he said made Newfoundlanders dependent upon the seal hunt. Now, many of them laugh at Greenpeace for attempting to make similarly abstract arguments the centrepiece of its efforts on the "tuna-dolphin" issue.

The majority of U.S. environmental groups engaged in the effort to save dolphins killed by the industrial tuna fishery take the same approach to the tuna-dolphin question that Greenpeace took in its anti-whaling and anti-sealing campaigns in the 1970s. They are keeping the issues simple and tightly focused. They are not afraid to use market pressure – boycotts – to achieve their goals. And they won't let social or economic factors get in the way of their one, overriding goal: saving the lives of dolphins.

These environmentalists know that their main weapon in support of the dolphin is the animal's own public image: cast in the popular imagination as the smartest and perhaps most lovable creature in the sea, these streamlined sea mammals have won themselves a soft spot in the collective psyche of North America and most of the world. It is this image that accounts for the horror and outrage that gripped the American public three decades ago, in the 1960s, when it became known that one of the main strategies for locating and catching tuna had resulted in the needless deaths of hundreds of thousands of dolphins. Because dolphins swim with tuna schools – travelling close to the ocean surface while the tuna swim below – industrial tuna-fishing fleets often seek out dolphins in the quest for their real quarry. Casting huge nets – sometimes a mile long – into the waters, they draw not only entire schools of tuna but also dolphins into their boats. Useless to the fishers, the dolphins wind up dying, collateral damage in this high-tech war at sea.

Soon after a scientist researching a master's thesis released this information about the dolphin kill in the 1960s, the wasting of dolphins as "by-catch" became a major public issue that demanded a political response. In 1972, as a result of protests by environmentalists and the dolphin-loving American public, the U.S. government passed the Marine Mammal Protection Act, restricting the ability of the domestic tuna fleet to fish in a manner harmful to dolphins.

The number of dolphin deaths declined after the act was passed, but the tuna-dolphin issue resurfaced with a vengeance at the end of the next decade. The U.S. environmental movement was enthusiastically onside when an amendment to the act was passed in 1988, internationalizing the scope of the legislation by banning from the U.S. market any tuna that had been dolphin-caught by foreign tuna fleets. In April 1990 the three largest U.S. tuna canners announced that they too would exert pressure over the practices of international tuna fleets by buying only tuna certified by independent, on-board observers to be "dolphin-safe." The mood among U.S. ecologists was buoyant. Greenpeace campaigner Traci Romine hailed the move as "a major victory, the most important event since the Marine Mammal Protection Act." Things were looking brighter and brighter for dolphins everywhere.[11]

But then, shortly after U.S. environmentalists uncorked the champagne to celebrate their new victories, Greenpeace had a change of heart. Having been flayed by Aboriginal and social justice groups for promoting a European seal-pelt boycott that helped destroy the economies of many northern Canadian Native communities in the 1970s and 1980s, Greenpeace began to consider the social consequences of an international boycott of dolphin-caught tuna. While its fellow environmentalists in the United States lauded the U.S. government and the big tuna canners for their far-reaching actions in defence of dolphins, Greenpeace was hearing a different story from its new bureaus in Latin America about the motivations of U.S. business and government and the predicament of just-established tuna fisheries in the Southern Hemisphere. The organization withdrew its support for the embargo.

When Greenpeace's Latin American staff apprised their Northern counterparts of how the issue looked from the South, they told them that this "victory" was not so much an environmental one, but rather an economic triumph for U.S. interests seeking to protect themselves from foreign competition. Although Latin American nations were indeed responsible for an increasing number of dolphin deaths, the Southern environmentalists maintained that these countries were forced to do so by irresistible economic pressures created outside their borders. Mexico and Peru, for instance, had invested heavily in purse-seine fishing technology to be able to fish in the waters off their coasts where, since the 1950s, the U.S. tuna fleet's technology had guaranteed that the United States could continue to scoop up a resource that the Latin Americans thought was theirs. In the 1980s those investments paid off, as the Latin American newcomers began to give the U.S. fishers stiff competition.

At the same time, a desperate economic crisis deepened the Latin Americans' dependency upon tuna fishing. Northern banks were squeezing the Third World for debt-servicing payments on its ruinous foreign debt. Since most of the tuna catch from Latin America was sold to canneries in the United States, the proceeds were a vital source of hard currency that could be used to keep the foreign bankers at bay. While Northern creditors may have smiled upon Latin American efforts to make a go of things in tuna fishing, however, U.S. tuna interests were decidedly hostile.

The Latin Americans saw the U.S. Congress pass its "dolphin-safe" law soon after the U.S. tuna lobby began to complain about the new Latin American competitors – proof enough to them that the legislation was not enlightened environmentalism but a protectionist move, pure and simple. Chilean Greenpeace campaigner Juan Carlos Cardenas said that the U.S. ban on foreign tuna was perceived in the South as a "declaration of war" and a transparently economic measure.[12] Greenpeace got the same message during its efforts to set up shop in Mexico, when a Mexican official accused the organization of being a front for the CIA.

What was obvious to the Latin Americans – but invisible to ecologists in the North – was that the U.S. ban created a no-win situation for the new tuna fisheries of the Southern hemisphere. Being offered the choice of cleaning up their act or being shut out of the

U.S. tuna market was really no choice at all: given their enormous indebtedness, the Southern tuna-fishing nations couldn't possibly raise the funds to convert to dolphin-safe fishing methods.

The boycott also raised emotional questions about national sovereignty. Cardenas argued that the amendment to the Marine Mammal Protection Act set a dangerous precedent for relations within the Americas, "for, through it, U.S. law is indirectly regulating Latin American resources. To us, the focus is very U.S.-centric, and if continued, would have led to severe contradictions between Greenpeace in the United States and in Latin America."[13]

Greenpeace's new position was that the larger economic and political issues had to be addressed to arrive at a just and durable solution. The situation was ironic: here was Greenpeace, an organization that had built its worldwide renown and its financial and institutional might upon the use of stark, unambiguous images and simple political imperatives like "Stop Whaling," now suddenly swimming against the tide it had helped create, trying to launch a nuanced and difficult debate in the face of a compelling set of images, and turning its back on what seemed like a sure victory for the environmental movement: the prospect of a boycott supported by industry and the world's most powerful government.

Greenpeace's break with its own tradition carried both rewards and costs. The decision to hold out for a longer-term solution to the tuna-dolphin issue helped cement its credibility in Latin America, where the organization hoped to establish a beachhead for its future expansion throughout the Third World. But it played havoc with its public image among supporters in the industrialized world, who had always turned to Greenpeace for clear images and black-and-white morality tales. On the tuna-dolphin issue, what the Northern public got from Greenpeace was a complex policy stand – which, at points, was also seemingly contradictory. Even other environmental groups were hard-pressed to understand and quick to condemn the policy.

★ ★ ★

Although the perceptual gulf between North and South remains a defining trait of the tuna-dolphin debate, it may have been Greenpeace's sensitivity to the Latin Americans' point of view that rescued the only forum for North-South dialogue on the tuna-dolphin issue from self-immolation.

The Inter-American Tropical Tuna Commission was headed towards dissolution at its May 1990 meeting, given the deep division between its members over the question of the U.S. embargo. Greenpeace – represented by members from both sides of the equator – kept the commission talking and looking for solutions. What gave member nations the hope of finding some common ground was a new Greenpeace proposal that rejected the U.S. boycott but called for an end to the dolphin kill based not only upon a transfer of new technology from North to South but also upon other economic arrangements that would make conversion feasible for the Latin American fleets. By the mid-1990s Greenpeace and the Southern participants in the Tuna Commission still had hopes of achieving that goal.

Far from being an isolated conflict, the clash over tuna-dolphin may be emblematic of the problems involved with exporting the programs and perspectives of Northern-based environmental organizations. The tuna-dolphin issue reveals a perceptual rift between North and South that not only complicates specific ecological causes, but also casts doubt upon the efficacy of a global environmental vocabulary. A simple environmental imperative ("Save the Dolphins") may enlist unqualified support in the North, but people in poorer parts of the world are much more likely to answer with subsidiary questions like "how?" and "at whose expense?" The fact that Northern environmental organizations are willing to ignore those questions merely shows that they are used to talking to a specific group of people.

Born of the electronic brain of Northern mass media, the modern ecology movement has crafted a message – encoded in the graphic language of TV – designed to appeal to the same middle-class, comfortable, yet concerned constituency that is so coveted by advertisers. One of the things the movement has been telling those followers is that ecology is *the* all-important issue: an issue that transcends and diminishes traditional politics and its mundane concerns; an issue that – by addressing the very survival of the planet – reaches beyond the petty distinctions that separate human beings in different lands and cultures.

On an abstract level, that statement may be true. The threat of environmental calamity is a concern that ultimately has an impact on everyone on the planet: we may all get fried if the ozone layer continues to disappear, or sent to heaven in a puff of smoke if a nuclear war breaks out. But how much you're likely to worry about those things – and, consequently, whether you'll position the environment as your number one concern, above all others – is sure to depend on where you're situated and what other problems you face in daily life.

Middle-class people in a relatively rich country are likely to have enough material comforts to be able to cast their sights on the larger questions in the world, without worrying about day-to-day survival. They may also be politically secure enough to take a stand on the environment without undue personal risk, and rich enough to make a donation to an organization like Greenpeace. But for those who count themselves among the world's poor majority, planetary survival may seem like a meaningless concept alongside the tangible struggles of putting a little food on the table, or of staying ahead of disease or some hostile army – all in hopes of being able to see the sun rise for another day.

And so the assumption (implied in the actions of the groups that supported the U.S. dolphin-caught tuna boycott) that success in preserving the environment is always more important than the subsidiary political or economic questions reveals the cultural biases and limitations of the movement. Although the message of environmentalists can travel unfettered across the globe through the electronic media, it may not resonate as something true and universal when it lands on foreign soil. Without reflecting local concerns and accommodating the local situational constraints, the environmental ethic may seem like something that's imposed from afar, just one more foreign import that the world is forced to accept in an era of global trade and satellite TV. The risk, in short, is that environmentalism can appear threatening to the very people that Northern ecologists are desperate to recruit as allies.

This is what the U.S. commentator Benjamin Barber warned about when he recently cited the environmental movement as one component of a phenomenon he has dubbed "McWorld." That's Barber's term for a new, Northern-spawned global culture "tied together by technology, ecology, communications and commerce." In Barber's view, the agents of McWorld – the primary icons of which are "MTV, Macintosh, and McDonald's" – are promoting a uniform, secular culture that re-creates human beings as mere consumers of goods and images, while assigning no role to other, more traditional aspects of citizenship. Barber feels the onward march of McWorld will militate against the prospects for future peace by constantly infuriating and inciting the forces that rise up to defend (in whatever part of the world) tribal, regional, or national identity threatened by this great monolith, McWorld. In Barber's view, the story of the near future is likely to be a patchwork of factional warfare, as these champions of local identity (which he refers to rhetorically as "Jihad") rise up against the threatening, dulling, influence of a global culture dedicated to recasting peoples and cultures as mere adjuncts of the world economy.[14]

But the problem with exporting environmentalism beyond its birthplace in Western Europe and North America is not just a cultural one. Many people in poor countries have come to resent Northern environmentalists for practical, rather than symbolic reasons. Amongst pundits in the South, it is common to view the environmental movement not as a politically neutral entity promoting universal, common-sense issues, but as a pawn in the global power game, an instrument of the Northern-based multinational corporations that own and control McWorld and its franchises across the globe. The celebrated Senegalese writer Samir Amin has said, for instance, that the control of the debate over environment is one of the five monopolies of Northern-based corporations and governments (along with monopolies over finance capital, weapons of mass-destruction, the international communications system, and high-technology patents), and these monopolies guarantee that the less developed world will remain subservient to the will of the more developed North. By controlling the dialogue on environment, Amin argues, the dominant powers of the North can dictate how different countries will use their resources and can therefore dictate the pace and direction of economic and social life in the Third World.[15] Benjamin Barber seems to concur: "This ecological consciousness has meant not only greater awareness but also greater inequality as modernized nations try to slam the door behind them, saying to developing nations, 'The world cannot afford your modernization; ours has wrung it dry.'"[16]

This is not to say that environmentalism never speaks to the conditions or social/political realities of the Third World. As the end of the century draws nearer, a new brand of socially aware Southern environmentalism appears to be assuming a critical place on the global landscape and influencing the thinking of longer-established environmental groups in the North. This movement draws its sense of urgency both from the catastrophic impact of environmental degradation on the poor, and from the rapid and immense ecological effect of economic globalization. Far from viewing the concerns of environmentalists and the Third World poor as mutually exclusive, this new brand of environmental thinking proposes that they are inextricably and immediately linked.

A few examples of how traditional Third World social justice issues intersect with ecological concerns are provided by Ricardo Navarro, president of El Salvador's Center for Appropriate Technology (CESTA), winner of the prestigious Goldman prize and a vice-president of the international wing of Friends of the Earth. At a 1996 speaking engagement in Ottawa, Navarro stressed for his Northern audience that, in his country, environmental degradation is on the verge of becoming an immediate, life and death issue for a majority of the population – and as such is an issue that has profound political implications.

"In El Salvador, the ecological problem is not the Panda Bear of the WWF," he said. "It is where do you find the energy to cook your food when the forest has been taken away from you? What we are experiencing now in El Salvador is that pollution is now sending people to hospitals, and lack of water, pollution of water, is generating political conflict. We are soon going to be killing each other because of lack of water in El Salvador."

In Navarro's view, the crises of poverty and ecological calamity – both of which he views as products of an illogical, growth-oriented global economic model – are mutually reinforcing. Poverty leads to environmental destruction, and environmental destruction leads to poverty. Consider two cases: in one, forests are chopped down in order to build cash-generating luxury resorts – with the result that the poor can no longer get firewood or food from the forest. In another case, poor Salvadoreans harvest sea turtle eggs in order to survive economically – and the consequence is that sea turtles will soon face extinction.

Navarro's organization, CESTA, proposes a wide range of practical means to address both the social and the ecological aspects of this pernicious equation, from introducing ecologically benign technologies such as solar ovens and peddle-powered air compressors to enhance the lot of the poor, to paying people outright to protect sea turtle eggs rather than to harvest them. All of those measures rest on the understanding, as Navarro says, that "We have to find ways to deal with the extremes of wealth and poverty if we want to survive."

Still, while the work of CESTA (among other organizations) demonstrates that environmentalism can be seen in the South as a movement with relevance to and interconnectedness with other aspects of life there, suspicions remain about the motives of Northern-based environmental organizations. It's the McWorld phenomenon, as noted by Barber.

However, although Barber specifically mentions Greenpeace as one manifestation of McWorld, the fact remains that this organization has done more than most Northern-based environmental outfits to address the analytical blind spots that normally raise hackles in the South. Which brings us back to the tuna-dolphin issue. Greenpeace has stood alone amongst Northern-based environmental groups in insisting that the issue does not begin and end with the killing of dolphins.

In summer 1992, when I spoke to Traci Romine – the Greenpeace official who had, not long before, publicly lauded the amendment to the Marine Mammal Protection Act – she talked up the new Greenpeace position with appeals both to long-term pragmatism and to a more soft-hearted consideration of what is fair and just. A soft-spoken, almost shy woman (an odd characteristic, I found, for someone working for Greenpeace) her gravelly voice started to ring with an indignant zeal when she addressed the issue of who should be held most responsible for the slaughter of the dolphins.

"Let's not forget," she said, launching into a historical litany that would surely have no place on the nightly news, "that the U.S. introduced this fishing practice – that's number one. If you look at the dolphin species in the Eastern Tropical Pacific, the U.S. fleet was responsible for 89 per cent of all the mortality that occurred in this ocean since the 1950s. What I mean is that, the scientific community now believes that eight million dolphins have died since the fishery began in 1959 and the U.S., in its industrial development of the fishery, is responsible for the deaths of 89 per cent of those dolphins."

Since her conversion to the anti-embargo position, Romine has come to accept the Latin Americans' contention that it was the presence of a devastatingly efficient, high-tech U.S. tuna fleet off their coastlines that prompted a response in kind. Those nations could have either forfeited the tuna in nearby waters to U.S. interests or adopted the same technology. In the jungle of international economics, the law is that you compete or die.

"The industry in Latin America," she concludes, "was essentially forced, driven, or chose, to adopt the same technologies and the same purse-seine fishing strategies in order to compete and sell tuna and get into the global markets and pay debts and build their economies and do all those things that nations want to do. How can you turn around, from the U.S., and put embargoes on countries without understanding that relationship, without looking at how it developed, and at minimum saying that we have a certain culpability, and that we should match our pressure with incentives? We should help create the transformation and the conversions that are needed to create environmental stability. We should put money into research. We should make sure new technologies that are environmentally sound are available to all nations. Our GNP is somewhere around twice or three times larger than the GNP of our neighbours to the South. If we are going to go around as a nation introducing certain development models, we have a responsibility to help bring about the conversions that are necessary when that model falls apart. So from the Latin American point of view – as much as I understand of it – there's a lot of validity in saying, 'Wait a minute. We had a standard of development that you imposed in our waters. We did what any competitor would do, and that is to make sure that our development matched what was plausible, and now we're being penalized.'"

To some environmentalists, this may all sound like an outpouring of bleeding-heart liberalism – some guilt-ridden apologia for Third World nations' misdeeds, offered at the expense of the dolphins. But Romine is quick to add that there are some hard-nosed, practical reasons for opposing the boycott in favour of more systemic solutions. She proposes that while a trade embargo arising from issue-specific public pressure may accomplish some of its immediate goals and make a lot of people feel better, in the long run it lets governments and industry off the hook for finding a solution to the wider problem of overfishing in the oceans. By looking at the economic and technological roots of the problem – and by seeking a political solution that makes it possible for all countries to replace a highly destructive fishing technology with a more conservationist one – environmentalists could establish a new code on the seas that would protect all the species – not just dolphins – threatened by industrial fishing.

"Greenpeace believes that this is a global problem in commercial, industrial fisheries," Romine says. "So what we've got to have is a global solution, meaning we need a multilateral system of control. The industries have got to start agreeing, the governments have got to start agreeing that a multilateral system of control, monitoring, enforcement, and regulation is the only thing that's going to ensure the environmental health is maintained in these diverse marine communities."

★ ★ ★

About a year after Traci Romine uttered those words, Greenpeace was still trying to make its case to the public – and to the rest of the environmental movement – that multilateral conventions and enforcement mechanisms were the only means that could adequately address the larger issues underlying the tuna-dolphin controversy. In summer 1993, Greenpeace International released a report entitled "In the race for tuna . . . dolphins aren't the only sacrifice: The impacts of commercial tuna fishing on oceans, marine life and human communities." The report prompted a near war in cyberspace, with accusations and counteraccusations hurled between Greenpeace and its competitors via e-mail. Greenpeace maintained that U.S. canneries' dolphin-safe labelling had "turned into a public relations marketing scheme by transnational tuna corporations" and that "attempting to solve one fraction of a global problem – with 'dolphin-safe' labels on tuna cans – has resulted in spilling the negative impact of commercial tuna fishing into waters outside the Eastern Pacific Ocean and onto species other than dolphins."

What purely market-based solutions do not address, the report says, is that there is a whole constellation of side effects from industrial tuna fishing that "range from the disappearance of previously self-sufficient artisanal communities, to the capture and death of marine species such as dolphins, sharks, and endangered sea turtles . . . to the lack of international systems to manage, monitor and control the tuna industry." To address those problems, Greenpeace calls for an institutional solution based upon either "the creation of a single body which assumes responsibility for the details of management of tuna-fishing around the world" or "the establishment of a global system to co-ordinate the activities of a series of regional tuna management bodies."

Prominent among the other recommendations is that tuna companies be forced to pay for the development of new tuna fishing gear that doesn't harm any other species and to make that technology available – without charging royalties – to fishing fleets from both rich and poor nations. This idea arises from Greenpeace's analysis that the introduction of new generations of more efficient fishing technology has created a vicious circle, in which fleets are driven to overfish in order to recoup the enormous cost of this technology and poor nations are drawn into that destructive cycle by the need to compete with fleets from richer countries.

In response to the report, two directors of the California-based Earth Island Institute (one of the most prominent players in the tuna-dolphin story), along with co-signers from five other U.S. environmental organizations, issued a blistering public statement denouncing the Greenpeace document as "inaccurate, naive, and damaging to the best interests of dolphins and the marine environment." Their problem was not with Greenpeace's promotion of international bodies to control the tuna fishery, or with the demand for new technology, but with Greenpeace's attempts to downplay the effectiveness of "dolphin-safe" tuna labelling. Greenpeace had suggested, for instance, that companies were getting around labelling requirements by fishing in oceans outside the Eastern Tropical Pacific (the only ocean in which dolphin-safe monitoring is enforced) and then taking their catch to distant ports where it would be impossible to determine where the tuna was caught and by what means. Earth Island and its allies responded that different sets of gear were needed to fish in different oceans, and that trans-shipping tuna around the globe would be too expensive and too risky a way of getting a dolphin-safe label on dolphin-caught tuna. They challenged Greenpeace to find examples of this practice.

"Surely, Greenpeace's contention that dolphin-safe monitoring is inadequate and that tuna companies around the world are routinely mislabelling tuna should make it easy for Greenpeace to document specific instances of mislabelling," the letter read. "After all, Earth Island Institute, EarthTrust and several other organizations with far smaller budgets have been able to uncover dolphin-unsafe and drift-net operations from time to time." The organizations refuted Greenpeace's suggestion that tuna companies were "spending millions of dollars in advertising to persuade consumers how environmentally conscious they are" in order to turn the tuna-dolphin issue into a public relations victory. "Untrue," declared the Earth Island letter. "The industry has spent absolutely insignificant amounts on any advertising of tuna, let alone their environmental image. Check the facts."

Greenpeace's critics saved their most vociferous commentary for what they felt would be the practical impacts of removing the public focus from dolphins and putting it onto the bigger issues. The critics interpreted remarks in the Greenpeace document that "dolphin-safe" labels did not address important questions such as overfishing for the tuna itself, the wasting of other species, and the destruction of traditional, non-technological fisheries as meaning that Greenpeace favoured replacing the "dolphin-safe" label with a more generic and encompassing "environmentally friendly" stamp. The letter defended the dolphin-safe program, saying it had been responsible for reducing the dolphin kill by the U.S. fleet from 12,463 in 1989 to 439 in 1992.

Classifying tuna in line with environmental impacts other than just the dolphin kill would be tantamount to applying impractically broad "standards that are impossible to enforce." Insisting on broader definitions of environmental friendliness "may be a good way to make cheap publicity," the Earth Island missive said. "The only problem is that they don't do any good, while obscuring truly workable solutions."

In her return volley, Greenpeace's International Oceans Campaign Co-ordinator, Isabel McCrea, denied that Greenpeace had intended to undermine the dolphin-safe labelling program or to have it replaced by another form of environmental labelling. Although she provided no new information to back up Greenpeace's claims that dolphin-safe monitoring was being circumvented, she reiterated the central contention that applying U.S. national laws to back up a marketplace embargo is an inadequate way to deal with a problem that involves a multitude of species in a number of oceans and jurisdictions. Monitoring of (mostly U.S.) vessels in the Eastern Tropical Pacific was making no impact on the Mediterranean driftnet fishery, or on driftnet fishers from Japan or Taiwan, she said. Instead, what had brought some fisheries outside of the U.S. purview into line were political resolutions. Contrary to Earth Island's contention that UN resolutions would be useless in forcing compliance, McCrea maintained that the Japanese had discontinued driftnet fishing (which generates enormous bycatch) as a result of diplomatic pressure to conform with UN resolution 44/225, and that the routine inclusion of international monitors on board boats in the tropical

Pacific was due not to market pressure, but to the signing of an inter-governmental agreement by those countries involved in purse-seine fishing in that area.

It seems the debate over the merits of dolphin-safe labelling, the U.S. embargo, and the potential of new diplomatic measures could continue indefinitely, supported on both sides by scientific data that is not likely to mean much to members of the general public (like myself) who don't have a detailed understanding of industrial fishing practices. Yet, setting aside the conflicting scientific claims, I can see a couple of obvious points: the divergent perspectives on tuna-dolphin are largely a product of differing geographic perspectives; and the debate, despite the cold scientific calculations, is being driven to a significant degree by a hot-blooded institutional rivalry between environmental groups.

This much became apparent as I listened to David Brower, the founder of the Earth Island Institute, who came to Ottawa in 1994 to address a meeting of the Canadian Environmental Network. Brower is a legend of the U.S. environmental movement. In over five decades of pioneering ecological work, he has been director of the Sierra Club and a founder of both Friends of the Earth and Earth Island. He has fought tirelessly against hydro dams, mining opera-tions, and other despoilers of wildlands in the United States. He has been responsible for drawing untold thousands into the movement through his speeches and his personal example of unrelenting opti-mism and dedicated hard work. At the Ottawa engagement, Brower again proved that it is his force of character – not just his track record – that has won him the adulation of his peers. Brower, age eighty-two at the time, was a gracious and good-humoured gentleman, quick with a joke, self-effacing and humane, and unflaggingly ener-getic in his desire to address new challenges and initiate new cam-paigns.

Yet when I asked him about the rift between Earth Island and Greenpeace over tuna-dolphin, Brower's buoyant mood seemed to collapse, and a wounded look passed across his face. The two groups would remain poles apart, he insisted, as long as Greenpeace calls the attempt to save dolphins and to get sensible tuna fishing under way "environmental imperialism." Brower said he was baffled by that label, but he suspected that it might just be an underhanded device for Greenpeace to recapture a larger share of the public relations spotlight after being upstaged by smaller groups like Earth Island on

the tuna-dolphin issue. Brower said he can't take Greenpeace's criticisms seriously because the group supported the U.S. tuna boycott
"until we got all the credit at Earth Island. They were very strange
on that one. They took all the credit they could, saying it was them –
not we – who had done it, and then when they finally realized that
we were getting the credit they reversed themselves."

This continuing turf war between Greenpeace and Earth Island
goes at least as far back as a 1988 press conference, called to
announce the U.S. tuna canners' "dolphin-safe" commitment.[17]
According to Earth Island director Dave Phillips, about eight Greenpeace people showed up for the meeting and proceeded to declare
the new policy a victory for Greenpeace. Phillips's claim (supported
by other credible observers) was that Greenpeace had essentially
hijacked the publicity wagon when the tuna ban was announced.
Phillips also charged that the Greenpeacers had handed out a video
of dolphin-unsafe tuna fishing, which though taken by Earth Island
employee Sam LaBudde was tagged with a Greenpeace credit.
Greenpeace apparently continued to refer to the tuna ban in its door-
to-door fundraising as "the kind of thing we work for," even though
Greenpeace opposed the ban. As media guru Herb Gunther (a former advisor to Greenpeace) told *Rolling Stone* magazine, Earth Island
ran a campaign against dolphin-caught tuna by mortgaging David
Brower's house and paying its campaigners meagre salaries of
$12,000 dollars a year. It clearly must have hurt when Greenpeace –
the wealthiest and best-known of environmental groups – came out
in opposition to their policy. For Greenpeace to start using the tuna
ban as grist for its fundraising mill, however, was sure to transform
their differences from a mere disagreement over policy into a blood
feud.

The biggest tragedy of all this, perhaps, is that Greenpeace clearly
broadened the policy debate around tuna-dolphin and that if relations between environmentalists had not been so badly poisoned by
the appearance of opportunism on Greenpeace's part, other environmental groups might be more inclined to listen to them. And that
would surely be of benefit to most North American environmentalists who, despite their dedication and their considerable expertise on
home turf, still exhibit a tunnel-vision that blinds them to the concerns and perspectives of the majority of the world's population.

At the Canadian Environmental Network gathering where David
Brower had come to speak, for instance, a classically Northern-

centric brand of environmental thinking was on display. Of the two other speakers who served as warm-up acts for Brower, one presented a slide-show about wilderness preservation; the other presented the findings of her scientific investigation into the consequences of ozone depletion on animals and marine life. Worthy and important as those topics are, I got the feeling that there should have been more, that there should have been some recognition of the social dimension of environmentalism, a dimension that lies at the centre of the ecological debate outside the industrialized world.

Absent from the proceedings was any discussion of the political and economic questions that Southern nations see as fundamental to solving the ecological crisis (and which were the major focus of the NGO forum at the Rio Summit) – questions about how to make it economically viable for desperately poor people *not* to pillage the environment for survival; about how to reign in the pollution-spewing, resource-devouring multinational corporations that have used the newly deregulated international trading regime to stomp carelessly across the globe; questions about how to empower humble people who want to protect their corner of the Earth. When the speakers did venture into politics, it was to offer the "write to your MP" type of solutions that for most of the world's population miss the point entirely.

David Brower's presentation did give a nod to the transnational nature of ecological crisis by announcing the formation of the Ecological Council of the Americas, an expanded version of the Canada-U.S. Environment Council, which Brower promised will "go all the way down to Tierra del Fuego." Founded about six years after Greenpeace decided to take the plunge into Latin America, the new Council is based on the same view that environmental decay is a global concern, but there is no indication that it shares Greenpeace's commitment to hiring staff locally or transferring the Southern perspective on the ecological crisis to the North.

Indeed, there was a disturbingly patronizing ring to Brower's words. Brower said the Council, which is being "started jointly by Canada and the United States," arose from the recognition that "we've got to learn how to figure out, for our own reasons as well as theirs, what to do about the people in the developing world." He dealt with the problem of being a Northern-based organization moving into the South by joking that although the Ecological Council of the Americas was a pretentious name, "It's not nearly as pretentious as the World Series, which consists only of the United States and Canada."

Brower's baseball joke scored well with the audience that night – especially in a year when the World Series wasn't being played for the first time since 1904 – but it didn't answer the underlying questions about how the Ecological Council would fare on foreign terrain. And that brings us back to the tuna-dolphin issue, surely a litmus test of the chances for North American environmentalists to build bridges to the wider world. After all, the same tuna boycott so enthusiastically endorsed in the United States has elicited enormous anger in the South. Do Northern ecologists understand that anger? Do they find any value in the argument that measures such as boycotts will only increase the misery of poor in countries that have become dependent on the tuna fishery?

I put those questions to David Brower – in a roundabout way – by asking him if he had any qualms about using market pressure against Latin American tuna fishers. "You've got to," he answered. "Market pressure makes quick changes. These people are going to go right ahead and do it unless there's something done besides what's been done already." As for the idea that the boycott would wind up hurting poor people who had few economic options, he answered that people in those countries should stop hurting dolphins.

Brower did not respond this way out of malicious insensitivity, or out of any commitment to a fundamentalist animal rights credo that puts animals' lives ahead of human life. It's just that he reads the world differently than opponents of the boycott. In his view, there's an easy way out. His solution is that the new tuna fishing nations of Latin America should appeal for international funds to convert to dolphin-safe technology. When they get the money, he believes, the dolphins will be safe and the people will be happy.

Whether this seems a workable solution or a pipe dream will, once again, probably be defined by the analyst's specific vantage point and experience. David Brower is a man who is used to speaking with powerful men like Jimmy Carter and Ted Turner. He considers them allies and speaks optimistically about "changing the consciousness" of corporate and government leaders so that they'll become leaders in the fight for the environment. Yet people south of the Rio Grande probably have a less benign view of the world leadership. For people who have, for example, very recently experienced the brutality of the "austerity programs" imposed by the International Monetary Fund at the behest of foreign banks and governments, the idea that the rich and powerful will selflessly ride to their rescue may seem a trifle fantastic.

Given this huge perceptual gulf, Greenpeace could make an enormous contribution to the movement: by cluing other Northern environmental groups into the realization that environmental issues look different from outside their world. This perspective might not be accepted, of course; it's even been a tough sell within Greenpeace, where many staff were worried that policies crafted to be diplomatically coherent might lose their public appeal.

In a February 1992 e-mail transmission, for instance, Greenpeace's fisheries campaigner in the United Kingdom pointed out to her counterparts abroad that serious contradictions in Greenpeace's policy stances had been brought to light by the 1992 GATT decision that declared the U.S. tuna embargo an unfair impediment to trade. Like other environmental organizations, Greenpeace had denounced the GATT position, citing it as an example of how the politics of global free trade can undermine national initiatives to protect the environment. But that denunciation appeared to be a direct contradiction of earlier Greenpeace policy: Greenpeace, after opposing the U.S. embargo, was now coming out against the ruling *that would overturn the embargo it had campaigned against*. This discrepancy was sure to create some confusion in the public mind, the U.K. campaigner said, and she also worried that Greenpeace's characterization of the tuna boycott as "protectionist and neocolonialist" would tie the organization's hands in the future.

"This ... bit of reasoning disturbs me," she wrote, "because to some extent any trade sanctions by richer countries can be construed that way. I need to know if that concern is going to be raised in other issues." She also saw Greenpeace's rejection of unilateral national action (to deal with an international issue) as a dangerous precedent that could lead the organization to future policy stances that would appear anti-environmental. "As a campaigner, I would like to support unilateral actions done by concerned countries," she wrote. "I do not care if their motives are protectionist or not, as long as it achieves our goals."

The organization's renegade stand against the U.S. tuna embargo had led it into a nightmarish web of conflicting policy imperatives. The case of the tuna-dolphin issue – and of fisheries campaigning in general – appears to have been a case in which Greenpeace's diplomatic goals went wildly out of sync with its media machine.

CHAPTER 10

THE BIG TRADE-OFF

FROM MEDIA CIRCUS TO DIPLOMATIC ARENA

GREENPEACE VETERANS WILL GO ON AT LENGTH ABOUT well-placed news stories – timed precisely to coincide with international meetings – that have worked to support their manoeuvres in the sheltered sphere of diplomacy. "It's really a left-right strategy," says Paul Hohnen, Greenpeace International's political director. "One hand tries to focus public attention on the issue, while the other hand – working with the politicians and sometimes with corporations – tries to translate that into real national and international legislative outcomes."

Like Hohnen, Michael M'Gonigle argues that Greenpeace may be unique among non-governmental organizations in its ability to channel the public discontent it arouses directly into the lobbying process. Yet he amends Hohnen's description of "left-right strategy" by adding that Greenpeace's capacity for scientific research has become a third and equal part of the process. "The lobbying tactics that Greenpeace uses are quite comprehensive, unlike other organizations," says M'Gonigle, who gave Greenpeace its first continuing presence in the rarefied realm of international deal-making by organizing its delegation to the International Whaling Commission in the 1970s.

Although M'Gonigle's initiative may have been the first attempt to establish a permanent and ongoing Greenpeace presence in diplomatic circles, there is plenty of evidence that, from the very beginning, the organization's founders had intended to use Greenpeace's media profile to exert diplomatic pressure. Patrick Moore says the first Greenpeace diplomatic initiative was when he and Jim Bohlen attended the U.S. Atomic Energy Commission hearings on the Amchitka test. Such tactics also played a major role at the outset of the campaign against French nuclear tests in the Pacific. Moore recalls himself and Jim and Marie Bohlen travelling to the United Nations in New York to lobby (mostly Third World) governments to have the French tests put on the agenda of the first world environment conference in Stockholm in 1973.

Meanwhile, another founding member of Greenpeace, Ben Metcalfe, spearheaded the European flank of Greenpeace's diplomatic efforts concerning the Stockholm conference and the French tests. Metcalfe's efforts included a highly publicized audience with the Pope and the chaining of Greenpeacers to Notre Dame Cathedral in Paris. There was a majority vote at Stockholm to ban atmospheric nuclear tests.

Because Greenpeace "has the big profile," M'Gonigle says, "it can co-ordinate a direct action with some major lobbying event and the release of a major report on, say, dioxin." This hybrid strategy has allowed the organization, on several occasions, to shed considerable light on a dark and furtive world in which battalions of anonymous bureaucrats in suits spend much of their time deciding what the future will look like for the rest of us.

This is no small accomplishment. The non-democratic nature of international regulating bodies is a galling affront to grassroots groups around the world, because many of them find their ability to act increasingly restricted by international trade treaties and the unelected officials who write them. M'Gonigle cites one example memorable for its grim absurdity: in 1988 a subgroup of GATT called the Codex Alimentarus ruled that Mexican hospitals could not teach new mothers about breastfeeding because, in their learned opinion, this constituted a non-tariff barrier to trade. In other words, an unelected and virtually invisible cabal of bureaucrats criminalized education to protect mothers and babies in order to advance the interests of the multinational corporations that manufacture infant formula.

Yet sometimes the good guys win. No one has of yet been able to hold the GATT (now transformed into the World Trade Organization) accountable to public opinion, but some lesser bodies have shown themselves vulnerable to pressure. M'Gonigle's mood shifts from bitter irony to restrained gloating as he tells a story about the London Dumping Convention, an international body that regulates the disposal of various types of wastes. At the London Dumping Convention's 1988 meeting, Greenpeace achieved a surprise victory by unleashing all its scientific, lobbying, and PR guns.

The big industrial countries – Japan, the former Soviet Union, France, the United States – dominated the London Dumping Convention's membership of seventy-five nations. According to M'Gonigle, smaller countries rarely came to the meetings. The first advantage that Greenpeace had as a participant at the Convention was its reputation for generating good headlines, a talent that creates discomfort for organizations that like to work in secrecy. "The organization meets every year, very quietly," M'Gonigle says, "and the press is not particularly interested in it, except in as far as Greenpeace is able to do something that generates press interest. So the public face of the London Dumping Convention is really what Greenpeace tells the press." In the case of the 1988 meeting Greenpeace made news by locating a ship burning waste in the North Sea.

In attempting to push the Convention to outlaw the incineration of toxic wastes at sea, though, Greenpeace talked to more parties than just the media. The organization's international celebrity allowed it to play kingmaker. Before this particular meeting Greenpeace put a little booklet together and sent it out to every country-member, to all the embassies. On the opening day of the meeting, M'Gonigle says, "Here were all these delegates who had never attended walking around with this little green book under their arms that briefed them on all the issues."

At the outset of the meeting, M'Gonigle says, it was almost inconceivable that the powerful industrial nations – which had maintained that incinerating toxic waste was not environmentally harmful – would have allowed the passage of a resolution that ended the practice. But a couple of lead delegations, including the Danes, had been convinced by Greenpeace's scientific research and were pushing for that kind of resolution.

"And some of these countries had Greenpeace representatives on the delegation," M'Gonigle says. "So there we were, in this international meeting, with Greenpeace representatives on various delegations – the second-largest delegation there was from Greenpeace – plus there were all these other countries that were looking to Greenpeace for leadership." The press, M'Gonigle says, was only interested in what Greenpeace had to say. "It was a very impressive display of organizational skill, and the phase-out of the disposal of industrial wastes at sea passed at that meeting against the strenuous opposition of Britain, France, the Soviet Union."

Greenpeace's diplomatic corps has assumed increasing prominence within the organization over the past few years. In some cases this contingent can work alone, without being backed up by direct-action stunts or media campaigns. "Not many people understand how we really work," David McTaggart said in 1991. "We would always prefer *not* to do actions, because of the money and the risk. We try to get the situation clear in our own heads first, do the science, then have quiet conversations with lots of people, from companies to presidents of countries. If they do whatever, that's all you'll hear about it. If nothing happens, then you go to the action."[1]

McTaggart cited the international moratorium on development in Antarctica as an example of where Greenpeace scored a major diplomatic coup entirely through backroom lobbying, without having to resort to headline-grabbing antics. "Antarctica was a perfect example of quiet activism," he said. "Setting up a base down there was like a dog peeing, staking out territory. If anyone had really had a legitimate claim to Antarctica, they would have run us out, and they didn't."

Greenpeace's backroom lobbying is also said to have influenced key policies in the former Soviet Union, an accomplishment that many Greenpeacers will attribute, in reverent whispers, to McTaggart's personal influence with Mikhail Gorbachev. McTaggart himself is not shy about accepting credit for helping to end the Cold War. "The unilateral Soviet moratorium on nuclear testing," he told one magazine, "was straight out of a briefing paper we submitted to Gorbachev. . . . The Soviet decision to stop whaling, and to support the creation of a world park in Antarctica are other areas where we've managed to get our foot in the door."[2]

Despite M'Gonigle's enthusiasm for Greenpeace's infiltration of the private club of international diplomacy (and for Greenpeace's skill at beating the diplomats on their own gaming tables once inside), others worry about putting too much stock in deal-making and international conventions. Agreements are only words on paper, they warn, and they often have little to do with what goes on in the real world. In the pages of *Mother Jones* magazine, Greenpeace Latin America campaigner Juan Carlos Cardenas shrugged off the organization's success in keeping the Inter-American Tropical Tuna

Commission at the table with the remark that this victory was just "palace politics." The real challenge, he said, is to nurture a Latin American environmental movement that has a broad base of public support. "Otherwise we will be co-opted by governments," Cardenas said.[3]

Other critics stress the need to respond with grassroots action when the politicians renege on their international commitments. In his book *Green Rage*, Christopher Manes recounts how Iceland subverted the spirit of the IWC's international moratorium on whaling by sanctioning the killing of several thousand whales for purposes of "scientific research" – a brazen exploitation of a loophole in the agreement. Efforts by mainstream environmental groups to have the United States boycott Icelandic products (and Japanese products, since Japan was the major consumer of Icelandic-caught whale products) ended in failure, Manes says.

But what did slow down the Icelandic whalers was the "direct-action" techniques of Paul Watson's Sea Shepherd Conservation Society, whose members allegedly destroyed an Icelandic whale research station and scuttled two of the four boats in Iceland's whaling fleet. Manes believes that although Greenpeace denounced Sea Shepherd's action as something akin to terrorism (presumably in part to protect its reputation as a responsible participant in international policy-making), the attack on the fleet did a lot to turn Icelanders against whaling. By Manes's account, when a young Icelander publicly stated that he had helped the foreigners scuttle the Icelandic boats (thereby violating a strongly held code of social behaviour in that tight-knit, law-abiding society) he triggered a debate among his countrymen over the activity that had driven this young man to be disloyal to the community. Many Icelanders, writes Manes, emerged from this period of soul-searching with the new belief that whaling is wrong. The issue became so uncomfortable for Iceland that when Paul Watson flew into the country to offer himself for trial, he was promptly deported so that the government could avoid further embarrassment.[4]

Mike Affleck believes that Greenpeace would be wise to balance its efforts in international diplomacy by redoubling its work at the grassroots. The international toxic trade campaign, a major focus of Greenpeace's activity throughout the early 1990s, was viewed as having achieved its goals when it became clear that the Basel Convention (finally ratified in September 1995) would ban the shipment of toxic wastes from the countries of the Organization for Economic Co-operation and Development (OECD) to Third World nations. "That campaign was considered a fantastic success," Affleck says. "And their terrific success happened at an international convention. The toxic trade campaign is in the same position that the ozone campaign was in after the 1990 meeting of the Montreal Protocol in London, where people were saying, 'We won. We've got phase-out dates, this thing is really going to happen.'" But an agreement, Affleck says, isn't enough. It has to be implemented, and that's still the problem. "If we stop at the political agreement, we're just stupid."

In the long run, Affleck fears that as Greenpeace gets absorbed more into the world of diplomatic abstractions, it could lose sight of the need for painstaking, unglamorous work on the ground – tracking toxic waste shipments or badgering companies that produce CFCs. "I think it's a real danger if Greenpeace considers political conventions the end point of every campaign," he says. "That the final culmination of every campaign is a worldwide convention that bans chlorine, or a convention that bans ozone-depleting substances. That would mean that all of our work gets directed through the political eye, and I don't think that's the right thing for us to be doing."

But it seems increasingly difficult to think of Greenpeace as a grassroots organization. A good portion of its work is now done either behind closed doors in diplomatic lobbying or through the mass media. One former Greenpeace staff member, David Peerla, believes that a major, hidden cost of Greenpeace's victories on specific issues is that its campaigning style tends to reinforce the sense of social isolation that ultimately works against grassroots social protest. Peerla doesn't quarrel with the idea that Greenpeace campaigns are often highly effective. His own experience confirms this.

From 1990 to 1992 Peerla, trained as a sociologist, led a Greenpeace campaign to publicize the destruction of British Columbia forests. Greenpeace's access to the European media allowed it to eventually help break a stalemate in a fight pitting environmentalists against labour. Peerla says that the forest companies, often through citizen groups they fund, had successfully contained environmentalists' challenges to logging by stoking the fears of forest workers and dependent communities over the question of job loss. The environmentalists' standard repertoire of tactics had only made that stalemate more entrenched.

"Environmentalists and labour are in an antagonistic situation in British Columbia, particularly in the direct, face-to-face confrontations when you're sitting on a blockade saying, 'You, worker, cannot go to work.' What we were doing was a little different. I never wanted to put my campaign in a direct confrontation with labour, because I thought it was a false antagonism. So I never organized any direct civil disobedience that prevented workers from going to work in the forest. My activities were quite outside their range – they were in another dimension where I was really confronting what I saw as the fundamental opponent, namely capital, the corporate sector. I was confronting them on their terrain, in their market. In the market, it's really the corporations versus us, and the labour movement has no role to play."

The strategy involved publicizing the destruction of the Canadian rainforest in the media of Belgium, Germany, and England. A spread in *The Observer* magazine entitled "Canadian Chainsaw Massacre" was among the biggest hits. European politicians toured B.C. clear-cuts, and Aboriginal leaders went on Greenpeace-sponsored tours through Europe. The campaign attacked the credibility of the B.C. government and threatened the sales of Canadian forest companies: there was a hint that a European boycott of B.C. wood would be next. Peerla says that forest companies, conditioned to using their transnational scope to rebuff their workers' demands (by threatening to move their operations out of province, for instance), were now getting a taste of their own medicine.

"The traditional labour movement – those people in Port Alberni, British Columbia – are stuck in that space," Peerla says. "We're not stuck in that space in the same way – we can operate in Germany, we can operate in the U.K., we can operate in Belgium. So that the worker in Port Alberni confronting the employer – the corporation MacMillan Bloedel who is active in all of those places – can only confront it on one terrain. Whereas we can confront Mac and Blo on all their terrains, or a much larger percentage of them – so that we have a much more flexible opposition than the spacialized, contained labour movement. And I think that's a very opportune formulation in this political climate."

But while Greenpeace's transnational scope and footloose style of campaigning may be *strategically* opportune, Peerla believes that these things are less effective in capturing the human heart, which in the long run may be just as important. A year after Peerla had spoken so enthusiastically about Greenpeace's ability to hunt down corporations around the globe, I interviewed him again. By the time of our second conversation Peerla had wound down his campaign (largely due to the effects of the recession on the finances of Greenpeace International) and left the organization. His remarks were noticeably more downbeat. The comparison between the organizing styles of labour unions (an old social movement) and Greenpeace (a new social movement born of the electronic age) emerged once again as a prominent theme, but this time the emphasis had shifted: Peerla had become much more concerned with what Greenpeace had lost with its leap into the mass media age than with what it had gained.

In traditional labour organizing, he argues, a real human being would go to a community and spend significant time there explaining the commitments and beliefs of the union movement and trying to get workers to sign on. This face-to-face process revolved around a sense of community and social solidarity and required an active and ongoing participation by the members. Union members are typically called upon to stand for office and vote for their leadership, and when it comes down to a test, they are expected to stand together – quite literally – by walking a picket line. None of this is required in a Greenpeace campaign.

Peerla describes a television-centred organizing style that can mobilize widespread public outrage on an issue but can't necessarily sustain it with the kind of ingrained commitment found in older social movements. At their worst Greenpeace campaigns may merely replicate the consumerist ethic of television, hawking the excitement of social activism – one more exotic item on the electronic menu that's beamed into most modern homes – in exchange for funds and signatures on petitions rather than for active involvement. So while union members are traditionally referred to as "brother" and "sister," Greenpeace supporters might more appropriately be seen as "consumers" or "customers" – people who aren't linked by surrogate family or community ties, but who buy a stake in the organization.

"The community in the Greenpeace world," Peerla says, "is a symbolic community linked through the exchange of words, images, and information in the electronic media. You have a vast array of individual supporters distributed all through Canada, all through the world – let's say, five million people – who all give money to Greenpeace. And their sense of belonging to Greenpeace is through the transaction of giving them money and also seeing the images that are produced by Greenpeace on TV. So they can say, 'Well, I gave them twenty-five bucks, and there they are hanging from this particular nuclear reactor challenging nuclear power.'"

In Peerla's view, this is Greenpeace's big trade-off. The price tag for its prominent profile in the world media (which, by extension, gives it a PR club it can use to beat on corporations, and a voice in international policy-making forums) is the continued erosion of the sense of community and of human contact, which were once the foundation of social activism. It has bred a *passive* form of activism, very much in line with the effects of television as a whole, the medium that in just over a generation has constructed a formidable barrier between the citizens of industrialized nations and the physical world around them. As the branches of the tree have stretched skyward, it seems, the roots may have gotten weaker.

"We recognize now," Peerla says, "that there is this generalized dissolution of face-to-face communities that's taking place in the world as we become more privatized, passive consumers of TV images. This is commonly referred to as the disappearance of the public sphere. Greenpeace, as an organization, perfectly reflects this. It does not contribute to re-creating a public sphere, to re-creating face-to-face communities. So the issue is whether or not this is a way that social change should be organized. I myself believe that the disappearance of face-to-face communities is a tragedy."

Also displaced by the rise of the media campaign is a certain sense of history – the consoling realization that today's efforts are part of a broader historical sweep, that the disconnected events in the present make solid sense as part of a broader picture. As David Peerla points out, all social movements in the past have attempted to provide a "master narrative" to link events and inform the daily struggles with historical sense: the traditional left and the labour movement have seen history as the unfolding struggle between the working class and capital; Third World movements generally see their stories as the fight against the forces and legacy of colonialism, for instance. But Greenpeace – bound by the stylistic boundaries of a small electric box – can deal with nothing but the present. Its mythology is composed of an infinite number of unconnected incidences – small dramas that can be told in two minutes or so on the television news – with no common villains and little thematic continuity other than being loosely based on the struggle to protect the environment.

Perhaps as a product of inhabiting the "acoustic space" described by Marshall McLuhan, Greenpeace does not feel bound to tell its stories as part of a linear unravelling of history or continuing clash of interests. Peerla says this is reflected, at the macro level, by the structure of the organization itself: it has no formal ideology, no texts to guide the way, and it does not celebrate its own historical high points as markers for the future – in the way the storming of the Bastille, the October Revolution, or the Winnipeg general strike was celebrated by others.

Instead, the form of Greenpeace mirrors the form of television; a continuous, amorphous flow. Meanwhile, at the micro level, the essence of Greenpeace becomes how it constructs its media events. The stunts are expensive, well-honed, and play precisely to the demands of television. At their centre is an emotionally compelling image, some captivating spectacle clearly rooted in the present tense, with non-essential information and historical context sheered away. Performing for a medium that measures audience loyalty in the number of jolts-per-minute, Greenpeace has been careful to keep up with the competition.

"What you are trying to do there," Peerla says, describing the construction of a Greenpeace media event, "is create a situation that usually involves suspense – so, for example, people are hanging off a tall building, or are in some kind of dangerous situation. Maybe they are handcuffed to the railroad tracks or – for example, an action that I was engaged in with others – someone's inside a box, and there's a railway car bearing down on this box containing people. So that's an inherently dramatic situation that's created. The cameras come and the campaigner is able to get out the message."

Although these theatrics make it onto the six o'clock news, at what price? "Of course, you have to simplify the message to such a degree that the question is whether you lose any kind of analytical basis. So you are contributing to this plotless nature of the world, so that people can't make sense of what the larger story is, if there is a larger story." This, Peerla points out, is a key weakness. In the midst of all the different Greenpeace actions, when people lose sight of the larger stories, of the "systematic villains," many of them will find it difficult to make sense of the connections between the issues.

If you believe that TV's status as a pre-eminent cultural and political force will remain into the foreseeable future, Peerla's contention – that allowing its fate to be bound up with the workings of television has robbed Greenpeace of a larger sense of history and purpose – is a bleak reading of the prospects for the environmental movement. There are those, however, who feel that the cathode box – and the mass culture it spawned – entered into decline in the early 1980s as the personal computer and its associated electronic information networks started to give people what they couldn't get from TV. And this may be good news for people who believe that environmental objectives are best served by an expansive view of the world and a more long-term sense of outcome.

Marshall McLuhan believed not only that every new medium made some aspect of the present culture obsolete, but also that it retrieved something from the past. What lost aspect of our culture did the personal computer – and, by extension, e-mail and the Internet – retrieve from some bygone era? A respect for print? A penchant for the personal conversation? You could probably make the case for both of those elements by looking at the case of EarthFirst!, an environmental organization born about a decade after Greenpeace, when the monolithic mass culture of the television age had begun to give way to the multimedia circus made possible by the PC. Cheap household computers demand different qualities from their users than does the tube in the rec room: for one, you have to be willing to read; for another, you might be more inclined to interact (either electronically or in the flesh) with other human beings than to passively accept the truth that Peter Mansbridge or Tom Brokaw deliver from on high.

It might not be surprising then that EarthFirst! – while it does, like Greenpeace, rely heavily on television exposure – has constructed an organizational mythology that involves a set of sacred printed texts, something that Peerla says is lacking within Greenpeace. In his book *Confessions of an Eco-Warrior*, EarthFirst! co-founder Dave Foreman draws heavily upon literary reference. Consider that EarthFirst!'s patented brand of hands-on activism – known as monkey-wrenching – was inspired by Edward Abbey's novel *The Monkeywrench Gang*. It is also striking that Foreman's memoirs repeatedly refer to the 1949 tract *A Sand County Almanac* – written by forest ranger and conservationist Aldo Leopold – for philosophical and moral guidance and a sense of historical lineage.

So EarthFirst! may have upstaged more established environmental groups in the 1980s not because of its effectiveness in getting on the nightly news, but because it offered its adherents the sense of belonging to a tradition that predated the television universe, as well as a set of intellectual precepts they could subscribe to. All of which is to suggest that the context for environmental work has changed substantially since Greenpeace was born; that the impression of permanent flux produced by television may have actually reignited the desire for permanence and long-range vision.

CHAPTER 11

AFTER THE COLD WAR

RETHINKING STRATEGIES FOR A NEW AGE

ON JANUARY 15, 1991, A CNN CREW IN BAGHDAD BEAMED out a live feed that would dominate the world's airwaves and become the defining historical image of a time that, to this day, remains obscured by the heavy cloak of press censorship. A blackened sky, a high-pitched mechanical whine, the staccato drumbeat of anti-air-craft guns, sudden explosions of light that revealed a cowering city: these were the ominous, dim testaments to a historic turning point. The Gulf War was on. A new era had begun.

For politicians, the press, the general population, and especially for antiwar activists, the Gulf War remains an uncomfortable memory. For many of us, that gruesome little war laid to rest the brief, euphoric dream that the aftermath of the Cold War would be a time of new prosperity (remember the peace dividend?) and global co-operation. But for the politicians who sought to reinstate business-as-usual and reignite their own political careers with some good old nationalist sabre-rattling, the Gulf War turned out to be a hollow vic-tory; a year after his 95 per cent wartime approval rating, U.S. Presi-dent George Bush had plummeted in the polls and was on his way out of office.

The media, as well, have little reason for dwelling on this phase in history. Their coverage of the Gulf War, stage-managed almost com-pletely by the military, pointed out the flaws in a news-gathering sys-tem desperately dependent upon the largesse of official sources; and it invited unflattering comparisons to Vietnam, where independent reporting did, eventually, triumph over official propaganda. Meanwhile, the crisis of self-image that the Gulf War would trigger in Northern peace groups, including Greenpeace, would be close to soul-shattering. Greenpeace's inability to counter pro-war propaganda cast doubt upon the organization's own internal structure, its relationship to the media, and its reading of politics and world events. After significant successes against nuclear weapons proliferation during the previous decade, Greenpeace found itself virtually disarmed during the war in the Persian Gulf.

Karen Mahon, a Canadian peace activist who found a home at Greenpeace Canada after leaving the Toronto Disarmament Network, was in Vancouver – the place where Greenpeace had launched itself in the 1970s by rallying enormous opposition to U.S. military plans, where the streets had once been packed with antiwar demonstrators – as the war between Iraq and the U.S.-led alliance was announced. "I was on the phone talking to the chair of our board about various other things, and someone came into the office to say, 'This is it; the U.S. has just bombed Baghdad,'" Mahon remembers. She pauses for a few seconds, as if summoning the emotion of the time. "And the devastation in the room was just unbelievable. This is something that we as peace activists had thought was unthinkable, and it took us a number of days to even sort out how to begin to react. We really were shocked the way one is when one encounters a personal tragedy."

The impact was magnified, Mahon says, because she and her co-workers had clung to the belief that the standoff in the Middle East would never progress to that point. "We went into the war thinking 'surely this couldn't happen' – we thought we'd come so far in our work towards peace, that after the events of the past five or six years, this kind of situation wasn't possible."

When Greenpeace did catch its breath, it took a leading role – within Canada – in directing the peace movement's response. But with Canada itself at war for the first time since World War II, Greenpeace found little of the public encouragement it could have expected in earlier disarmament campaigns. Bomb threats were more likely.

"Throughout the war we did everything we could," Mahon says. "We pulled out every trick in the bag. We formed international alliances, we had protests outside of MPs' offices, we climbed the Royal York [hotel, in Toronto] where Prime Minister Mulroney was speaking, with a tape-recording saying 'Stop the War,' listing the environmental impacts, the human impacts of the war. And we didn't see ourselves as having that much impact. As the war continued, we became more and more isolated."

Why had the Greenpeace contingents in the Toronto and Vancouver offices – some of them veterans of peace movement politics – so badly misjudged the prospects for going to war, and so badly misjudged the public response to its announcement? The answers probably have a lot to do with context. Greenpeace's anti-nuclear successes in the 1980s resulted largely from being able to take on a single, specific aspect of the issue. Greenpeace didn't have to challenge the entire logic of the nuclear arms race – that process was already under way: over thirty years of Cold War had allowed people the time to question the costs, consequences, and fundamental logic of a seemingly endless superpower standoff. The Gulf War required starting from square one. To oppose the Gulf War was to oppose a moral hypothesis that was fresh; that appeared to stand up to scrutiny; and that was receiving saturation endorsement in the media of many countries. The only way of campaigning against the war would have been on the grounds that killing thousands of innocent people, that ripping apart families and destroying the emotional and material fabric of a whole society, is morally wrong. But that's a lot like campaigning against the very concept of war: a tough sell when faced with the strong, highly focused script being used to convey the immediate events. To many people this conflict wasn't at all like the Cold War. Saddam Hussein was clearly a monster who was brutally repressing his own people and invading other nations. So let's bomb the Iraqis to Kingdom Come.[1]

Steve Shallhorn, a veteran campaigner, has worked mostly on the "peace" side of the Greenpeace amalgam – first as an architect of the Nuclear Free Seas Campaign during the 1980s, later as an organizer struggling to build a strategy for the Gulf War. More recently he began working on the Greenpeace campaign against land mines, which represents the organization's first attempt to lobby against conventional weapons. Shallhorn readily concedes that, after a very precise series of campaigns aimed at penetrating the chinks in the logic of the Cold War, Greenpeace was not equipped to deal with a dramatic shift in the strategic framework when the Gulf War arose. "Greenpeace had been able to campaign against nuclear weapons, during the Cold War, without getting caught up in Cold War patterns," he says. "The Gulf War posed a lot of problems for Greenpeace, because we were still trying to come to terms with the coming down of the Berlin Wall, the collapse of the Warsaw pact, and what this meant for us."

During the Cold War, Greenpeace skirted the quagmire of geopolitical abstraction by focusing on the material impact of the technology, which members hoped would bring home the tangible dangers of the arms race to ordinary people. The nuclear free seas campaign, which Shallhorn describes as "a very classic Greenpeace campaign" (by virtue of its boat-based, direct-action components and its focus on bringing important research to public light) was a case in point: it drew public attention towards the soft underbelly of the nuclear weapons establishment and generated vast international outrage. With a third of the world's nuclear weapons based on ships, Greenpeace was able to pose questions about safety that couldn't be reasonably answered. The less structured chain of naval command meant that a ship's captain out of contact with his superiors could give an order that might trigger a nuclear war. Greenpeace's research also showed that superpower vessels had often engaged in provocative and dangerous forms of gamesmanship at sea, raising the spectre that this underwater bravado could get out of hand and "go ballistic." The record of accidents and near accidents also predicted a fair likelihood of a disastrous accident involving nuclear weapons, and it was entirely possible that such a disaster could occur near to a large population centre.

"Virtually every country with a coastline would regularly have port visits by warships, in particular by warships carrying nuclear weapons," Shallhorn says. "We were able to show that for about sixty days per year, there were nuclear warships in the middle of Canadian cities, whether it was Halifax or Vancouver, or occasionally some of the Great Lakes ports, including Montreal and Toronto."

With the public's attention captivated by the danger of nuclear calamity being as close as the nearest dock, Greenpeace was able to create arresting images to get the message out. Again, it was "classic" Greenpeace. Visiting warships were buzzed by Greenpeace rubber dinghies. Some ships would have banners draped on them. All of the efforts were intended "to identify, in the public mind, a visiting warship with a nuclear weapon," says Shallhorn. The issue allowed Greenpeace to win public sympathy by demonstrating its own determination and courage.

On one occasion, in 1989, Greenpeace acted on a tip it had received from inside the U.S. nuclear weapons program and was able to crash the test launch of a submarine-based Trident missile fifty miles off the coast of Florida. "We launched some of our rubber inflatable speed boats," remarks Shallhorn, who took part in the action. The Greenpeace boats were able to place themselves above the USS *Tennessee* as it was submerged. "You could tell where the submarine was from the mast. We were able to attach our nuclear-free seas banners right onto the submerged submarine. The only way that the mission commander could launch the missile would be to incinerate the people who were in these boats above the submarine, and faced with that choice they cancelled the test. It was a great sight to see the submarine submerge and go back to port with its tail between its legs."

Generating a powerful image of courage, conviction, and resistance, this Greenpeace action helped to publicly expose a dangerous escalation in the Cold War arms race that otherwise would have proceeded in silence. Was similar image-making possible during the Gulf War? Would it even be possible to issue a clear message in such an ambiguous political situation? And how can you "expose" the military when they are loudly trumpeting their own activities, bombarding the public with propaganda?

According to Shallhorn, in the lead-up to the war the one vehicle for protest under serious consideration was for Greenpeace to send a boat into the Gulf to serve as both a possible conference centre for various parties to seek peace and a broadcasting site – the one media focal point in the area that would not be controlled by the military. Eventually they decided they couldn't do this, out of a concern for the safety of the ship. "The gulf was mined," Shallhorn says. "There was considerable military presence there, and while in the past Greenpeace had confronted military power on the high seas, there was an uneasiness that this time there was a higher level of military readiness and a lower set of rules of engagement for the military forces in the area."

Another problem, according to Shallhorn, was to identify who Greenpeace could involve in the process, "and a feeling that events were too large and too fast-moving for an organization like Greenpeace to influence. Perhaps we were not strong enough, and at the same time there was the possibility that we could be used, or painted into a corner, by one or the other of the sides' propaganda machine."

Others say that the organizational confusion within Greenpeace was the primary factor in scuttling plans for a ship in the Gulf. "The organization couldn't come to terms with that war at all, it was split by it," says Andy Booth in Bristol. "The North American, South American offices wanted massive action by the organization, they wanted to send a boat to the Gulf to intervene. The European offices said, 'no way, it's not an issue for the organization.' It brought up the whole discussion as to whether the organization is an environmental group, or an environment and peace group, and that was never resolved."

Across the ocean in Syracuse, New York, Mike Affleck agrees that Greenpeace was too divided within itself to take a strong stand against the Gulf War. "In part, that is just a part of the fundamental problem, that Greenpeace doesn't have a position on war; we don't have a principle on war and peace." But while Booth characterizes North America as being solidly in favour of antiwar action, Affleck says that within the United States there was extensive discussion on whether coming out against the Gulf War would damage Green-peace's donor base. "In times such as now, when Greenpeace financing is a big issue, it's unwise to take an unpopular stance, so the organization gets compromised by its own difficulties," he says.

Booth argues that in Europe the anxiety was not so much over finances as over public image. "People believed our public profile was not as an antiwar organization. They pointed to the demise of organizations like the CND in the UK – which was a big antiwar organization that collapsed at the end of the Cold War, it collapsed, it disappeared – and they said, 'This could happen to us. Why are we getting involved in this issue?' You looked around the organization and suddenly you realized that not everybody is pacifist."

According to Booth, Greenpeace should have campaigned hard on the Gulf War because it would have "galvanized" the organization – provided it with a sense of moral centre and a new role for the 1990s – and besides, it had the skills that would have given it the best shot at success of any peace group. He doesn't believe that the danger to its ship is what kept Greenpeace out of the Gulf. "There were people who were willing to take the risk," he says. "That wasn't the issue. It was mainly that, policy-wise, Greenpeace couldn't get its act together."

What Greenpeace wound up doing in lieu of launching a direct campaign against the war was to campaign against its *environmental side effects* – though most of this work came after the war was over. The result was an unsatisfying attempt to balance the concerns of both sides within Greenpeace: an antiwar document that has the feel of being put together by a market-research company. The four-page executive summary of Greenpeace's report on the Gulf War ultimately comes off as somewhat absurd because of what it fails to say. While cataloguing a list of ecological ills that included oiled house martins and disturbances in the sex ratios of sea turtles, the document does not once refer to the multitude of human beings who were killed as massive amounts of munitions rained down onto Iraq.

While many Greenpeacers learned about the limitations of their own organization during the Gulf War, others had a change of heart about the nature of the media. John Maté was an anti-nuclear campaigner at the Greenpeace Vancouver office from 1989 to 1992. A former family therapist, he had also worked at organizing benefit performances for social change organizations. The Gulf War was a torturous period for him: at the time his daughter was studying in Israel and living on a kibbutz, and many of his friends were Israelis who believed that the war was morally sound. "But I had to go with what I thought was the right thing to do," he says, "and from my perspective this war was fought more for George Bush's political agenda than for the liberation of Kuwait. And it was a war that would result in many innocent women and children being killed."

Maté did not believe that people who came out against the war got a fair hearing in the Vancouver media, particularly after Canada officially became a combatant. He was suspicious of how *The Vancouver Sun* packaged the antiwar message. Maté says that he himself was erroneously quoted as calling for "guerilla action," a phrase that appeared in the paper next to a large picture of a U.S. federal office being trashed in San Francisco. He complains that his attempts to publicize a speaking engagement by retired Rear Admiral Eugene Carroll of the Centre for Defense Information in Washington were completely shut down by the Vancouver media. Carroll, who had once been in charge of U.S. forces in the Middle East as well as commander of the *USS Midway*, should have been considered an eminent expert on Middle East conflict, in anybody's books. Although it can be a dangerously wrong-headed exercise to read conspiracy theories into the fluid and unpredictable process of putting newspapers together, Maté feels his perceptions conform to a broader, statistically verifiable trend that occurred across North

America during the war. He cites a Fairness and Accuracy in Reporting (FAIR) study that shows the peace message was virtually banished from the media in the months during which support for the Gulf War was being drummed up: between August 8 and January 3, of 2,855 minutes of television coverage of the Gulf crisis, only 29 minutes were devoted to the opposition to the military buildup.

To John Maté the lesson from this period is clear. While Greenpeace had built its entire strategy on the McLuhanesque proposition that getting a place in the public eye was a question of penetrating the technological logic of the medium, Maté believes that under many circumstances this isn't enough: when it comes down to the crunch, the owners of mass media can shut you down or shut you up if they don't like your message. In times of warfare, news organs feel an obligation to reproduce – or at least to not challenge – the propaganda of the state. This impulse is most likely strengthened by the fact that both mass communications and weapons manufacturing are big business – in some cases, the *same* big business.

In this matter Maté turns for guidance not to McLuhan but to Noam Chomsky, who notes that through cross-ownership of corporations many of the entities that control major broadcasting outfits also own companies that have grown wealthy, for instance, producing weapons systems. So it's not illogical to expect that these interlocking institutional interests might have the effect of sidelining the peace movement from media play. Chomsky has also shown how coverage can be moulded by the sheer volume of propaganda that institutions like the military are able to generate. Maté retrieves some telling statistics, cited by Chomsky in the book *Manufacturing Consent*, to illustrate the enormous PR power of the U.S. Air Force, just one branch of the U.S. military. In 1979-80, the air force distributed 690,000 copies per week of its own newspapers; issued 45,000 headquarters news releases and 615,000 hometown news releases; gave 6,600 news media interviews; held 3,200 news conferences; conducted 500 news media orientation flights; delivered 11,000 speeches; held 50 meetings with editorial boards . . . well, you get the picture.[2]

Given this constant barrage of "news" from the official sources, Maté feels that alternative organizations – even those as steeped in the ways of news production as Greenpeace – are unable to compete. The purpose of this deluge of material, readily reproduced by journalists looking for quick copy, is to "massage the psyche of the public" – to set the emotional and intellectual tone and context in which the events of the world are reported. Unable to match the volume of material generated by "the other side," critics of the establishment are also handicapped by having to challenge an entire worldview in sixty seconds, or within the few lines of counterpoint that are often tagged at the end of stories.

So Maté believes that Greenpeace has to look elsewhere for its competitive advantage; its images in the media have to be bolstered by the kind of longer-term activist work that can shift the paradigms in people's heads. While protesting a nuclear port visit, he says, it's important not to do it just while the cameras are there, but to maintain a long-term presence so that people – even reporters – ask questions and start to think more deeply about the issues. People, he believes, are searching for context, meaning, and personal connection; not sound bites. Maté has given up on the idea that getting on the nightly news is hitting the jackpot: it may be just as important to get a well-reasoned story out through alternative media as it is to plant one or two images among the avalanche of images on TV.

"Greenpeace has to be very careful about not confusing getting its name mentioned in the press with actually educating the public on a certain issue," Maté says. "Real change takes much longer than a ten-second sound bite. I don't think there's enough of a critical view of the media within Greenpeace."

★ ★ ★

The Gulf War has not been the only recent event to raise these kind of critical questions about the social function of mass media; and John Maté is not alone among Greenpeace alumni in questioning the media's institutional constraints – in considering the matters of ownership, corporate power, and their influence over content. This theme became a prominent one as I returned to gather impressions from two influential figures in the formation of Greenpeace, whose help I sought in understanding how the media and its role in society might have changed since 1971 – and what those changes might mean for the future.

Ben Metcalfe, one of the originals, was chiefly responsible for infusing the media politics into Greenpeace's organizational strategy. Close to a quarter-century later, Metcalfe indeed did feel that conditions had changed sufficiently to warrant a thorough rethinking. The media environment today, Metcalfe believes, is dominated by fear and apathy. The fear is both personal – people are constantly reminded that they could at any moment lose their jobs, so they should work harder and keep their mouths shut – and societal, with constant images of violence in the outside world telling people that they'd best stay home, where it's safe.

Metcalfe believes that this fear and apathy have undermined the strategy of image-based campaigning by, in effect, devaluing the currency. While in the past images of violence or injustice could have been used to provoke moral outrage or a rebellion of conscience (as happened, perhaps, during the Vietnam War), today those images just contribute to a sense of numbness that feeds public apathy.

"One of the things that the media has done, consciously or unconsciously," says Metcalfe, reflecting on things in his cabin in the British Columbia woods, "is to saturate the people with these things so that they can no longer react in what you might call a moral sense, in a moral way. They've either got to look at it as entertainment or not look at it at all. After they see the events in Rwanda, they are saturated with violence and suffering, but then they go off to get more of the same as entertainment, the Arnold Schwarzeneggers bring it to them. Hollywood helps create this apathy in people, and this fear."

An example, Metcalfe believes, is how the movies have gradually "accommodated" the Mafia through gangster films that portray those criminals as terrifying, almost unstoppable agents of brutality, whose presence in our culture is a given, "something we just have to live with." War is conducted along a similar principle: its primary function now is to strike fear into the souls of human beings, to crush the will to disobey. "The strategy in war changed by creating huge, unbearable firepower," Metcalfe says. "The firepower now on a battlefield is unbearably terrifying. You saw it in the Gulf War. They put up a curtain of flame and metal that no man could stand psychologically, mentally. Terror is the thing."

The dual strains of fear instilled in middle-class North Americans – the active fear of losing one's livelihood; the passive, paralysing, fear of the world as a place of unsurmountable and inevitable violence – work together in a way that almost forecloses on the possibility of mass, moral resistance, Metcalfe says. Caught in this pincer movement, most people just count their blessings and keep their heads down.

"I don't think you could make a movie now for the big cinema and achieve any kind of vibration in the people – it would all be taken as entertainment," Metcalfe says. "You could show the slaughter in Tiananmen Square, body by body, shot by shot, and Mr. Clinton would still say, and justify it, that yes, trade is more important. The people are not criminal, but they are justifiably shortsighted sometimes. Because they don't want to suffer unemployment. They don't want to scramble for their mortgage or live on the street with a shopping cart."

Metcalfe argues that it is possible to dispel this vague haze of anxiety. What's required is to start pointing fingers; to show that the fears are deliberately planted and of political utility. He does not believe that the economic and environmental chaos that currently besets the world has arisen through chance or as a result of a blind mechanism. He thinks there are conscious decisions being made by people who stand to profit: that the same people who hold the gun of unemployment to the heads of an increasingly insecure workforce (in order to drive down wage costs and generate a mood of compliance) are the same people who are deforesting British Columbia and Indonesia and carting toxic waste to poor people's backyards. These policies are not computer-generated. They spring from the heads of people who hold seats on the boards of major corporations, who dictate the policies of government and the marketplace that the rest of us must live by.

Metcalfe believes that it is time to resurrect the strategy of the "muckrakers" of the nineteenth and early twentieth centuries, who cast an unflattering light on the American Robber Barons – the Carnegies, Morgans, Rockefellers – and in the process paved the way for social reform. The important thing is to make it personal, to hold the decision-makers accountable. "They didn't go after the Mafia in Chicago without naming Al Capone," he says. "The fact of the matter is, that if what is happening to the world today is criminal, then there are people who are criminals doing it. They are the people who have the power at the board level, and at the ownership level to do it or to stop doing it. It's not the abstraction of the corporation; it's individuals. And I'm not simplifying things. It *is* that simple."

So you target the modern-day Robber Barons – whose financial and political reach dictates the shape of our world – and you bring their activities out of the shadows. But how? The best way, Metcalfe says, is the old way. "Anyone can start a newspaper and disturb the shit," he says. "If real writers, young men and young women who are intent upon saying what's happening in the world, got together, they could be like a bunch of bakers getting together to create a bread company. The newspaper is still a working, efficient thing. You put out the sheet when you have some money, and give it away. The virus will spread."

★ ★ ★

The second person I wanted to revisit from the early days was Marshall McLuhan, who – even if unknowingly – had a lot to do with the founding and success of Greenpeace. Because McLuhan had long since died, he wasn't available for an interview. The next best option was to speak to one of the keepers of his legacy.

Nelson Thall, once McLuhan's chief archivist, is now the director of the think tank division of the McLuhan Centre for Global Communications in Toronto, set up by Marshall McLuhan's family. Thall, I found, can retrieve a McLuhan aphorism about as effortlessly as a country pastor can bring a Biblical quotation to his lips. When I approached him, Thall hadn't heard that Greenpeace's founders were fans of McLuhan, but the connection was no surprise to him given McLuhan's observation decades earlier about the satellite giving rise to the planetary consciousness from which sprang beatniks, hippies, and, yes, environmentalists.

"Sputnik created Beatnik," Thall explains to me, quoting his mentor. "Basically, the effect of the satellite as a technology was to turn the planet into a stage, to make people see the planet as Spaceship Earth." Beatnik culture, by McLuhan's reckoning, was a subliminal expression of this new realization that the world was small – that electric technology had made it possible to be in instantaneous contact with virtually any other place on the globe. The composite effect of this planetary shrinkage was to "retribalize" humanity; and thus the Beatnik, Thall says, "was the first tribal image that came out as a result of the satellite. The young don't dress, the young wear costume, because the planet got turned into a stage as a result of the satellite. The Beatnik image of long hair and jeans and beard is costume."

The environmental movement was another natural expression of this "paradigm shift" brought about by the shrinking, tribalizing effect of satellite technology, he says. "If you see the planet as a big,

big thing, you don't mind polluting it. But if you see it all as your backyard, you've got to keep it livable."

Given that satellite technology made ecological consciousness possible, it seems an appropriate intuition that Greenpeace should have chosen to communicate its pro-environmental message using the mass communications media. Twenty-five years later, communications technology, environmental issues, and the world in general have changed a lot. I ask Thall if, today, environmental politics and television are perhaps not such a good fit; if television is too simple-minded a medium to convey the current environmentalists' complex messages. Thall rejects the entire premise of my question: he reminds me that, after all, the medium is the message, so content is entirely beside the point. It's what the technological process does to us and says to us that's important. "The content, McLuhan used to say, is like the juicy bit of meat carried by the burglar to distract the watchdog of the mind. McLuhan was the first to find that the media have no content; the user is the content."

It is interesting though, that Thall short-circuits the political implications of that statement when he goes on to tell me that the elite has clamped down on television by imposing a restrictive format upon it. "You find that most television is scripted in advance," he says, "although it shouldn't be scripted in advance because its real power is to deliver the immediate now. The establishment locked down, shut out live TV in the sixties, because it was too dangerous for them. It was too much of a threat to allow live TV because people could get on and say things directly, they could talk over the heads of the electric bureaucrats."

The distinction between format and content in this case is entirely beyond me: why would it be a threat to have people speaking directly to the public if they weren't saying something dangerous? Is it not content, ultimately, that the establishment has sought to control? Never mind – we'll let the semantical distinctions pass. Thall's basic point is what's important: that, as we proceed further into the electronic age, the range of debate allowed on mass media has gotten smaller – that those with money and power are going out of their way to make sure that television does not fulfil its revolutionary (or even democratic) potential.

This message is reinforced in a dramatic way as Thall begins to talk about the limited options he has for sharing what he considers an essential message of McLuhan's inquiries. In his own work as a consultant to business, Thall confides, the content of his analysis is indeed restrained by what his clients are prepared to hear. Personally, Thall accepts his mentor McLuhan's contention that new media have such powerful transformative powers over the societies in which they are unleashed that "there must be a technological prohibitive rather than a technological imperative" – in other words, that society, rather than the marketplace, should control the pace of technological change.

"If McLuhan were here today he would say 'these things have to be made illegal until society decides what its effects should be.' Virtual reality is going to kill more people than all the hand guns in North America. Every new technology scrubs off a layer of our identity, and violence is a quest for identity." But do Thall's corporate clients listen to such pleas for restraint? No way. "We don't get hired to talk about that," he says. "We have to work in the commercial world, and the commercial world isn't interested in the areas that we've been talking about. So we bite our tongues and go ahead and do the job that has to be done, but behind the scenes we say, 'Oh boy, we don't like what we see.'" It seems that Thall's job, essentially, is to tell industry how to do things that he thinks should not be done.

★ ★ ★

Nelson Thall's observation that television came under much tighter control after the experience of the 1960s sheds light upon an apparent paradox in Greenpeace's experience. Recent Greenpeace media campaigns have had the most significant impact in places outside of that Northern sphere in which communications is the biggest business (some might argue that media is the leading economic sector in postindustrial nations), where vast bureaucracies control programming decisions and spin-doctors have attached themselves like barnacles to the mass media ship.

To "control" television is a costly process. In countries of the Third World and Eastern Europe, where media is generally a lot poorer and less "sophisticated," and where democracy is most often a recent innovation, Greenpeace is a sensation. In countries of the North Greenpeace sometimes seems like just part of the landscape. The paradox is that as mass communications get bigger, richer, and more sophisticated, they want less and less to do with the complex issues that environmental groups are now immersed in. And this raises a larger debate about whether TV, as a medium, needs to be retooled to bring it into sync with the demands of today's world. The problem may not be the strategies of public interest groups like Greenpeace; the problem may be the media themselves.

"The thing to ask ourselves," author and television documentarist Michael Ignatieff recently remarked to an audience of CBC reporters, "is whether the formats – whether the grammar of television particularly – make it possible to tell the truth. All the time disciplines of television now – 23 minute news programs, 90 second reports – seem to me in question with the kind of stories you're dealing with. You're going to Rwanda, for God's sake, at enormous expense, to send back 90 seconds or two minutes and five – you've got 147 words or whatever it is, to tell these stories about a massacre involving half a million human beings, in a tribal context that your viewers don't know a thing about. The grammar of television is breaking down, and it should break down, if it is honest about its obligation to tell the truth."[3]

Ignatieff went on to say that the time constraints of TV almost inevitably lead to the complex stories – such as the war in Bosnia – being shoehorned into simple narrative structures, preformulated at head office, that are inadequate vessels for the crises of the post-Cold War world. "We are all operating within very powerful narrative conventions," he said. "Good guy conventions/bad guy conventions. Victim conventions/aggressor conventions. None of which may apply, for instance, in the Bosnian case. . . . The narrative conventions are so strong, that it's very difficult to simply move upstream from them.

"Good journalism," according to Ignatieff, "is about questioning not only your sources but the narrative conventions that are driving you from home office," which means "simply changing the narrative drive of the world news machine itself." Although Ignatieff framed his remarks in the context of the increasing complexity of geopolitical stories in the aftermath of the Cold War, they apply equally to environmental issues, very few of which have seemed straightforward in the 1990s.

A significant body of opinion then, insists that it is partly the fault of the media themselves that social change groups have trouble reaching the public in this age of more complex concerns; whether because of corporate clampdown, or simply because of tightened formats, dictated by technology and increased competition. Others suggest that part of the problem originates on the supply side: that Greenpeace could have more impact within this new media environment if it had more imagination. As one insider told me: "Even people within Greenpeace were bored of our actions. If I saw one more banner hanging, I was ready to vomit."

Stefan Weber of Greenpeace Switzerland believes that every new issue can be simplified; think about it hard enough, he tells me, and you can find the haiku that's at the heart of a complex novel. The Swiss office, for example, illustrated the problems with genetic engineering by commissioning the artist Andre Heller to construct hot air balloons; one was a plant with a Scorpion tail, another was a flying fish. These images struck the public as "bizarre and absurd," Weber says, but that was appropriate because "the reality of it was equally bizarre and absurd."

After long internal discussions about what Greenpeace could do to get its PR machine back on track, it appeared in 1995 that the organization was finally emerging from a long drought. The spaces between media hits in the North had been growing, but that year two huge successes – the campaign against the Brent Spar oil platform in the North Sea, and the campaign against renewed French nuclear testing in the South Pacific – put Greenpeace back on the map.

After devoting an ocean of ink to the crisis *within* Greenpeace, to how Greenpeace had seemed to have lost its timing as a media spectacle-maker, the press was again trumpeting a winner. In August, after the Brent Spar campaign, *The Economist* magazine marvelled at how Greenpeace could operate according to local conditions in a multitude of countries yet still co-ordinate a coherent international campaign. *The Wall Street Journal* devoted several thousand words to dissecting how Greenpeace's mastery of the sound bite and the TV picture had "humiliated" Shell, one of the world's leading oil companies.

The real resurrection of Greenpeace would begin a few weeks later with the announcement that France was going to shatter the global moratorium on nuclear testing by resuming its test program in the South Pacific. Greenpeace was immediately able to raise an enormous outcry against the tests, which reminded me of a comment that *The Guardian*'s environment editor, John Vidal, had made back in March. In the midst of describing how Greenpeace had lost its lustre – and (so he maintained) much of its relevance in Britain – Vidal suddenly qualified his remark by saying, "But then again, all you would need is some God-awful thing like Chernobyl, and suddenly the thing would surge."

The new French tests appeared to be, in symbolic terms, a kind of a cataclysm, if a lesser one, and true to Vidal's prophecy they rocketed Greenpeace back to superstar status. The Greenpeace protest against the first French test was the top item on the TV news around the world and appeared on the front page of just about every newspaper. It prompted open outrage among members of the European Parliament and sparked an effective global boycott of French products. For years Greenpeace veterans like David McTaggart had been haranguing the organization to get back to basics – to concentrate on concrete issues that could be communicated simply and clearly; to choose battles that could be won. Apparently this advice was eventually accepted, and the resulting payoff in public profile was enormous.

Perhaps this is the most appropriate role for an organization like Greenpeace; perhaps its ability to capture headlines on a massive scale, to stir outrage at brazen assaults on the environment, and so to trigger the economic and political pressure needed to hold the aggressor in check makes it uniquely capable of springing into action in times of crisis. There can be little doubt, as well, that this type of performance will be required in the future: given a seemingly endless supply of governmental and corporate miscreants – given that polluters are continually seeking out new frontiers around the world – it may be that environmentalists are destined to spend most of their time fighting a rearguard action, keeping watch over the planet, ready to sound the alarm when the most offensive acts are about to be committed.

I glance at a stack of recent magazines and find that Greenpeace, the watchdog, has found no shortage of criminals to bark at after its rebirth in the South Pacific. In Nigeria Greenpeace helped to publicize the murder of Ken Saro-Wiwa, assassinated by the state for helping to expose the chemical despoliation of his country by foreign oil companies. In New Zealand the *Greenpeace MV* set sail to protest another nuclear test, this time not by the French but by the Chinese. In Canada Greenpeace warns that a plan to generate power from surplus Soviet nuclear warheads is a PR exercise to justify building more nuclear power plants. The list of current environmental crimes could go on and on, and is sure to get only longer in the coming years, for these are dark times.

But many environmentalists – some of them former Greenpeacers – now believe that a rearguard action is not enough: that our future depends upon the building of a new vision of an ecologically sane world, a vision based on the shared knowledge of people from across the globe and from differing intellectual traditions, and addressing fundamental structural questions such as the nature of our economic system and the need for democratic input into initiatives that have an impact on the environment. It is no longer enough to be against what is bad – the bigger challenge is to replace the evil with an image of good and a new sense of common cause. As the most geographically, culturally, and politically diverse of environmental organizations, Greenpeace has provided a platform for just this sort of meeting of minds to take place.

Many people wonder – after the organization's long period of internal feuding – how much more dialogue can take place within Greenpeace, whether the atmosphere has been so poisoned that reasoned debate is impossible. Still, the past suggests that Greenpeace is nothing if not resilient. To write the organization off now would be to ignore its considerable history of crisis and rebirth.

In a way, whether Greenpeace survives – and in what form, with what functions – is almost beside the point. Greenpeace became an institution because of its uncanny ability to understand mass media, to operate as an appendage of the mass media system. Many of its shortcomings are consequently the shortcomings of the media themselves.

So the question becomes, how do mass media need to change to expand beyond their present limitations – to situate issues within a broader context, to embrace the underlying dimensions of a seemingly simple problem, to be more than just reactive, to become a conduit for new ideas and insights? In the closing years of the millennium it seems as though these questions are being asked not just by environmentalists and political malcontents: there is a growing, generalized discontent with the brand of hot-button politics practised through the television news especially, and cynicism about the quality of information that pours through that tiny cable every day.

Yet replacing the current status quo with something healthier is not a simple matter. I have, for instance, quoted pundits with diametrically opposite views of what to do to turn things around. Ben

Metcalfe calls for a return to the muckraking tradition, arguing that simplifying the issues – which in many cases comes down to asking the old question "who profits?" – will provide the antidote to all the obfuscatory spin-doctoring that so often makes it onto the newswires and TV reports unchallenged. Michael Ignatieff believes, by contrast, that the news media need to embrace complexity rather than simplify issues – that evil in the world is most often produced by a murky mixture of random events, colliding agendas, and morally ambiguous decision-making rather than by conscious planning.

Deciding which approach is correct would be as difficult as defining where investigative journalism ends and crazy conspiracy theorizing begins; there are flaws, as well as advantages, to both approaches. The side that you lean towards depends on your individual worldview.

Then there are those who hold to the idea, à la McLuhan, that the shape of tomorrow's world depends more on how the globe is wired up than on what travels along the wires. The medium is the message. This belief underlies a lot of the current Internet mania. To say that new forms of communications such as the Net will lead to a better informed citizenry and a reinvigorated democratic process is a logical thing: computer networking seems a lot more participatory, a lot less passive, than television-watching. There is more information available, often distributed via specialized and sophisticated news groups, and more and more people seem to be buying into the technology.

But that argument only goes so far. The corporate takeover of cyberspace – the attempt to find commercial applications for these brilliant new digital technologies – suggests that the Internet will soon look a lot like the Home Shopping Network. And besides, while computer networking has created a new, quasi-public platform for groups with ideas to express but with insufficient funds to get those ideas on television, the action at that higher level is still more important: TV remains the centrifugal force in our culture; it is the town square where the news is announced to the multitudes, while other media are just backstreets and alleyways in which small groups mutter amongst themselves. Television – along with, to a lesser extent perhaps, the print news services – is still a mass media, with the potential of creating immediate political ripples, of prodding politicians into action.

Of course, the mainstream media rarely live up to that potential. Mostly, they are sound and fury signifying not very much at all, if anything. Emptiness and illusion. A drug. Brain-candy. A way to sell things, or to build markets for things. Which is why many people would say that it is not worth it to spend major cash chasing a few minutes on TV. Why not concentrate on alternative media, or on the communities of committed individuals who have hooked up through the Internet, or on nurturing the grassroots?

But choosing one medium or milieu over another would be wrong. Perhaps the future lies in recognizing the connections between various media, in studying the architecture that makes one house out of a series of rooms. Human beings receive information from a number of sources beyond the mass media – through word of mouth, from local and special-interest media, or simply from what we see around us, the activities we engage in. We gain knowledge from a mutual recognition of the conditions we deal with every day, from our personal histories, from our community histories. This is how many of our underlying opinions are formed, how our cultural assumptions are solidified. If the images on television are out of sync with the things we've learned and are learning, the information in those images loses credibility. The levels of information are interrelated; they influence and shape each other. This means that it is impossible to separate what happens in the Big Media, the mainstream media, from what happens at the grassroots.

If our world really is unified by a global electronic nervous system – if ideas and impulses pass through us at the speed of electricity – then the regions, cities, and neighbourhoods that are now plugged into and increasingly controlled by the image factories of Hollywood or New York, Toronto or London, are also, simultaneously, organisms with the potential to project their own experience into the global brain. In the face of globalization, we experience a paradox: local reality takes on a universal appeal. Bombarded by images that are manufactured and generic, we crave to know about the minutiae of daily life, about what's going on in places that are linked to us but somehow different. What we seek to know is partly physical. What is happening to the water, the air, the animals in the places that we live in? What is happening in places where other people live? What is it like to walk the streets on the other side of the globe?

As we are absorbed more and more into a two-dimensional reality of electric images, these questions about our physical environment seem likely to captivate us all the more. Which indicates that – as we prepare to enter a new millennium – we will be hearing a lot more from the organizations and individuals treading the same rough path that Greenpeace has helped to open up and mark out over the past quarter-century.

NOTES

CHAPTER 2. FROM THE CONTROL TOWER

1 A friend commented that this concept is what the producers of the television program *Star Trek: The Next Generation* were driving at when they created the Borg, an entity physically encased in a huge box floating through space. The Borg takes over human bodies, which once under its control become Zombies that see through prosthetic eyes and move with the aid of external wiring – their individual consciousness subsumed by the large Borg consciousness. They wander around muttering things like "you will become one with the Borg" and "resistance is futile." This, my friend believes, is an apt metaphor for the intrusion of the communications establishment into our own lives and for its redesign of human biology.

2 For the sake of shorthand and not upsetting conventional wisdom, I'm crediting the "global village" remark to McLuhan, even though Nelson Thall, who was once McLuhan's chief archivist, says that McLuhan was not its originator. According to Thall, McLuhan borrowed the concept from the 1930s tract *Men without Art*, in which Wyndham Lewis wrote that the world had become a global village. After citing Lewis, Thall says, McLuhan commented that the world since then had become a theatre. The idea, in any case, is that electronic media are making the world smaller and smaller.

3 *The Way It Is*, CBC Radio, Nov. 26, 1967.

4 Bob Hunter, *The Greenpeace Chronicle* (London: Pan books, 1980). This book, an account of the organization's first seven years, was never published in Canada.

5 *Bringing back the Future*, CBC Radio, April 1, 1973.

6 *As It Happens*, CBC Radio, Oct. 28, 1971.

7 "The Amchitka Bomb Goes Off," *Time*, Nov. 15, 1971.

8 "Amchitka's Flawed Success," *Time*, Nov. 15, 1971.

CHAPTER 4. GLOBAL VILLAGE OR DIVIDED PLANET?

1 Greenpeace campaigns have almost always followed this pattern. Activities against the Amchitka nuclear test, whaling, sealing, land mines, among others, were already taking place before Greenpeace became involved with them, with other groups having done substantial research and laying the groundwork. As Greenpeace International's former communications director, Andy Booth, told me, "All [a Greenpeace campaign] does is take information, package it, and target it – with political objectives. It's an information recycling operation." In the case of pesticide poisoning, for instance, a public interest group had researched and published a book on the issue six years earlier: David Weir and Mark Schapiro, *Circle of Poison: Pesticides and People in a Hungry World* (San Francisco: Institute for Food and Policy Development, 1981).

2 Michael M'Gonigle, "Recasting the National Debate," *Canadian Forum*, September 1991.

3 Michael M'Gonigle and Ben Parfitt, *Forestopia: A Practical Guide to the New Forest Economy* (Madeira Park, B.C.: Harbour Publishing, 1994).

4 Laurie Adkin, "Counter-Hegemonic and Environmental Politics in Canada," in *Organizing Dissent: Contemporary Social Movements in Theory and Practice*, ed. William Carroll (Toronto: Garamond Press 1992).

5 Stephen Dale, "Ecologist's Opinions on Debt Provoke Passionate Debate," *NOW* (Toronto), Nov. 2-8, 1989. Adams wrote to the newspaper to complain that she had been taken out of context, but I believe that her remarks were virtually impossible to misinterpret.

6 Raymond Bonner, *At the Hand of Man: Peril and Hope for Africa's Wildlife* (New York: Alfred A. Knopf, 1993).

7 Bonner, *At the Hand of Man*, p.112.

8 Dave Foreman, *Confessions of an Eco-Warrior* (New York: Harmony Books, 1991), p.204.

CHAPTER 5. BEHIND THE MASK: CONFLICT, CRISIS, AND CREATIVITY BEHIND THE MEDIA IMAGE

1 Arnold uses the word "potential" partly because nobody, at this point, has been killed by a tree-spike. In one widely publicized case in Cloverdale, California, in 1987 (cited in Klint's film) a mill worker suffered a broken jaw when a saw shattered after hitting a spike. Despite this incident, Earth First! founder Dave Foreman continues to support tree-spiking. In his book *Confessions of an Eco-Warrior* Foreman maintains that the saw broke only because it was in poor repair; that the tree was spiked by a non-environmentalist who offered no warning that the action was being taken; and that the company was at fault because it failed to take safety measures against any kind of foreign objects found in trees. According to Foreman, there are numerous deaths occurring each year due to the dangerous nature of forestry work; this one injury, he says, doesn't compare. He argues: "Responsible tree-spiking (done as a last resort after legal means, civil disobedience, and lesser forms of monkeywrenching have failed; and only with full warning to the land-managing agency and timber harvesters) is justified and ethical."

Former Greenpeacer Paul Watson also condones tree-spiking and other forms of "eco-tage." But it's interesting to note that, according to Watson's own version of events, the reason he was expelled from Greenpeace in 1977 was his colleagues' objection to his having undertaken an act of property destruction. Watson was given the heave-ho from Greenpeace, he says, because he grabbed a Newfoundland sealer's hakapik (club) and threw it into the water. Greenpeace's official history states it somewhat differently: the authors say Watson "was accused of creating dissension over campaign tactics on the whaling issue." See Michael Brown and John May, *The Greenpeace Story* (Scarborough, Ont.: Prentice-Hall Canada), p.50,

In any case, Ron Arnold's suggestion about Greenpeace being an outfit of "potential murderers" is far-fetched on several counts, notably: (1) no one has ever been killed by a tree-spike; (2) Greenpeace does not condone tree-spiking; and (3) the idea takes guilt by association to ridiculous lengths.

2 The June 1993 issue of *The Public Eye*, the publication of Political Research Associates of Cambridge, Massachusetts, a public interest investigative organization, documents some of the funding sources and political connections of wise use. According to the report, Ron Arnold was until recently a registered agent for the American Freedom Coalition, a political offshoot of Reverend Sun Myung Moon's Unification Church. Arnold and the wise use movement have also received support from Alan Gottlieb's Centre for the Defense of Free Enterprise, a fundraising body for right-wing causes.

3 *The Ottawa Citizen*, June 9, 1993.

4 *The Winnipeg Free Press*, June 10, 1993.

5 Bruce Livesay, "The Politics of Greenpeace: The Green Giant in Hot Water," *Canadian Dimension*, Vol.28, No.4 (August-September 1994).

6 Natasha Nita, "Greenpeace Stops $800,000 Pledges to HQ," *The Australian* (Sydney), May 28, 1993.

7 "Greenpeace Runs out of Steam," *The Independent Monthly* (Surry Hills, New South Wales, Australia), July 1994.

8 "A Consumer Guide to Charity," *Esquire*, December 1987.

9 "Greenpeace in 'Twinkie Land' Rift," *The Guardian* (London), Oct. 19, 1994.

10 Bronwen Maddox, "Campaigners All at Sea," *Financial Times* (London), Nov. 12, 13, 1994.

11 "Greenpeace Split as Campaigners Fight to Save Jobs," Reuters, Oct. 28, 1994.

12 *The Guardian*, Oct. 19, 1994.

13 Tom Horton, "The Green Giant," *Rolling Stone*, Sept. 5, 1991. Bohlen did, however, serve on the board of Greenpeace Canada during the 1980s.

14 In addition to his journalistic output, Metcalfe is also the author of two books: one a collection of essays about his clinical experiments with LSD in the late 1950s; the other a biography of Roderick A. Brown, magistrate, writer, and "my mentor as a fly-fisherman," he says.

15 I was unable to ask McTaggart for his side of this story despite repeated requests to Greenpeace's PR people for an interview with him.

16 See Stephen Probyn and Michael Anthony, "The Cartel that Ottawa Built," *Canadian Business*, November 1977. The authors document how the Trudeau

Canadian Business, November 1977. The authors document how the Trudeau government took a leading role in a uranium-producers cartel that managed to quadruple uranium prices between 1972 and 1976 (the same period during which McTaggart was beaten by French agents and then embroiled in a protracted legal challenge against France). France and Canada joined with South Africa and Australia in the price-fixing scheme, run out of an office in Paris. Canada's participation had the backing of cabinet.

CHAPTER 6. CIVIL WARS AND SEAL HUNTS

1 *The Journal*, CBC television, March 21, 1991.
2 Joyce Nelson, "Pulp and Propaganda," *The Canadian Forum*, July/August 1994.
3 See Bob Hunter's two columns, *eye* (Toronto), Feb. 18, 23, 1993. To the uninvolved reader the columns, which deal with Patrick Moore's work for the B.C. Forest Alliance, appear to be somewhat less than vitriolic. While Hunter does use the word "Judas," he does not appear to be accusing Moore but rather reporting, in a comic vein, on how some ex-colleagues have been dealing with him: "Poor Dr. Moore has been called the Judas of the eco-movement, and even old friends are afraid to acknowledge him in public. People make the sign of the eco-cross in front of him, and cover their hippie-children's eyes." Hunter seems to have a certain affection for Moore: "I have a conflict of interest here because Moore is an old buddy, and because I am certain he cannot possibly be an evil person." Hunter also says that Moore is "an intellectual and tactician of considerable stature, and his 'defection,' if that's what it is, to the industry side of the argument is bad news indeed for the environmental movement." In terms of the substance of Moore's conclusions about forest practices and the "sustainability" of the forest industry, Hunter mostly bases his case on an exchange of charges and countercharges between Moore and the World Wildlife Fund (WWF). While Hunter understandably comes out on the side of the WWF, he is not dismissive of Moore's ideas, acknowledging that nobody's view of the issue is "divinely ordained" and that statistics can tell conflicting stories.

CHAPTER 7. THE QUEST FOR COVERAGE: IN TECHNOLOGY WE TRUST

1 In "Creation of the E-nation," *Canadian Geographic*, November/December 1995, writer Rosa Harris-Adler notes an earlier example of how new technology changed the style of news reporting. Sending news copy from afar by telegraph, she wrote, led to the death of the ornate prose that had been common in newspaper reporting and ushered in a new succinct and uniform reporting style. The expense of the telegraph – as well as the need to standardize the prose to accommodate the wide number of newspapers that began to subscribe to the wire services – led to this change.
2 Roger Bolton, "Agenda Benders," in "Whose News: Democracy and the Media," special issue (in collaboration with Channel Four television), *The New Statesman and Society*, March 1995, pp.4-6.
3 Nick Bell, "Three Is a Crowd," *Television Business International*, July/August 1994.
4 David Bryer (Director of Oxfam UK-I), "Humanitarian Intervention: Military and Non Military Responses to Global Emergencies – An NGO View," speech

given at the Wilton Park Conference, Wiston House Conference Centre, Steyning, West Sussex, March 1, 1994.

5 Bell, "Three Is a Crowd."

6 Gregg Easterbrook, "Here Comes the Sun," *The New Yorker*, April 10, 1995.

CHAPTER 8. MASS MEDIA AND MASS ACTION: THE CHALLENGE OF A NEW ENVIRONMENTALISM

1 Robert Braile, "Blowin' in the Wind: Is Mainstream Environmentalism Sustainable?" *Utne Reader*, No.67 (January-February 1995).

2 Paul Brown, "Greenpeace Protesters Face Internal Discipline," *The Guardian*, reprinted in *The Ottawa Citizen*, Feb. 14, 1995.

CHAPTER 9. MANUFACTURING EVENTS: SWASHBUCKLERS, SCIENTISTS, AND DOLPHIN-TUNA TURF WARS

1 "Activist May Get Hero's Welcome," *The Globe and Mail*, July 31, 1993.

2 Hunter, *The Greenpeace Chronicle*, p.232.

3 Ibid., p.415.

4 Ibid., p.180.

5 Ibid., pp.188-89.

6 David Nicolson Lord, "Even Rainbow Warriors Change," *The Independent* (London), Nov. 4, 1994.

7 *Sunday Morning*, CBC Radio, Jan. 15, 1978.

8 Ibid.

9 Marshall McLuhan and Bruce R. Powers, *The Global Village: Transformations in World Life and Media in the 21st Century* (New York: Oxford University Press, 1989).

10 *As It Happens*, CBC Radio, April 1, 1973.

11 This section draws heavily on Bob Ostertag's account, in "Greenpeace Takes over the World," *Mother Jones*, March/April 1991.

12 Ostertag, "Greenpeace Takes over the World," p.85.

13 Ibid.

14 Benjamin Barber, "Jihad versus McWorld," *Atlantic Monthly*, March 1992.

15 Presentation at the International Development Research Centre, Ottawa, February 1992.

16 Barber, "Jihad versus McWorld."

17 For details on the following story, see Horton, "The Green Giant."

CHAPTER 10. THE BIG TRADE-OFF: FROM MEDIA CIRCUS TO DIPLOMATIC ARENA

1 Quoted in Horton, "The Green Giant."

2 Quoted in Ostertag, "Greenpeace Takes over the World," p.33.

3 Quoted in Ostertag, "Greenpeace Takes over the World," p.85.

4 Christopher Manes, *Green Rage: Radical Environmentalism and the Unmaking of Civilization* (Boston: Little, Brown and Company, 1990).

CHAPTER 11. AFTER THE COLD WAR: RETHINKING STRATEGIES FOR A NEW AGE

1 According to Paul William Roberts, "Saddam's Inferno," *Harper's*, May 1996, the combined toll of the war and continued embargo remained immense for ordinary Iraqis five years after the end of the war. Paradoxically, economic crisis and the ripping apart of families have made it even easier for Saddam to control demoralized Iraqis. According to Roberts, "The only people not affected by the embargo are Saddam and his inner circle."

2 Edward S. Herman and Noam Chomsky, *Manufacturing Consent: The Political Economy of the Mass Media* (New York: Pantheon Books, 1988), pp.19-20.

3 CBC National Journalism Symposium, Ottawa, May 27-29, 1994.

INDEX

DATE DUE